Lecture Notes in Computer Science   13290

More information about this series at https://link.springer.com/bookseries/558

Emanuele De Angelis · Wim Vanhoof (Eds.)

Logic-Based Program Synthesis and Transformation

31st International Symposium, LOPSTR 2021
Tallinn, Estonia, September 7–8, 2021
Proceedings

Editors
Emanuele De Angelis (iD)
IASI-CNR
Rome, Italy

Wim Vanhoof (iD)
University of Namur
Namur, Belgium

ISSN 0302-9743   ISSN 1611-3349 (electronic)
Lecture Notes in Computer Science
ISBN 978-3-030-98868-5   ISBN 978-3-030-98869-2 (eBook)
https://doi.org/10.1007/978-3-030-98869-2

This Springer imprint is published by the registered company Springer Nature Switzerland AG
The registered company address is: Gewerbestrasse 11, 6330 Cham, Switzerland

Preface

This volume contains a selection of the papers presented at LOPSTR 2021, the 31st International Symposium on Logic-Based Program Synthesis and Transformation held during September 7–8, 2021, as a hybrid (blended) meeting, both in-person (at the Teachers' House in Tallinn, Estonia) and virtually, and co-located with PPDP 2021, the 23rd International Symposium on Principles and Practice of Declarative Programming.

Previous LOPSTR symposia were held in Bologna (2020 as a virtual meeting), Porto (2019), Frankfurt am Main (2018), Namur (2017), Edinburgh (2016), Siena (2015), Canterbury (2014), Madrid (2013 and 2002), Leuven (2012 and 1997), Odense (2011), Hagenberg (2010), Coimbra (2009), Valencia (2008), Lyngby (2007), Venice (2006 and 1999), London (2005 and 2000), Verona (2004), Uppsala (2003), Paphos (2001), Manchester (1998, 1992, and 1991), Stockholm (1996), Arnhem (1995), Pisa (1994), and Louvain-la-Neuve (1993). More information about the symposium can be found at: http://saks.iasi.cnr.it/lopstr21/.

The aim of the LOPSTR series is to stimulate and promote international research and collaboration on logic-based program development. LOPSTR is open to contributions in logic-based program development in any language paradigm. Topics of interest cover all aspects of logic-based program development, all stages of the software life cycle, and issues of both programming-in-the-small and programming-in-the-large, including synthesis; transformation; specialization; composition; optimisation; inversion; specification; analysis and verification; testing and certification; program and model manipulation; machine learning for program development; verification and testing of machine learning systems; transformational techniques in software engineering; and applications and tools. LOPSTR has a reputation for being a lively, friendly forum for presenting and discussing work in progress. Formal proceedings are produced after the symposium so that authors can incorporate this feedback in the published papers.

In response to the call for papers, 16 contributions were submitted from authors in 10 different countries. One of the submissions was withdrawn by the authors, and each of the remaining submissions was reviewed by three Program Committee members or external referees. The Program Committee accepted one full paper for immediate inclusion in the formal proceedings; nine more submissions were selected for presentation at the symposium. In addition, the symposium program included the joint PPDP-LOPSTR invited talks by Harald Søndergaard (University of Melbourne, Australia) and Stephen Wolfram (Wolfram Research, UK). After the symposium, the authors of the contributions accepted for presentation were invited to revise and extend their submissions. Then, after another round of reviewing, the Program Committee accepted seven more full papers for inclusion in the formal proceedings. In addition to the eight accepted papers, this volume includes the paper contributed by the invited speaker Harald Søndergaard: "String abstract domains and their combination".

Thanks to Springer's sponsorship, LOPSTR 2021 featured a best paper award. The Program Committee assigned the award to "Disjunctive Delimited Control" by Alexander Vandenbroucke and Tom Schrijvers.

We want to thank the Program Committee members, who worked diligently to produce high-quality reviews for the submitted papers, as well as all the external reviewers involved in the paper selection. We are very grateful to the Local Organization Committee, chaired by Niccolò Veltri, for the great job they did in managing the hybrid in-person and virtual event. We are grateful to EasyChair for providing support to deal with the submission and reviewing process. Special thanks go to all the authors who submitted their papers to LOPSTR 2021, without whom the symposium would have not be possible. Emanuele De Angelis is member of the INdAM Research group GNCS. Wim Vanhoof is a member of the Namur Digital Institute (NADI).

February 2022   Emanuele De Angelis
                                                           Wim Vanhoof

Organization

Program Chairs

Emanuele De Angelis   Institute for Systems Analysis and Computer Science "A. Ruberti" – National Research Council, Italy

Wim Vanhoof   University of Namur, Belgium

Program Committee

Roberto Amadini	University of Bologna, Italy
Sabine Broda	University of Porto, Portugal
Maximiliano Cristiá	CIFASIS-UNR, Argentina
Włodzimierz Drabent	IPI PAN, Poland, and Linköping University, Sweden
Catherine Dubois	Samovar, ENSIIE, France
Gregory Duck	National University of Singapore, Singapore
Fabio Fioravanti	University of Chieti-Pescara, Italy
Jeremy Gibbons	University of Oxford, UK
Gopal Gupta	University of Texas at Dallas, USA
Geoff Hamilton	Dublin City University, Ireland
Michael Hanus	Kiel University, Germany
Bishoksan Kafle	IMDEA Software Institute, Spain
Maja Kirkeby	Roskilde University, Denmark
Temur Kutsia	RISC, Johannes Kepler University of Linz, Austria
Michael Leuschel	University of Düsseldorf, Germany
Pedro López-García	IMDEA Software Institute and Spanish National Research Council, Spain
Jacopo Mauro	University of Southern Denmark, Denmark
Fred Mesnard	Université de la Réunion, France
Alberto Momigliano	University of Milan, Italy
Jorge A. Navas	SRI International, USA
Naoki Nishida	Nagoya University, Japan
Alicia Villanueva	Universitat Politècnica de València, Spain

Local Organizing Committee

Niccolò Veltri (General Chair)   Tallinn University of Technology, Estonia
Ruth Laos   Tallinn University of Technology, Estonia
Kristel Toom   Tallinn University of Technology, Estonia
Tarmo Uustalu   Reykjavik University, Iceland and Tallinn
                                 University of Technology, Estonia

Additional Reviewer

Nelma Moreira

Contents

String Abstract Domains and Their Combination

Harald Søndergaard[✉]

School of Computing and Information Systems, The University of Melbourne,
Melbourne, VIC 3010, Australia
harald@unimelb.edu.au

Abstract. We survey recent developments in string static analysis, with
an emphasis on how string abstract domains can be combined. The paper
has formed the basis for an invited presentation given to LOPSTR 2021
and PPDP 2021.

1 Introduction

String manipulating programs are challenging for static analysis. The primary
problem in static analysis, of finding a good balance between precision and efficiency, is particularly unwieldy for string analysis. For static reasoning about
strings, many facets are of potential relevance, such as string length, shape, and
the set of characters found in a string. Hence abstract interpretations of string
manipulating programs tend to either employ an expressive but overly expensive
abstract domain, or else combine a number of cheaper domains, each designed
to capture a specific aspect of strings.

Much of the interest in the analysis of string manipulation is due to the
fact that web programming and the scripting languages that are supported
by web browsers make heavy use of strings. In the absence of static typing,
strings, because of their flexibility, often end up being used as a kind of universal data structure. Moreover, scripting languages usually determine object
attributes dynamically, treating an object as a lookup table that can associate
any sort of information with an attribute, that is, with a string. And attributes
may themselves be constructed dynamically. All this contributes to making the
construction of robust, secure programs difficult. Hence much research on string
analysis comes from communities that work with languages such as JavaScript,
PHP and Python. The dynamic nature of these languages calls for combinations
of non-trivial static and dynamic analysis, a continuing challenge.

This survey focuses on abstract interpretation. Much of it is based on Amadini et al. [2,3], from whom we take the concept of a "reference" abstract domain.
We provide a Cook's Tour of string abstract domains, discuss how to combine
domains, and show how reference domains can help domain combination, in
theory and in practice.

© Springer Nature Switzerland AG 2022
E. De Angelis and W. Vanhoof (Eds.): LOPSTR 2021, LNCS 13290, pp. 1–15, 2022.
https://doi.org/10.1007/978-3-030-98869-2_1

2 Preliminaries

We start by summarising the main mathematical concepts underpinning abstract interpretation. Readers familiar with abstract interpretation and finite-state automata can skip this section.

A *poset* is a set, equipped with a partial order. A binary relation $\sqsubseteq$, defined on a set D, is a *partial order* iff it is reflexive, transitive and antisymmetric. Two elements $x, y \in D$ are *comparable* iff $x \sqsubseteq y$ or $y \sqsubseteq x$. A poset D is a *chain* iff, for each pair $x, y \in D$, x and y are comparable.

An element $x \in D$ is an *upper bound* for set $D' \subseteq D$ iff $x' \sqsubseteq x$ for all $x' \in D'$. Dually we may define a *lower bound* for D'. An upper bound x for D' is the *least upper bound* for D' iff, for every upper bound x' for D', $x \sqsubseteq x'$. We denote it (when it exists) by $\bigsqcup D'$. Dually we may define the *greatest lower bound* and denote it by $\bigsqcap D'$. We write $x \sqcup y$ for $\bigsqcup \{x, y\}$ and $x \sqcap y$ for $\bigsqcap \{x, y\}$.

Let $\langle D, \sqsubseteq \rangle$ and $\langle D', \leq \rangle$ be posets. A function $f : D \to D'$ is *isotone* iff $\forall x, y \in D : x \sqsubseteq y \Rightarrow f(x) \leq f(y)$. A function $f : D \to D$ is *idempotent* iff $\forall x \in D : f(f(x)) = f(x)$. Function f is *reductive* iff $\forall x \in D : f(x) \sqsubseteq x$; it is *extensive* iff $\forall x \in D : x \sqsubseteq f(x)$. A function which is isotone and idempotent is a *closure operator*. If it is also reductive, it is called a *lower closure operator* (lco). If it is extensive, it is called an *upper closure operator* (uco).

A poset $\langle D, \sqsubseteq \rangle$ is a *lattice* iff every finite subset $X \subseteq D$ has a least upper bound and a greatest lower bound—written $\bigsqcup X$ and $\bigsqcap X$, respectively. The lattice is *complete* iff the condition applies to every subset, finite or not. It is *bounded* iff it has a unique least element (often written $\bot$) and a unique greatest element (often written $\top$). We write the bounded lattice D as $\langle D, \sqsubseteq, \bot, \top, \sqcap, \sqcup \rangle$. A complete lattice is necessarily bounded.

Abstract interpretation is a *declarative* approach to static program analysis. An analysis is almost completely described by its associated *abstract domain*: the set $\mathcal{A}$ of abstractions of computation states used by the analysis. The abstract domain is usually a *bounded lattice* $\langle \mathcal{A}, \sqsubseteq, \bot, \top, \sqcap, \sqcup \rangle$. In our case, an element of $\mathcal{A}$ will be a *string property*. Strings are constructed from some unspecified alphabet Σ. Hence each element (or *abstract string*) $\hat{s} \in \mathcal{A}$ denotes a set of concrete strings $\gamma(\hat{s}) \in \mathcal{P}(\Sigma^*)$ via a *concretization function* γ such that $\hat{s} \sqsubseteq \hat{s}'$ iff $\gamma(\hat{s}) \subseteq \gamma(\hat{s}')$. Often γ has an adjoined function $\alpha : \mathcal{P}(\Sigma^*) \to \mathcal{S}$, the *abstraction function*, that is, we have a *Galois connection*: $\alpha(S) \sqsubseteq \hat{s}$ iff $S \subseteq \gamma(\hat{s})$. In this case both α and γ are necessarily isotone, $\alpha \circ \gamma$ is an lco, and $\gamma \circ \alpha$ is a uco. Moreover, every concrete operation $f : \mathcal{P}(\Sigma^*)^k \to \mathcal{P}(\Sigma^*)$ has a unique best counterpart on $\mathcal{S}$, namely $\lambda(\hat{s_1}, \ldots, \hat{s_k}) \cdot (\alpha \circ f)(\gamma(\hat{s_1}), \ldots, \gamma(\hat{s_k}))$. Hence we can essentially identify a program analysis with the *abstract domain* it uses.

We use standard notation and terminology for automata [24]. A deterministic finite automaton (DFA) R with alphabet Σ is a quintuple $\langle Q, \Sigma, \delta, q_0, F \rangle$, where Q is the (non-empty) set of states, $q_0 \in Q$ is the start state, $F \subseteq Q$ is the set of accept states, and $\delta : (Q \times \Sigma) \to Q$ is the transition function. The language recognised by R is written $\mathcal{L}(R)$. We use $\mathcal{L}_R(q)$ to denote the language recognised by $\langle Q, \Sigma, \delta, q, F \rangle$, that is, by a DFA identical to R, except q is considered the start state. We let $\delta^* : (Q \times \Sigma^*) \to Q$ be the generalised transition function defined by

$$\delta^*(q, \epsilon) \quad = q$$
$$\delta^*(q, x\ w) = \delta^*(\delta(q, x), w)$$

Let $q \to q'$ stand for $\exists x \in \Sigma(\delta(q, x) = q')$. The DFA $\langle Q, \Sigma, \delta, q_0, F \rangle$ is *trim* iff δ is a *partial* deterministic function on $Q \times \Sigma$, and for all $q \in Q \backslash \{q_0\}$, there is a $q' \in F$ such that $q_0 \to^+ q \wedge q \to^* q'$.

3 String Abstract Domains

A *string abstract domain* approximates concrete domain $\langle \mathcal{P}(\Sigma^*), \subseteq, \varnothing, \Sigma^*, \cap, \cup \rangle$. Figure 1 shows Hasse diagrams for some example string domains. We discuss them in Sect. 3.2, but first we look at some simple but general string domains.

3.1 Programming Language Agnostic String Abstract Domains

Exactly which strings a variable may be bound to at a given program point is an undecidable problem. For a simple program such as

```
x = "foo"
if (*)
    x = "zoo"
```

it is easy to tell that x, upon exit, will take its value from the set $\{foo, zoo\}$. But in general we have to resort to finite descriptions of (possibly infinite) string sets, and reason with those. For example, we may approximate a set of strings by the characters they use. Then

$$\alpha_{chars}(\{foo, zoo\}) = \{f, o, z\}$$
$$\gamma_{chars}(\{f, o, z\}) \quad = \{w \in \Sigma^* \mid chars(w) \subseteq \{f, o, z\}\}$$

Abstraction usually *over-approximates*; our description $\{f, o, z\}$ may have been intended to describe $\{foo, zoo\}$, but is applies to an infinity of other strings, such as zoffo.

Let us list some examples of string domains. $\mathcal{CI} = \{\perp_{\mathcal{CI}}\} \cup \{[L, U] \mid L, U \in \mathcal{P}(\Sigma), L \subseteq U\}$ is the Character Inclusion domain. It provides *pairs* of character sets, the first of which hold characters that *must* be in any string described, the second characters that *may* be there. An example is given in the table on the right.

Domain	$\gamma(\{foo, zoo\})$
$\mathcal{CI}$	$[\{o\}, \{f, o, z\}]$
$\mathcal{SS}_2$	$\{foo, zoo\}$
$\mathcal{SL}$	$[3, 3]$
$\mathcal{PS}$	$\langle \epsilon, oo \rangle$

The String Set domain $\mathcal{SS}_k$ provides string sets up to cardinality k, representing all larger sets as $\top$. The String Length domain $\mathcal{SL}$ provides pairs $[lo, hi]$ of natural numbers that give lower and upper bounds on the length of strings described, again exemplified in the table. Let us describe the Prefix/Suffix domain $\mathcal{PS}$ in some formal detail (for more detailed definitions of the other domains, see for example [3]).

$\mathcal{PS} = \{\bot_{\mathcal{PS}}\} \cup (\Sigma^* \times \Sigma^*)$. The meaning of an element of form $\langle p, s\rangle$ is the set of strings that have p as prefix and s as (possibly overlapping) suffix. Formally,

$$\gamma(\bot_{\mathcal{PS}}) = \emptyset$$
$$\gamma(\langle p, s\rangle) = \{p \cdot w \mid w \in \Sigma^*\} \cap \{w \cdot s \mid w \in \Sigma^*\}$$

The largest element $\top_{\mathcal{PS}} = \langle \epsilon, \epsilon\rangle$ where ϵ is the empty string. $\sqsubseteq$, $\sqcup$ and $\sqcap$ are defined in terms of longest common prefix/suffix operations. Let $lcp(S)$ and $lcs(S)$ be the longest common prefix (respectively, suffix) of a string set S. Then $\langle p, s\rangle \sqsubseteq_{\mathcal{PS}} \langle p', s'\rangle$ iff $lcp(\{p, p'\}) = p' \wedge lcs(\{s, s'\}) = s'$, and $\langle p, s\rangle \sqcup_{\mathcal{PS}} \langle p', s'\rangle = \langle lcp\{p, p'\}, lcs\{s, s'\}\rangle$. The meet operation $\sqcap_{\mathcal{PS}}$ is induced—for details see Costantini $et\ al.$ [9]. The abstract catenation operation is particularly simple in the case of $\mathcal{PS}$: $\langle p, s\rangle \odot_{\mathcal{PS}} \langle p', s'\rangle = \langle p, s'\rangle$, with $\bot_{\mathcal{PS}}$ as an annihilator. The abstract version of substring selection (from index i to j) is defined

$$\langle p, s\rangle[i..j]_{\mathcal{PS}} = \begin{cases} \langle p[i..j], p[i..j]\rangle & \text{if } j \leq |p| \\ \langle p[i..|p|], \epsilon\rangle & \text{if } i \leq |p| \leq j \\ \top_{\mathcal{PS}} & \text{otherwise} \end{cases}$$

Most of these abstract operations have $O(|p| + |s|)$ cost.

Many other, often more sophisticated, string abstract domains have been proposed. For example, the $string\ hash$ domain [20] ($\mathcal{SH}$) is a flat domain of hash values (integers) obtained through application of some string hash function.

3.2   Language Specific String Domains

Aspects of some scripting languages necessitate greater care in string analysis. For example, it may be important to distinguish strings that are valid representations of "numerical entities" such as "-42.7" or "NaN". Figures 1(a–c) shows string abstract domains used by three different analyzers for JavaScript. A string set such as {foo, NaN} is represented as $\top$, $NotSpecial$, or $NotUnsigned$, by the respective tools, all with different meanings.

Note that it is very difficult for a program analyzer to maintain precision in the presence of dynamic typing and implicit type conversion. Arceri $et\ al.$ [4] retain some agility in their JavaScript analyzer through the use of a $tuple\ of$ $abstractions$ for each variable x: ($x\ qua$ number, $x\ qua$ string, ...), so that the relevant abstraction can be retrieved across conversions.

Amadini $et\ al.$ [3] performed a comparison of a dozen common string abstract domains, shown in Fig. 1(d). Figure 1 also identifies the (non-extreme) elements of some domains not discussed so far, namely $\mathcal{NO}$, $\mathcal{NS}$, $\mathcal{UO}$, and the Constant String domain $\mathcal{CS}$. The details of these are not essential for this presentation, except we note that elements of $\mathcal{CS}$ are single strings, $\bot_{\mathcal{CS}}$, or $\top_{\mathcal{CS}}$, with the obvious meanings. The main message to take away is that potentially useful string domains are $legion$.

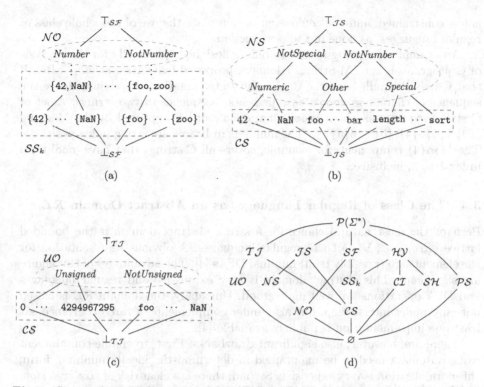

Fig. 1. String abstract domains used by different tools for JavaScript analysis: (a) SAFE [19], (b) JSAI [18], (c) TAJS [16]; (d) domains compared experimentally in Amadini *et al.* [3] ($\mathcal{HY}$ is the "hybrid" domain of Madsen and Andreasen [20])

3.3 Regular Expression-Like Domains

The "Bricks" domain of Costantini *et al.* [8] captures (sequences of) string sets with multiplicity. A *brick* is of form $[S]^{i,j}$ where S is a finite string set. $[S]^{i,j}$ represents the set $\bigcup_{i \le k \le j}\{w_1 \cdot w_2 \cdots w_k \mid (w_1, w_2, \ldots, w_k) \in S^k\}$. For example, $\{ab, c, abab, cab, cc\}$ can be approximated by the brick $\{ab, c\}^{1,2}$. Elements of the *Bricks* domain are sequences of bricks, with the sequencing representing language catenation. The "Dashed Strings" of Amadini *et al.* [1] offer a variant of this using sequences of blocks $[S]^{i,j}$ which are like bricks, except S is a finite set of characters.

More expressive fragments of regular expressions are sometimes used [6,21]. For example, Park *et al.* [21] approximate string sets by "atomic" regular expressions. These are regular expressions generated by the grammar

$$S \to \text{`}\epsilon\text{'} \mid \text{`}\Sigma^*\text{'} \mid A\ S \mid \text{`}\Sigma^*\text{'}A\ S \qquad A \to \mathsf{a}_1 \mid \ldots \mid \mathsf{a}_n$$

where $\Sigma = \{\mathsf{a}_1, \ldots, \mathsf{a}_n\}$ (we use quotes to stress that in this grammar, ϵ and Σ^* are *terminals*, not meta-symbols). The abstract domain used by Choi *et al.* [6]

is less constrained, and one could even contemplate the use of the whole class of regular languages, as done in the next section.

An example of a string abstract domain designed specifically for the analysis of C programs is the "M-Strings" domain, proposed by Cortesi *et al.* [7]. Recall that C uses the null character \0 to indicate termination of a string. Hence the sequence of characters zooo\0ba represents a sequence of two strings. A set of C string sequences such as {zooo\0ba, dooo\0da} is captured by the M-string $\langle\{0\}\top\{1\}o\{4\}, \{5\}\top\{6\}a\{7\}\rangle$. The numbers in braces are string index positions. The $\{1\}o\{4\}$ component, for example, covers all C strings that have 'ooo' from index 1 to 3, inclusive.

3.4   The Class of Regular Languages as an Abstract Domain $\mathcal{RL}$

Perhaps the most natural choice for a string abstract domain is the bounded lattice $\langle Reg, \subseteq, \varnothing, \Sigma^*, \cap, \cup\rangle$ of regular languages. A obvious representation for the elements are (possibly trim) minimal DFAs [4]. The advantages of this choice are significant: This abstract domain is very expressive and regular languages and DFA operations are well understood. Unusually, the domain $\mathcal{RL}$ is closed not only under intersection, but also under complement—a rare occurrence. At least one implementation is publicly available [4].

There are, however, also significant drawbacks: First, to enable containment tests, automata need to be maintained in deterministic, ideally minimal, form; this normalisation is very expensive. Second, there is a clear risk of *size explosion*, as DFA size is unbounded; for $\mathcal{L}(R) \cap \mathcal{L}(R')$ and $\mathcal{L}(R) \cup \mathcal{L}(R')$ it can be as bad as $|R| \cdot |R'|$. Finally there is the termination problem. Unlike other abstract domains discussed so far, $\mathcal{RL}$ has infinite ascending chains, so that Kleene iteration may not terminate without "widening".

4   Widening

Where an abstract domain has infinite ascending chains, termination is usually ensured by defining a *widening* operator ∇. This is an upper bound operator $(a \sqsubseteq a\nabla b$ and $b \sqsubseteq a\nabla b)$ with the property that, for any sequence $\{a_1, a_2, \dots\}$, the sequence $b_1 = a_1, b_{i+1} = b_i\nabla a_{i+1}$ stabilises in finitely many steps [10].

The design of widening operators is a difficult art. Done well, widening can be very powerful, but there is usually no single natural design that presents itself. For highly expressive domains it often becomes hard to balance convergence rate with preservation of precision.

Bartzis and Bultan [5] pioneered the design of widening for automata. We will explain their widening with an example—for exact definitions, the reader is referred to the original papers discussed in this section.

Example 1. Consider this pseudo-code (from [2]) involving a while loop:

```
x = "aaa"
while (*)
```

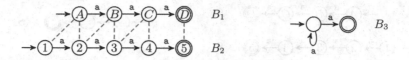

Fig. 2. DFA widening a la Bartzis and Bultan [5]

```
if (length(x) < 4) x = "a" + x
```

When the loop is first entered, the variable has the value aaa. After one iteration, the value is aaaa. Figure 2 shows the (trim, deterministic) automata for these values, $B_1 = \langle Q_1, \Sigma, \delta_1, q_{01}, F_1 \rangle$ and $B_2 = \langle Q_2, \Sigma, \delta_2, q_{02}, F_2 \rangle$. The idea now is to weaken B_2 by merging some of its states. Which states to merge is determined by similarity with B_1 as follows. Consider the relation

$$\rho = \left\{ (q_1, q_2) \in Q_1 \times Q_2 \;\middle|\; \begin{array}{l} (a) \mathcal{L}_{B_1}(q_1) = \mathcal{L}_{B_2}(q_2), \textbf{ or} \\ (b) q_1 \in (Q_1 \setminus F_1), q_2 \in (Q_2 \setminus F_2), \text{ and for some} \\ w \in \Sigma^*, q_1 = \delta_1^*(q_{01}, w) \text{ and } q_2 = \delta_2^*(q_{02}, w) \end{array} \right\}$$

For our example, we have $\rho = \{(A, 2), (B, 3), (C, 4), (D, 5), (A, 1), (B, 2), (C, 3)\}$. Now the idea is to form the reflexive transitive closure of $\rho^{-1} \circ \rho$, to create an equivalence relation on Q_2. The result of widening will be the corresponding quotient automaton—states of B_2 that belong to the same equivalence class are merged. For our example there are two classes, $\{1, 2, 3, 4\}$ and $\{5\}$, and the resulting automaton is B_3 shown in Fig. 2.   □

Two comments are relevant. First, the automata that result from this type of widening are usually non-deterministic, and in an implementation, widening needs to be followed by determinisation. Moreover, as shown by D'Silva [14], widening is generally sensitive to the shape of the resulting DFA, and for best results, minimisation is also required. Second, as pointed out by Bartzis and Bultan [5], the method as described is not strictly a widening, as it does not guarantee stabilisation in finite time. Bartzis and Bultan mention that a guarantee can be secured by dropping the "q_1 and q_2 are reject states" part of the condition (b) in the set comprehension above, but the cost is an intolerable loss of precision; their discussion ([5] page 326) underlines the tension between precision and convergence. For our example, the automaton that results when the condition is weakened recognises a^*, rather than the more precise $\mathcal{L}(B_3) = a^+$.

D'Silva [14] conducted a deeper study of a variety of families of widening for automata. These generalise the Bartzis-Bultan approach in a number of ways, including the way relevant state equivalence classes are identified. For example, in the "k-tails" approach, the relation ρ is determined by considering only strings of length k or less. Let $\mathcal{L}_R^k(q) = \{w \in \mathcal{L}_R(q) \mid |w| \leq k\}$. Then for automata S_1 and S_2, $(s_1, s_2) \in \rho$ iff $\mathcal{L}_{S_1}^k(s_1) = \mathcal{L}_{S_2}^k(s_2)$.

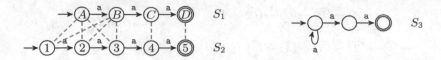

Fig. 3. 1-tails widening a la D'Silva [14]

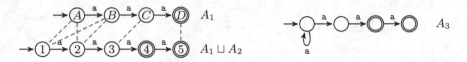

Fig. 4. Widening a la Arceri *et al.* [4]

Example 2. Consider again Example 1. The automata are shown (renamed) in Fig. 3. In this case, $\rho = \{(A,1),(A,2),(A,3),(B,1),(B,2),(B,3),(C,4),(D,5)\}$ and $(\rho^{-1} \circ \rho)^*$ induces three equivalence classes, $\{1,2,3\}$, $\{4\}$, and $\{5\}$. Hence the result of widening is S_3, shown in Fig. 3.   □

Again, D'Silva warns that the methods discussed may not always be widenings in the classical sense, as the convergence guarantees that are on offer are conditional on a variety of parameters.

D'Silva's ideas have been adopted for practical string analysis by Arceri, Mastroeni and Xu [4]. Here the decision about which states to merge is based on the k-tails principle just exemplified, but Arceri *et al.* replaces the induced widening operator ∇_k by ∇ defined by $A_1 \nabla A_2 = A_1 \nabla_k (A_1 \sqcup A_2)$.

Example 3. Figure 4 shows the result for our running example. As comparison is now against $A_1 \sqcup A_2$, we have $\rho = \{(A,1),(A,2),(B,1),(B,2),(C,3),(D,5)\}$, and $(\rho^{-1} \circ \rho)^*$ induces four equivalence classes, $\{1,2\}$, $\{3\}$, $\{4\}$ and $\{5\}$. The result of widening is A_3 in Fig. 4. Once S_3 and A_3 are determinised and minimised, they are identical (and more precise than B_3).   □

5   Combining Domains

The study by Amadini *et al.* [3] included *combinations* of different string abstract domains, but it focused on *direct products* of the domains involved.

5.1   Direct Products

Suppose the n abstract domains $\langle \mathcal{A}_i, \sqsubseteq_i, \perp_i, \top_i, \sqcap_i, \sqcup_i \rangle$ $(i = 1, \ldots, n)$ all abstract a concrete domain $\mathcal{C}$. Their *direct product* is $\langle \mathcal{A}, \sqsubseteq, \perp, \top, \sqcap, \sqcup, \rangle$ with:

- $\mathcal{A} = \mathcal{A}_1 \times \cdots \times \mathcal{A}_n$
- $(a_1, \ldots, a_n) \sqsubseteq (b_1, \ldots, b_n)$ iff $a_i \sqsubseteq_i b_i$ for all $i \in [1..n]$
- $\perp = (\perp_1, \ldots, \perp_n)$ and $\top = (\top_1, \ldots, \top_n)$

- $(a_1, \ldots, a_n) \sqcap (b_1, \ldots, b_n) = (a_1 \sqcap_1 b_1, \ldots, a_n \sqcap_n b_n)$
- $(a_1, \ldots, a_n) \sqcup (b_1, \ldots, b_n) = (a_1 \sqcup_1 b_1, \ldots, a_n \sqcup_n b_n)$
- $\gamma(a_1, \ldots, a_n) = \bigcap_{i=1}^{n} \gamma_i(a_i)$ and $\alpha(c) = (\alpha_1(c), \ldots, \alpha_n(c))$

The direct product generally induces a concretisation function which is not injective.

Example 4. Consider string analysis using $\mathcal{SL} \times \mathcal{CI}$. Of the two descriptions $([3,3], [\{a,b,c\}, \{a,b,c\}])$ and $([0,3], [\{a,b,c\}, \{a,b,c,d\}])$, the former is strictly smaller than the latter, by the component-wise ordering of the direct product. But $\gamma([3,3], [\{a,b,c\}, \{a,b,c\}]) = \gamma([0,3], [\{a,b,c\}, \{a,b,c,d\}])$; each represents the string set $\{abc, acb, bac, bca, cab, cba\}$. The components of the second description are unnecessarily imprecise. □

In an analysis based on the direct product, no exchange of information happens between the component domains, often leading to an unwanted loss of precision.

5.2 Reduced Products

The *mathematical* solution is to force γ to be injective. Consider the equivalence relation $\equiv$ defined by

$$(a_1, \ldots, a_n) \equiv (b_1, \ldots, b_n) \text{ iff } \gamma(a_1, \ldots, a_n) = \gamma(b_1, \ldots, b_n)$$

The *reduced product* $\mathcal{A}' = \mathcal{A}_1 \otimes \ldots \otimes \mathcal{A}_n$ is the quotient set of $\equiv$:

$$\mathcal{A}_1 \otimes \cdots \otimes \mathcal{A}_n = \{[(a_1, \ldots, a_n)]_\equiv \mid a_1 \in \mathcal{A}_1, \ldots, a_n \in \mathcal{A}_n\}$$

Define (the injective) $\gamma : \mathcal{A}' \to \mathcal{C}$ and $\alpha : \mathcal{C} \to \mathcal{A}'$ by

$$\begin{aligned} \gamma([(a_1, \ldots, a_n)]_\equiv) &= \bigcap_{i=1}^{n} \gamma_i(a_i) \\ \alpha(c) &= [(\alpha_1(c), \ldots, \alpha_n(c))]_\equiv \end{aligned}$$

If a greatest lower bound exists (say $\mathcal{A}_1, \ldots, \mathcal{A}_n$ are complete lattices) then $[(a_1, \ldots, a_n)]_\equiv$ is identified with its minimal representative: $\sqcap([(a_1, \ldots, a_n)]_\equiv)$. Moreover, if each (γ_i, α_i) is a Galois connection then so is (γ, α).

Reduced products are easy to define but generally hard to realise. Algorithms for the required operations are far from obvious. Moreover, an incremental approach to analysis where many abstract domains are involved does not appear possible. To quote Cousot, Cousot and Mauborgne [12], "The implementation of the most precise reduction (if it exists) can hardly be modular since in general adding a new abstract domain to increase precision implies that the reduced product must be completely redesigned". Section 6 suggests a remedy.

5.3 Paraphrasing: Translating Approximate Information

It is natural to propose some kind of information exchange to translate insight from one component of a domain product to other components, in order to calculate minimal representatives of equivalence classes. Let us call this improvement of one component using information from another *paraphrasing*.

As an example, $[\{a,b,c\},\{a,b,c,d\}] \in \mathcal{CI}$ can be seen as an "$\mathcal{SL}$ para-phraser" $\lambda v.\ v \sqcap_{\mathcal{SL}} [3,\infty]$ which tightens an $\mathcal{SL}$ component appropriately. More generally, the $\mathcal{SL}$ paraphraser corresponding to $[L,U] \in \mathcal{CI}$ is $\lambda v.\ v \sqcap_{\mathcal{SL}} [|L|,\infty]$.

Here is another example of a paraphraser. We can view $\langle p,s \rangle \in \mathcal{PS}$ as a $\mathcal{CI}$ paraphraser $P^{\mathcal{CI}}_{\mathcal{PS}}\langle p,s \rangle : \mathcal{CI} \to \mathcal{CI}$:

$$P^{\mathcal{CI}}_{\mathcal{PS}}\langle p,s \rangle(v) = \begin{cases} [L \cup X, U] & \text{if } v = [L,U] \text{ and } L \cup X \subseteq U \\ & \text{where } X = chars(p) \cup chars(s) \\ \bot_{\mathcal{CI}} & \text{otherwise} \end{cases}$$

Granger [15] proposed an important "local increasing iterations" technique to improve the precision of abstract interpretation. Granger's technique can also be used to improve the direct product of domains—it effectively uses paraphrasing systematically and repeatedly. Let us call the results *Granger products*.

However, when many abstract domains are involved, we soon run into a combinatorial problem. If we have n abstract domains, we can have $n(n-1)$ paraphrasers $P^j_i : \mathcal{A}_i \to \mathcal{A}_j \to \mathcal{A}_j$, so even for small n, a large number of "translation tools" are needed. The strain of juggling many different kinds of information, delivered through different abstract domains, becomes prohibitive. As we have seen, this is typically the situation we are faced in string analysis. Note that if paraphrasers of type $(\mathcal{A}_1 \times \cdots \times \mathcal{A}_k) \to \mathcal{A}_j \to \mathcal{A}_j$ are allowed (for $k > 1$), the number of possible paraphrasers is well beyond quadratic.

5.4   One-on-One Paraphrasing

Even if each one-on-one paraphraser $P^j_i(a_i)$ is an lco, it may have to be applied repeatedly. The combined effect of paraphrasing until no more tightening is possible comes down to computing the *greatest fixed point* of P defined by

$$P(a_1,\ldots,a_n) = \begin{pmatrix} a_1 \sqcap \prod_{i \in [1..n]} P^1_i(a_i)(a_1) \\ \vdots \\ a_n \sqcap \prod_{i \in [1..n]} P^n_i(a_i)(a_n) \end{pmatrix}$$

This is the approach suggested by Granger [15], and further developed by Thakur and Reps [25].

However, sometimes one-on-one paraphrasing falls short [2]:

Example 5. Let $\Sigma = \{a,b,c,d\}$ and consider the combination of abstractions

$$x = [5,6] \in \mathcal{SL} \qquad y = [\Sigma,\Sigma] \in \mathcal{CI} \qquad z = \langle ab, aba \rangle \in \mathcal{PS}$$

A system of optimal paraphrasers for this example leads to an equation system whose solution is simply (x,y,z).

That is, application of P provides no improvement (in this case P acts as the identity function). To see this, note that the knowledge (in y) that a string s uses the whole alphabet does not allow us to improve on x, nor on z. Conversely, neither x nor z can improve on y, since y is as precise as $\mathcal{CI}$ will allow. And, x and z clearly cannot improve on each other.

In contrast, in $P = \mathcal{SL} \otimes \mathcal{CI} \otimes \mathcal{PS}$, (x, y, z) denotes $\varnothing$, since no string satisfies all three constraints. To see this, note that the combination of y and z allows only strings of length 7 or more—strings must have form $\mathsf{ab}\Sigma^*\mathsf{c}\Sigma^*\mathsf{d}\Sigma^*\mathsf{aba}$ or $\mathsf{ab}\Sigma^*\mathsf{d}\Sigma^*\mathsf{c}\Sigma^*\mathsf{aba}$. $\qquad\square$

The example shows that sometimes no amount of (repeated) one-on-one paraphrasing will lead to the optimal reduction. Nor is this kind of paraphrasing enough, in general, to implement optimal transfer functions. Amadini *et al.* [2] have suggested an alternative that involves the use of what they call a reference domain.

6   Reference Abstract Domains

When a large number of abstract domains $\mathcal{A}_1, \ldots, \mathcal{A}_n$ need to be combined, we may look for a way of obtaining the effect of a reduced product, while avoiding the combinatorial explosion of paraphrasing. Amadini *et al.* [2] propose the use of an additional domain that can act as a *mediator* among the n given domains, a "reference" domain. This domain should be as expressive as each $\mathcal{A}_i$. This way it is, if anything, "closer" to the concrete domain than the reduced product is. In the diagram on the right, $\mathcal{C}$ is the concrete semantic domain and $\mathcal{P}$ is the reduced product of the n domains $\mathcal{A}_1$ to $\mathcal{A}_n$. For an abstract domain $\mathcal{R}$ to fill the role of reference domain, it must be located as suggested in the diagram.

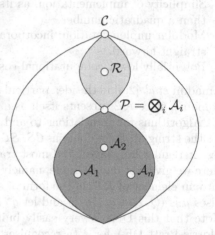

We can then achieve the effect of using $\mathcal{P}$ by recasting each of the n components in $\mathcal{RL}$, taking the greatest lower bound of the results in $\mathcal{RL}$, and translating that back into the n abstract domains $\mathcal{A}_1, \ldots, \mathcal{A}_n$. The combined effect of this amounts to the application of a "strengthening" function (an lco) $\mathbb{S} : (\mathcal{A}_1 \times \ldots \times \mathcal{A}_n) \to (\mathcal{A}_1 \times \ldots \times \mathcal{A}_n)$.

The same idea was present already in work on symbolic abstraction by Reps and Thakur [22], albeit in a rather different form. The authors cast the problem of symbolic abstraction in logical terms, associating abstract domains with different logic fragments. In that setting, a reference domain is simply a sufficiently expressive fragment.

Example 6. Take the case of abstract domains for linear arithmetic constraints. The well-known polyhedral domain [13] is very expressive and also expensive. Instead we may want to combine two cheaper analyses, namely intervals [11] and Karr's domain of affine equations [17]. However, reduced products of numeric abstract domains, while mathematically straightforward, are difficult to implement. Noting that *translations* between each cheap domain and the polyhedral domain are inexpensive, we may choose to use the latter as reference domain. For example, assume we have

$$x \in [5, \infty], z \in [1, 10] \text{ and } 2x - y = 8, x + 2z = 7$$

We translate each to polyhedral form and calculate the meet there:

$$(5 \le x, 1 \le z, z \le 10) \sqcap (2x - y = 8, x + 2z = 7)$$

Then we translate the result ($x = 5, y = 2, z = 1$) back into the interval domain, as well as into Karr's domain. Note how each component is strengthened.   □

In the presence of a large number of incomparable abstract domains, a suitable reference domain offers several advantages:

- Simplicity of implementation, as its requires $2n$ translation functions rather than a quadratic number.
- Modular implementation; incorporating yet another domain $\mathcal{A}_{n+1}$ is mostly straight-forward.
- Potentially lower computational cost at runtime.

Amadini *et al.* [2] find the idea particularly useful in the context of string abstract domains, since $\mathcal{RL}$ presents itself as a natural candidate for reference domain.

Algorithms for translations to and from $\mathcal{RL}$ are given by Amadini *et al.* [2], for the string abstract domains $\mathcal{CS}$, $\mathcal{SL}$, $\mathcal{CI}$, and $\mathcal{PS}$. Trim DFAs are used to represent regular languages, and most translations turn out to be straightforward. Here we give just one example, namely the translation of an element $\langle p, s \rangle \in \mathcal{PS}$ into an element of $\mathcal{RL}$, in the form of a trim DFA. Assume the DFA that recognises p is $\langle Q, \Sigma, \delta, q_0, \{q_f\} \rangle$ and let q^* be the unique state for which $\delta(q^*) = q_f$. Note that this DFA is very easily built. Let $\langle Q', \Sigma, \delta', q'_0, \{q'_f\} \rangle$ be the Knuth-Morris-Pratt DFA for s (a recogniser of $\Sigma^* s$). Again, this DFA is easily built directly, rather than going via an NFA (see for example [23] page 765). The DFA for $\langle p, s \rangle$ is $\langle (Q \cup Q') \backslash \{q_f\}, \Sigma, \delta[q^* \mapsto \delta^*(q'_0, p)] \cup \delta', q_0, \{q'_f\} \rangle$.

Example 7. Let $\Sigma = \{a, b, c\}$ and consider $\langle ab, ba \rangle \in \mathcal{PS}$ (denoting $ab\Sigma^* \cap \Sigma^* ba$). Figure 5 shows the DFA for ab (left), the KMP DFA for ab (middle), and their assembly into a DFA for the prefix/suffix description $\langle ab, ba \rangle$.   □

Translating back to prefix/suffix form is no harder. Given a trim DFA, one can extract the longest prefix in $O(|Q|)$ time, by following transitions from the start state, stopping when an accept state is reached, or when fan-out exceeds 1. Collecting the longest prefix is slightly more complicated [2] and requires $O(|\delta||Q|)$ time.

Example 8. Let us now combine $\mathcal{PS}$, $\mathcal{CI}$, $\mathcal{SL}$ and $\mathcal{CS}$ analysis, using $\mathcal{RL}$ to provide the precision of a reduced product. In the context of $\Sigma = \{a, b, c\}$, consider the description

$$\langle \langle ab, ba \rangle, [\{a, b\}, \{a, b, c\}], [0, 3], \top_{\mathcal{CS}} \rangle \in (\mathcal{PS} \times \mathcal{CI} \times \mathcal{SL} \times \mathcal{CS})$$

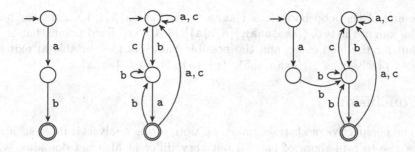

Fig. 5. Constructing a trim DFA for $\langle ab, ba \rangle \in \mathcal{PS}$

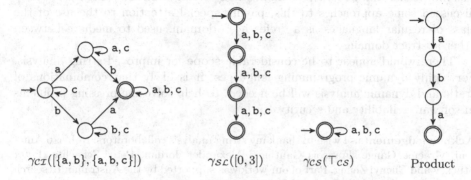

$\gamma_{\mathcal{CI}}([\{a, b\}, \{a, b, c\}])$ $\gamma_{\mathcal{SL}}([0, 3])$ $\gamma_{\mathcal{CS}}(\top_{\mathcal{CS}})$ Product

Fig. 6. Simpler descriptions as DFAs. The rightmost DFA is the product of the three on the left, together with the DFA from Fig. 5

The DFA for $\gamma_{\mathcal{PS}}(\langle ab, ba \rangle)$ is the one we just calculated (Fig. 5 right). The other three are shown in Fig. 6, together with the product of all four. This product automaton recognises $\{aba\}$. The refined information is then sent back to the elementary domains, to yield $\langle \langle aba, aba \rangle, [\{a, b\}, \{a, b\}], [3, 3], aba \rangle$. Notice the improved precision, especially for the $\mathcal{CS}$ component which has been strengthened from Σ^* to the singleton $\{aba\}$.   □

The generated product automata are not, in general, minimal, and we do not avoid the cost of minimisation. Keeping automata trim pays off by simplifying some translation operations, and the cost of trimming is low—linear in the size of a DFA.

Let us finally revisit the example that we started from. Our last example shows how simple abstract domains, when synchronised through an expressive reference domain, can yield a precise result. In Sect. 4, the use of widening led to an imprecise result such as aaa* to be produced. Here we avoid widening altogether.

Example 9. Consider again the while loop from Example 1. Assume analysis uses the direct product $\mathcal{PS} \times \mathcal{CI} \times \mathcal{SL}$, but utilises $\mathcal{RL}$ as reference domain. At the first entry of the loop, the description of the variable is $\langle \langle aaa, aaa \rangle, [\{a\}, \{a\}], [3, 3] \rangle$.

At the end of the loop body it is $\langle\langle \text{aaaa}, \text{aaa}\rangle, [\{a\}, \{a\}], [4, 4]\rangle$. Analysis finds that the join of the two, $\langle\langle \text{aaa}, \text{aaa}\rangle, [\{a\}, \{a\}], [3, 4]\rangle$, is a fixed point, that is, an invariant for the loop entry, and the possible values of the variable at exit are identified precisely as $\gamma(\langle\langle \text{aaaa}, \text{aaa}\rangle, [\{a\}, \{a\}], [4, 4]\rangle = \{\text{aaaa}\}$. $\qquad\square$

7   Conclusion

From the perspective of abstract interpretation, string analysis is interesting, as it gives rise to a plethora of natural but very different abstract domains, with very different degrees of expressiveness. A particular challenge is how to manage this multitude, that is, how to combine many string abstract domains. We have discussed some approaches to this, paying special attention to the use of the class of regular languages as a "reference" domain, used to mediate between other abstract domains.

There would appear to be considerable scope for improved string analysis. For highly dynamic programming languages, it is likely that combinations of static and dynamic analysis will be needed, to help solve the pressing problems in software reliability and security.

Acknowledgements. I wish to thank my string analysis collaborators: Roberto Amadini, Graeme Gange, François Gauthier, Alexander Jordan, Peter Schachte, Peter Stuckey and Chenyi Zhang. Part of our work was supported by the Australian Research Council through Linkage Project LP140100437.

References

1. Amadini, R., Gange, G., Stuckey, P.J.: Dashed strings for string constraint solving. Artif. Intell. **289**, 103368 (2020)
2. Amadini, R., et al.: Reference abstract domains and applications to string analysis. Fund. Inform. **158**, 297–326 (2018). https://doi.org/10.3233/FI-2018-1650
3. Amadini, R., et al.: Combining string abstract domains for JavaScript analysis: an evaluation. In: Legay, A., Margaria, T. (eds.) TACAS 2017. LNCS, vol. 10205, pp. 41–57. Springer, Heidelberg (2017). https://doi.org/10.1007/978-3-662-54577-5_3
4. Arceri, V., Mastroeni, I., Xu, S.: Static analysis for ECMAScript string manipulation programs. Appl. Sci. **10**, 3525 (2020)
5. Bartzis, C., Bultan, T.: Widening arithmetic automata. In: Alur, R., Peled, D.A. (eds.) CAV 2004. LNCS, vol. 3114, pp. 321–333. Springer, Heidelberg (2004). https://doi.org/10.1007/978-3-540-27813-9_25
6. Choi, T.-H., Lee, O., Kim, H., Doh, K.-G.: A practical string analyzer by the widening approach. In: Kobayashi, N. (ed.) APLAS 2006. LNCS, vol. 4279, pp. 374–388. Springer, Heidelberg (2006). https://doi.org/10.1007/11924661_23
7. Cortesi, A., Lauko, H., Olliaro, M., Ročkai, P.: String abstraction for model checking of C programs. In: Biondi, F., Given-Wilson, T., Legay, A. (eds.) SPIN 2019. LNCS, vol. 11636, pp. 74–93. Springer, Cham (2019). https://doi.org/10.1007/978-3-030-30923-7_5
8. Costantini, G., Ferrara, P., Cortesi, A.: Static analysis of string values. In: Qin, S., Qiu, Z. (eds.) ICFEM 2011. LNCS, vol. 6991, pp. 505–521. Springer, Heidelberg (2011). https://doi.org/10.1007/978-3-642-24559-6_34

9. Costantini, G., Ferrara, P., Cortesi, A.: A suite of abstract domains for static analysis of string values. Softw. Pract. Exp. **45**(2), 245–287 (2015)
10. Cousot, P.: Principles of Abstract Interpretation. MIT Press, Cambridge (2021)
11. Cousot, P., Cousot, R.: Abstract interpretation: a unified lattice model for static analysis of programs by construction or approximation of fixpoints. In: POPL 1977, pp. 238–252. ACM Publications (1977). https://doi.org/10.1145/512950.512973
12. Cousot, P., Cousot, R., Mauborgne, L.: A framework for combining algebraic and logical abstract interpretations, September 2010. Working paper https://hal.inria.fr/inria-00543890
13. Cousot, P., Halbwachs, N.: Automatic discovery of linear restraints among variables of a program. In: Proceedings of the Fifth ACM Symposium on Principles of Programming Languages, pp. 84–97. ACM Publications (1978). https://doi.org/10.1145/512760.512770
14. D'Silva, V.: Widening for automata. Diploma thesis, University of Zürich (2006)
15. Granger, P.: Improving the results of static analyses of programs by local decreasing iterations. In: Shyamasundar, R. (ed.) FSTTCS 1992. LNCS, vol. 652, pp. 68–79. Springer, Heidelberg (1992). https://doi.org/10.1007/3-540-56287-7_95
16. Jensen, S.H., Møller, A., Thiemann, P.: Type analysis for JavaScript. In: Palsberg, J., Su, Z. (eds.) SAS 2009. LNCS, vol. 5673, pp. 238–255. Springer, Heidelberg (2009). https://doi.org/10.1007/978-3-642-03237-0_17
17. Karr, M.: Affine relationships among variables of a program. Acta Inform. **6**, 133–151 (1976). https://doi.org/10.1007/BF00268497
18. Kashyap, V., et al.: JSAI: a static analysis platform for JavaScript. In: FSE 2014, pp. 121–132. ACM Publications (2014). https://doi.org/10.1145/2635868.2635904
19. Lee, H., Won, S., Jin, J., Cho, J., Ryu, S.: SAFE: formal specification and implementation of a scalable analysis framework for ECMAScript. In: FOOL 2012 (2012). https://doi.org/10.1145/2384616.2384661
20. Madsen, M., Andreasen, E.: String analysis for dynamic field access. In: Cohen, A. (ed.) CC 2014. LNCS, vol. 8409, pp. 197–217. Springer, Heidelberg (2014). https://doi.org/10.1007/978-3-642-54807-9_12
21. Park, C., Im, H., Ryu, S.: Precise and scalable static analysis of jQuery using a regular expression domain. In: DSL 2016, pp. 25–36. ACM Publications (2016). https://doi.org/10.1145/2989225.2989228
22. Reps, T., Thakur, A.: Automating abstract interpretation. In: Jobstmann, B., Leino, K.R.M. (eds.) VMCAI 2016. LNCS, vol. 9583, pp. 3–40. Springer, Heidelberg (2016). https://doi.org/10.1007/978-3-662-49122-5_1
23. Sedgewick, R., Wayne, K.: Algorithms, 4th edn. Pearson Education, London (2011)
24. Sipser, M.: Introduction to the Theory of Computation, 3rd edn. Thomson Course Technology (2012)
25. Thakur, A., Reps, T.: A method for symbolic computation of abstract operations. In: Madhusudan, P., Seshia, S.A. (eds.) CAV 2012. LNCS, vol. 7358, pp. 174–192. Springer, Heidelberg (2012). https://doi.org/10.1007/978-3-642-31424-7_17

Data Type Inference for Logic Programming

João Barbosa$^{(\boxtimes)}$, Mário Florido, and Vítor Santos Costa

Faculdade de Ciências, Universidade do Porto, Porto, Portugal
{joao.barbosa,amflorid,vscosta}@fc.up.pt

Abstract. In this paper we present a new static data type inference algorithm for logic programming. Without the need for declaring types for predicates, our algorithm is able to automatically assign types to predicates which, in most cases, correspond to the data types processed by their intended meaning. The algorithm is also able to infer types given data type definitions similar to data definitions in Haskell and, in this case, the inferred types are more informative, in general. We present the type inference algorithm, prove it is decidable and sound with respect to a type system, and, finally, we evaluate our approach on example programs that deal with different data structures.

Keywords: Logic Programming · Types · Type Inference

1 Introduction

Types are program annotations that provide information about data usage and program execution. Ensuring that all types are correct and consistent may be a daunting task for humans. However, this task can be automatized with the use of a type inference algorithm which assigns types to programs.

Logic programming implementers have been interested in types from early on [Zob87, DZ92, Lu01, FSVY91, YFS92, MO84, LR91, SBG08, HJ92, SCWD08]. Most research approached typing as an over-approximation (a superset) of the program semantics [Zob87, DZ92, YFS92, BJ88, FSVY91]: any programs that succeed will necessarily be well-typed. Other researchers followed the experience of functional languages and took a more aggressive approach to typing, where only well-typed programs are acceptable [MO84, LR91]. Over the course of the last few years it has become clear that there is a need for a type inference system that can support Prolog well [SCWD08]. Next, we report on recent progress on our design, the YAP^T type system[1]. We will introduce the key ideas and then focus on the practical aspects.

Our approach is motivated by the belief that programs (Prolog or otherwise) are about manipulating data structures. In Prolog, data structures are denoted

---

[1] This work is partially funded by the portuguese Fundação para a Ciência e a Tecnologia and by LIACC (FCT/UID/CEC/0027/2020).

E. De Angelis and W. Vanhoof (Eds.): LOPSTR 2021, LNCS 13290, pp. 16–37, 2022.
https://doi.org/10.1007/978-3-030-98869-2_2

by terms with a common structure and, being untyped, one cannot naturally distinguish between failure and results of type erroneous calls. We believe that to fully use data structures we must be able to discriminate between failure, error, and success. Thus our starting point was a three-valued semantics that clearly distinguishes type errors from falsehood [BFC19].

There, we first define the YAP^T *type system* that relates programs with their types. This defines the notion of *well-typed* program as a program which is related to a type by the relation defined by the type system. Here we present the YAP^T *type inference* algorithm which is able to automatically infer data type definitions. Finally we show that our type inference algorithm is sound with respect to the type system, in the sense that the inferred type for a program makes the program *well-typed*.

We shall assume that typed Prolog programs operate in a context, e.g., suppose a programming context where the well-known append predicate is expected to operate on lists:

```
append([],X,X).
append([X|R],Y,[X|R1]) :- append(R,Y,R1).
```

This information is not achievable when using type inference as a conservative approximation of the success set of the predicate. The following figure shows the output of type inference in this case, where ti is the type of the *i-th* argument of append, "+" means type disjunction and "A" and "B" are type variables (Fig. 1):

```
t1 = [] + [A | t1]              t1 = [] + [A | t1]
t2 = B                          t2 = [] + [A | t2]
t3 = B + [A | t3]               t3 = [] + [A | t3]
```

Fig. 1. (1) Program approximation; (2) Well-typing

Types t2 and t3, for the second and third argument of the left-hand side (1), do not filter any possible term, since they have a type variable as a member of the type definition, which can be instantiated with any type. And, in fact, assuming the specific context of using append as list concatenation, some calls to append succeed even if *unintended*[2], such as append([],1,1). The solution we found for these arguably over-general types is the definition of *closed types*, that we first presented in [BFSC17], which are types where every occurrence of a type variable is constrained. We also defined a closure operation, from open types into closed types, using only information provided by the syntax of the programs themselves. Applying our type inference algorithm with closure to the append predicate yields the types on the right-hand side (2), which are the *intended types* [Nai92] for the append predicate.

---

[2] Accordingly to a notion of *intended meaning* first presented in [Nai92].

Our type inference algorithm[3] works for pure Prolog with system predicates for arithmetic. We assume as base types *int*, *float*, *string*, and *atom*. There is an optional definition of type declarations (like data declarations in Haskell) which, if declared by the programmer, are used by the type inference algorithm to refine types. We follow a syntax inspired in [SCWD08] to specify type information. One example of such a declaration is the list datatype

```
:- type list(A) = [] + [A | list(A)].
```

In order to simplify further processing our type system and type inference algorithm assume that predicates are in a simplified form called *kernel Prolog* [VR90]. In this representation, each predicate in the program is defined by a single clause (H :- B), where the head H contains distinct variables as arguments and the body B is a disjunction (represented by the symbol ;) of queries. The variables in the head of the clause occur in every query in the body of that clause. We assume that there are no other common variables between queries, except for the variables that occur in the head of the clause, without loss of generality. In this form the scope of variables is not limited to a single clause, but is extended over the whole predicate definition and thus type inference is easier to perform. In [VR90] a compilation from full Prolog to kernel Prolog is defined. Thus, in the rest of the paper, we will assume that predicate definitions are always in kernel Prolog.

2   Types

Here we define a new class of expressions, which we shall call *types*. We first define the notion of *type term* built from an infinite set of type variables $TVar$, a finite set of base types $TBase$, an infinite set of constants $TCons$, an infinite set of function symbols $TFunc$, and an infinite set of type symbols, $TSymb$. *Type terms* can be:

- a type variable ($\alpha, \beta, \gamma, \cdots \in TVar$)
- a constant ($1, [\,], 'c', \cdots \in TCons$)
- a base type ($int, float, \cdots \in TBase$)
- a function symbol $f \in TFunc$ associated with an arity n applied to an n-tuple of type terms ($f(int, [\,], g(X))$)
- a type symbol $\sigma \in TSymb$ associated with an arity n ($n \geq 0$) applied to an n-tuple of type terms ($\sigma(X, int)$).

Type variables, constants and base types are called *basic types*. A *ground type term* is a type variable-free type term. Type symbols can be defined in a *type definition*. Type definitions are of the form:

$$\sigma(\alpha_1, \ldots, \alpha_k) = \tau_1 + \ldots + \tau_n,$$

---

[3] Implementation at https://github.com/JoaoLBarbosa/TypeInferenceAlgorithm.

where each τ_i is a type term and σ is the type symbol being defined. In general these definitions are polymorphic, which means that type variables $\alpha_1, \ldots, \alpha_k$, for $k \geq 0$, include the type variables occurring in $\tau_1 + \ldots + \tau_n$, and are called *type parameters*. If we instantiate one of those type variables, we can replace it in the parameters and everywhere it appears on the right-hand side of the definition. The sum $\tau_1 + \ldots + \tau_n$ is a *union type*, describing values that may have one of the types $\tau_1, \ldots, \tau_n$. The '+' is an idempotent, commutative, and associative operation. Throughout the paper, to condense notation, we will use the symbol $\bar{\tau}$ to denote union types. We will also use the notation $\tau \in \bar{\tau}$ to denote that τ is a summand in the union type $\bar{\tau}$.

Note that type definitions may be recursive. A *deterministic type definitions* is a type definition where, on the right-hand side, none of τ_i start with a type symbol and if τ_i is a type term starting with a function symbol f, then no other τ_j starts with f.

Example 1. Assuming a base type *int* for the set of all integers, the type list of integers is defined by the type definition $list = [\,] + [int \mid list]$[4].

Let $\vec{\tau}$ stand for a tuple of types $\tau_1 \times \cdots \times \tau_n$. A functional type is a type of the form $\vec{\tau_1} \rightarrow \tau_2$. A *predicate type* is a functional type from a tuple of the type terms defining the types of its arguments to bool, i.e. $\tau_1 \times \ldots \times \tau_n \rightarrow bool$. A *type* can be a *type term*, an *union type*, or a *predicate type*.

Our type language enables parametric polymorphism through the use of type schemes. A *type scheme* is defined as $\forall_{X_1} \ldots \forall_{X_n} T$, where T is a predicate type and $X_1, \ldots, X_n$ are distinct type variables. In logic programming, there have been several authors that have dealt with polymorphism with type schemes or in a similar way [PR89, BG92, Hen93, Zob87, FSVY91, GdW94, YFS92, FD92, Han89]. Type schemes have type variables as generic place-holders for ground type terms. Parametric polymorphism comes from the fact these type variables can be instantiated with any type.

Example 2. A polymorphic list is defined by the following type definition:

$$list(X) = [\,] + [X \mid list(X)]$$

Notation. Throughout the rest of the paper, for the sake of readability, we will omit the universal quantifiers on type schemes and the type parameters as explicit arguments of type symbols in inferred types. Thus we will assume that all free type variables on type definitions of inferred types are type parameters which are universally quantified.

Most type languages in logic programming use tuple distributive closures of types. The notion of tuple distributivity was given by Mishra [Mis84]. Throughout this paper, we restrict our type definitions to be deterministic. The types described this way are tuple distributive.

---

[4] Type definitions will use the user friendly Prolog notation for lists instead of the list constructor.

Sometimes, the programmer wants to introduce a new type in a program, so that it is recognized when performing type inference. It is also a way of having a more structured and clear program. These declarations act similarly to data declarations in Haskell.

In our algorithm, types can be declared by the programmer in the following way:- type $type\_symbol(type\_vars) = type\_term_1 + \ldots + type\_term_n$. One example would be:

```
:- type tree(X) = empty + node(X, tree(X), tree(X)).
```

In the rest of the paper we will assume that all constants and function symbols that start a summand in a declared type cannot start a summand in a different one, thus there are no overloaded constants nor function symbols. Note that there is a similar restriction on data declarations in functional programming languages.

2.1 Semantics

In [BFC19] we defined a formal semantics for types. Here we just give the main intuitive ideas behind it:

- The semantics of base types and constant types are predefined sets containing logic terms, for instance, the base type *int* is the set of all integers and the semantics of *bool* is the set of the values *true* and *false*;
- Tuples of types, $(\tau_1, \ldots, \tau_n)$, are sets of tuples of terms such that the semantics of each term belongs to the semantics of the type in the corresponding position;
- $f(\tau_1, \ldots, \tau_n)$ is the set of all terms with main functor f and arity n applied to the set of tuples belonging to the semantics of $(\tau_1, \ldots, \tau_n)$;
- The semantics of union types is the disjoint union of the semantics of its summands;
- The semantics of type symbols is the set of all terms that can be derived from its definition;
- The semantics of functional types, such as predicate types, is the set of functions that when given terms belonging to the semantics of the input types, output terms belonging to the semantics of output types. For instance the semantics of $int \times float \rightarrow bool$, contains all functions that, given a pair with an integer and a floating point number, output a boolean.
- The semantics of parametric polymorphic types is the intersection of the semantics of its instances (this idea was first used by Damas [Dam84] to define the semantics of type schemes).

In [BFC19] we defined a type system and proved that it is sound with respect to this semantics of types. Here we define a type inference algorithm and prove that it is sound with respect to the type system, thus, using these two results, we can conclude that the type inference algorithm is also sound with respect to the semantics.

2.2   Closed Types

Closed types were first defined in [BFSC17]. Informally, they are types where every occurrence of a type variable is constrained. If a type is not closed, we say that it is an *open type*. The restrictions under the definition of closed type can be compressed in the following three principles:

- Types should denote a set of terms which is strictly smaller than the set of all terms
- Every use of a variable in a program should be type constrained
- Types are based on self-contained definitions.

The last one is important to create a way to go from open types to closed types. We defined what is an unconstrained type variable as follows:

Definition 1 (Unconstrained Type Variable). *A type variable* α *is* unconstrained *with respect to a set of type definitions* T, *notation* unconstrained(α, T), *if and only if it occurs exactly once as a summand in the set of all the right-hand sides of type definitions in* T.

Unconstrained type variables type terms with any type, thus they do not really provide type information. We now define *closed type definition*, which are type definitions without type variables as summands in their definition.

Definition 2 (Closed Type Definitions). *A type definition* $\sigma = \bar{\tau}$ *is closed, notation* closedTypeDef(σ), *if and only if there are no type variables as summands in* $\bar{\tau}$.

The definition for closed types uses these two previous auxiliary definitions. Closed types correspond to closed records or data definitions in functional programming languages. The definition follows:

Definition 3 (Closed Types). *A type definition* $\sigma = \bar{\tau}$ *is closed with respect to a set of type definitions* T, *notation* closed(σ, T), *if and only if the predicate defined as follows holds:*

$$closed(\sigma, T) = \begin{cases} \neg unconstrained(\alpha, T) & \text{if } \bar{\tau} = \alpha \text{ and } \alpha \text{ is a type variable} \\ closedTypeDef(\sigma) & \text{otherwise} \end{cases}$$

Example 3. We recall the example in the Introduction, of the following types for the **append** predicate, where t_n is the type of *nth* predicate argument:

```
t1 = [] + [A | t1]
t2 = B
t3 = B + [A | t3]
```

Type t3, for the third argument of **append**, is open, because t3 has a type variable as a summand, thus it does not filter any possible term, since the type variable can be instantiated with any type. An example of a valid closed type for **append** is:

```
t1 = [] + [A | t1]
t2 = [] + [A | t2]
t3 = [] + [A | t3]
```

The next step is to transform open types into closed types. Note that some inferred types may be already closed. For the ones that are not, we defined a *closure* operation, described in detail in [BFSC17]. This closure operation is an optional post-processing step on our algorithm.

To close types, we calculate what we call the proper variable domain of every type variable that occurs as a summand in a type definition. The proper variable domain corresponds to the sum of the proper domains of each type that shares a type term with the open type we are tying to close. The proper domain of a type is the sum of all summands that are not type variables in its definition. We then replace the type variable with its proper variable domain.

We have tested the closure algorithm on several examples and for the examples we tried, the results seem very promising.

3   Examples

There are some flags in the type inference algorithm that can be turned on or off:

- *basetype* (default: *on*) - when this flag is turned on, we assume that each constant is typed with a base type, when it is turned off, we type each constant with a constant type corresponding to itself;
- *list* (default: *off*) - this flag adds the data type declaration for polymorphic lists to the program when turned on;
- *closure* (default: *off*) - when this flag is turned on, the closure operation is applied as a post-processing step on the algorithm.

In the following examples pi is the type symbol for the type of the *ith* argument of predicate p and we assume that all free type variables on type definitions are universally quantified and that the type of arguments of built-in arithmetic predicates is predefined as $int + float$.

Example 4. Let us consider the predicate *concat*, which flattens a list of lists, where *app* is the *append* predicate:

```
concat(X1,X2) :- X1=[], X2=[];
        X1=[X|Xs], X2=List, concat(Xs,NXs), app(X,NXs,List).

app(A,B,C) :- A=[], B=D, C=D;
        app(E,F,G), E=H, F=I, G=J, A=[K|H], B=I, C=[K|J].
```

The types inferred with all the flags *off* correspond to types inferred in previous type inference algorithms which view types as an approximation of the success set of the program:

```
concat :: concat1 x concat2
concat1 = [] + [ t | concat1 ]
concat2 = C + [] + [ B | concat2 ]
t = [] + [ B | t ]

app :: app1 x app2 x app3
app1 = [] + [ A | app1 ]
app2 = B
app3 = B + [ A | app3 ]
```

Now the types inferred when turning on the closure flag are:

```
concat :: concat1 x concat2
concat1 = [] + [ concat2 | concat1 ]
concat2 = [] + [ B | concat2 ]

app :: app1 x app2 x app3
app1 = [] + [ A | app1 ]
app2 = [] + [ A | app2 ]
app3 = [] + [ A | app3 ]
```

Note that these types are not inferred by any previous type inference algorithm for logic programming so far, and they are a step towards the automatic inference of types for programs used in a specific context, more precisely, a context which corresponds to how it would be used in a programming language with data type declarations, such as Curry [Han13] or Haskell.

Example 5. Let *rev* be the reverse list predicate, defined using the *append* definition used in the previous example:

```
rev(A, B) :- A=[], B=[] ;
        rev(C, D), app(D, E, F), E=[G], A=[G|C], B=F.
```

The inferred types with all flags off is (the types inferred for append are the same as the one in the previous example):

```
rev :: rev1 x rev2
rev1 = [] + [ A | rev1 ]
rev2 = [] + [ t | rev2 ]
t = B + A
```

If we turn on the *list_flag*, which declares the data type for Prolog lists, the type inference algorithm outputs the same types that would be inferred in Curry or Haskell with pre-defined built-in lists:

```
rev :: rev1 x rev2
rev1 = list(A)
rev2 = list(A)

list(X) = [] + [ X | list(X) ]
```

We now show an example of the minimum of a tree.

Example 6. Let *tree_minimum* be the predicate defined as follows:

```
tree_min(A,B) :- A=empty, B=0 ;
        A=node(C,D,E), tree_min(D,F), tree_min(E,G),
        Y=[C,F,G], minimum(Y,X), X=B.


minimum(A,B) :- A=[I], B=I;
        A=[X|Xs], minimum(Xs,C), X=<C, B=C ;
        A=[Y|Ys], minimum(Ys,D), D=<Y, B=D.
```

The inferred types with all flags off, except for the *basetype_flag*, are:

```
tree_min :: tree_min1 x tree_min2
tree_min1 = atom + node(tree_min2, tree_min1, tree_min1)
tree_min2 = A + int + float

minimum :: minimum1 x minimum2
minimum1 = [ minimum2 | t ]
minimum2 = A + int + float
t2 = [] + [ minimum2 | t2 ]
```

If we now add a predefined declaration of a tree data type and turn on the *list_flag*, the algorithm outputs:

```
tree_minimum :: tree_minimum1 x tree_minimum2
tree_minimum1 = tree(tree_minimum2)
tree_minimum2 = int + float

minimum :: minimum1 x minimum2
minimum1 = list(minimum2)
minimum2 = int + float

tree(X) = empty + node(X, tree(X), tree(X))
list(Y) = [] + [ Y | list(Y) ]
```

4   Type System

Here we define the notion of *well-typed* program using a set of rules assigning types to terms, atoms, queries, sequences of queries, and clauses. This is generally called a *type system* and ours follows the definition in [BFC19] with some differences in the notation for recursive types: here we explicitly add a set of (possibly recursive) type definitions instead of the fix-point notation for types used in the paper mentioned above. These small differences do not alter the soundness of the type system.

We first write the following subtyping relation from [BFC19].

Definition 4 (Subtyping). *Let ϕ be a substitution of types for type variables. Let $\sqsubseteq$ denote the subtyping relation as a partial order (reflexive, anti-symmetric and transitive) defined as follows:*

- *$\tau \sqsubseteq \tau\prime$ if $\exists \phi.\phi(\tau\prime) = \tau$ (Instance)*
- *$\tau \sqsubseteq \bar{\tau}$ iff $\tau \in \bar{\tau}$ (Subset)*
- *$f(\tau_1, \ldots, \tau_n) \sqsubseteq f(\tau\prime_1, \ldots, \tau\prime_n)$ iff $\tau_1 \leq \tau\prime_1, \ldots \tau_n \leq \tau\prime_n$ (Complex term construction/destruction)*
- *$\delta_1 \sqsubseteq \delta_2$ iff, assuming $\delta_1 \sqsubseteq \delta_2$, we get $\bar{\tau}_1 \sqsubseteq \bar{\tau}_2$, where $\delta_1 = \bar{\tau}_1$ and $\delta_2 = \bar{\tau}_2$ are the type definitions for δ_1 and δ_2 (Recursive Type Unfolding)*
- *$\tau \sqsubseteq \delta$ iff $\tau \sqsubseteq \bar{\tau}$ and $\delta = \bar{\tau}$ is the type definition for δ (Right Unfolding)*
- *$\delta \sqsubseteq \tau$ iff $(\tau) \sqsubseteq \tau$ and $\delta = \bar{\tau}$ is the type definition for δ (Left Unfolding)*
- *$\tau \sqsubseteq \tau_1 + \tau_2$ iff $\tau \sqsubseteq \tau_1$ or $\tau_2 \sqsubseteq \tau$ (Addition)*
- *if $\tau\prime \sqsubseteq \tau$, then $\tau \to bool \sqsubseteq \tau\prime \to bool$ (Contravariance)*

Subtyping of functional types is contravariant in the argument type, meaning that the order of subtyping is reversed. This is standard in functional languages and guarantees that when a function type is a subtype of another it is safe to use a function of one type in a context that expects a function of a different type. It is safe to substitute a function f for a function g if f accepts a more general type of argument than g. For example, predicates of type $int + float \to bool$ can be used wherever an $int \to bool$ was expected.

Let us now give some auxiliary definitions: an *assumption* is a type declaration for a variable, written $X : \tau$, where X is a variable and τ a type. We define a *context* Γ as a set of assumptions with distinct variables as subjects (alternatively *contexts* can be defined as functions from variables to types, where $domain(\Gamma)$ stands for its domain). Since Γ can be seen as a function, we use $\Gamma(X) = \tau$ to denote $(X : \tau) \in \Gamma$. A set of type definitions, Δ, is a set of type definitions of the form $\sigma = \bar{\tau}$, where each definition has a different type symbol on the left-hand side. It can also be defined as a function from σ to $\bar{\tau}$. We will therefore use the notation $\Delta(\sigma) = \bar{\tau}$ to denote $(\sigma = \bar{\tau}) \in \Delta$.

Our type system is defined in Fig. 2 and statically relates *well-typed* programs with their types by defining a relation $\Gamma, \Delta \vdash_P p : \tau$, where Γ is a context, Δ a set of type definitions, p is a term, an atom, a query, a sequence of queries, or a clause, and τ is a type. This relation should be read as expression p has type τ, given the context Γ and type definitions Δ, in a program P. We will write $\Gamma \cup \{X : \tau\}$ to represent the context that contains all assumptions in Γ and the additional assumption $X : \tau$ (note that because each variable is unique as a subject of an assumption in a context, in $\Gamma \cup \{X : \tau\}$, Γ does not contain assumptions with X as subject). We will write a sequence of variables $X_1, \ldots, X_n$ as $\overrightarrow{X}$, and a sequence of types as $\overrightarrow{\tau}$. We assume that clauses are normalized and, therefore, every call to a predicate in the body of a clause contains only variables.

Note that we have a different rule for recursive clauses and non-recursive clauses. Whenever we have a recursive clause, its type is derived assuming every recursive call has the same type as the head of the clause. This corresponds to the monomorphic restriction described in [Hen93], where the authors prove that

$VAR \qquad \Gamma \cup \{X : \sigma\}, \Delta \cup \{\sigma = \tau_1 + \ldots + \tau_n\} \vdash_P X : \tau_i$

$CST \qquad \Gamma, \Delta \vdash_P c : \tau, \text{ where } basetype(c) = \tau$

$CPL^{(a)} \qquad \dfrac{\Gamma, \Delta \vdash_P t_1 : \tau_1 \quad \ldots \quad \Gamma, \Delta \vdash_P t_n : \tau_n}{\Gamma, \Delta \vdash_P f(t_1, \ldots, t_n) : \tau}$

$UNF \qquad \dfrac{\Gamma, \Delta \vdash_P t_1 : \tau \quad \Gamma, \Delta \vdash_P t_2 : \tau}{\Gamma, \Delta \vdash_P t_1 = t_2 : bool}$

$CLL^{(b)} \qquad \dfrac{\Gamma \cup \{\overrightarrow{Y} : \overrightarrow{\sigma\prime}\}, \Delta \vdash_P (p(Y_1, \ldots, Y_n) : -body.) : bool}{\Gamma \cup \{\overrightarrow{X} : \overrightarrow{\sigma}\}, \Delta \cup \{\overrightarrow{\sigma} = \overrightarrow{\tau}\} \vdash_P p(X_1, \ldots, X_n) : bool}, \text{ where } \forall i. \sigma_i \sqsubseteq \sigma_i\prime$

$CON \qquad \dfrac{\Gamma, \Delta \vdash_P g_1 : bool \quad \Gamma, \Delta \vdash_P g_n : bool}{\Gamma, \Delta \vdash_P g_1, \ldots, g_n : bool}$

$CLS^{(c)} \qquad \dfrac{\Gamma, \Delta \vdash_P b_1 : bool \quad \ldots \quad \Gamma, \Delta \vdash_P b_m : bool}{\Gamma, \Delta \vdash_P (p(\overrightarrow{X}) : -b_1; \ldots; b_m.) : bool}$

$RCLS^{(d)} \quad \dfrac{\Gamma \cup \{\overrightarrow{X} : \overrightarrow{\tau}, \overrightarrow{Y_1} : \overrightarrow{\tau}, \ldots, \overrightarrow{Y_{k_n}} : \overrightarrow{\tau}\}, \Delta \vdash_P p(\overrightarrow{X}) : -b_1; \ldots; b_{m+n}. : bool}{\Gamma \cup \{\overrightarrow{X} : \overrightarrow{\tau}, \overrightarrow{Y_1} : \overrightarrow{\tau}, \ldots, \overrightarrow{Y_{k_n}} : \overrightarrow{\tau}\}, \Delta \vdash_P}$

$$(p(\overrightarrow{X}) : -b_1; \ldots; b_m;$$
$$b_{m+1}, p(\overrightarrow{Y_{11}}), \ldots, p(\overrightarrow{Y_{1k_1}});$$
$$\vdots$$
$$b_{m+n}, p(\overrightarrow{Y_{n1}}), \ldots, p(\overrightarrow{Y_{nk_n}}).) : bool$$

(a) Where $basetype(f) = \tau_1\prime \times \ldots \times \tau_n\prime \to \tau$, and $\tau_i \sqsubseteq \tau_i\prime$.
(b) Where the clause defining predicate p is in P.
(c) This rule is for non-recursive predicates only.
(d) This rule is for recursive predicates. Note that all variables in recursive calls in a certain sequence of goals have the same type as the variables in the head in that clause.

Fig. 2. Type System

if we allow polymorphic recursion, i.e. recursion with different instances of the same polymorphic type, then inference is not decidable.

Also note that the type for a predicate call is a subtype of the type for the clause defining it. This captures the fact that we can call a polymorphic predicate with a type that is an instance of the general type scheme, or if the input type of the predicate is a union type, we can call it with only some of the summands of that union.

5   Type Inference

We have seen how to define the notion of *well-typed* program using a set of rules which assign types to programs. Here we will present a type inference algorithm which, given an untyped logic program, is able to calculate a type which makes the program well-typed.

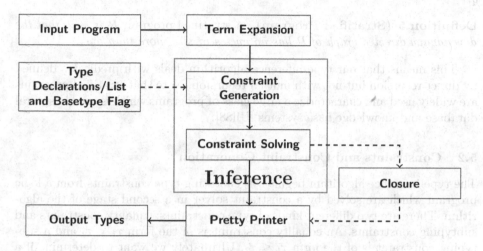

Fig. 3. Type Inference Algorithm Flowchart

Our type inference algorithm is composed of several modules, as described in Fig. 3. On a first step, when consulting programs, we apply term expansion to transform programs into the internal format that the rest of the algorithm expects. Secondly, we have the type inference phase itself, where constraint generation is performed, and a type constraint solver outputs the inferred types for a given program. There is also a simplification step that is performed during inference, to assure that the type definitions are always deterministic and simplified. After this, we either directly run a type pretty printer, or go through closure before printing the types.

Thus the type inference algorithm is composed of four main parts with some auxiliary steps:

- Term expansion
- Constraint generation
- Constraint solving
- Closure (optional).

Without closure or type declarations our algorithm follows a standard approach of types as approximations of the program semantics. Using our algorithm to infer well-typings (which filter program behaviour instead of approximating it) is possible either by using explicit type declarations or by using the closure step. Using one of the latter approaches, instead of the standard one, yields better results as can be seen in the example Sect. 3.

5.1   Stratification

We assume that the input program of our algorithm is *stratified*. To understand the meaning of stratified programs, let us define the *dependency directed graph* of a program as the graph that has one node representing each predicate in the program and an edge from q to p for each call from a predicate p to a predicate q.

Definition 5 (Stratified Program). *A stratified program P is such that the dependency directed graph of P has no cycles of size more than one.*

This means that our type inference algorithm deals with predicates defined by direct recursion but not with mutual recursion. Note that stratified programs are widely used and characterize a large class of programs which is used in several database and knowledge base systems [Ull88].

5.2   Constraints and Constraint Generation

The type inference algorithm begins by generating type constraints from a logic program which are solved by a constraint solver in a second stage of the algorithm. There are two different kinds of type constraints: equality constraints and subtyping constraints. An equality constraint is of the form $\tau_1 = \tau_2$ and a subtyping constraint is of the form $\bar{\tau}_1 \leq \bar{\tau}_2$. Ultimately we want to determine if a set of constraints C can be instantiated affirmatively using some substitution S, that substitutes types for type variables. For this we need to consider a notion of *constraint satisfaction* $S \models C$, in a first order theory with equality [Mah88] and the extra axioms in Definition 4 for subtyping.

Definition 6 (Constraint satisfaction). *Let $\equiv$ mean syntactic type equality and $\sqsubseteq$ the subtyping relation defined in Definition 4. $S \models C$ is defined as follows:*

1. *$S \models \tau_1 = \tau_2$ if and only if $S(\tau_1) \equiv S(\tau_2)$;*
2. *$S \models \bar{\tau}_1 \leq \bar{\tau}_2$ if and only if $S(\bar{\tau}_1) \sqsubseteq S(\bar{\tau}_2)$;*
3. *$S \models C$ if and only if $S \models c$ for each constraint $c \in C$.*

The constraint generation step of the algorithm will output two sets of constraints, Eq (a set of equality constraints) and $Ineq$ (a set of subtyping constraints), that need to be solved during type inference.

Let us first present two auxiliary functions to combine contexts. Contexts can be obtained from the disjunction, or conjunction, of other contexts. For this we define two auxiliary functions, $\oplus$ and $\otimes$, to define the result of disjunction, or conjunction, respectively, of context. These definitions are used by the constraint generation algorithm. They are defined as follows:

Definition 7. *Let Γ_i be contexts, and Δ_i be disjoint sets of type definitions defining the type symbols in Γ_i, respectively. Let V be the set of variables that occur in more than one context.*
$\oplus((\Gamma_1, \dots, \Gamma_n), (\Delta_1, \dots, \Delta_n)) = (\Gamma, \Delta)$, where:

$\Gamma(X) = \sigma\prime$, where $\sigma\prime$ is a fresh type symbol, for all $X \in V$, and $\Gamma(X) = \Gamma_i(X)$, for all $X \notin V \wedge X \in domain(\Gamma_i)$;
$\Delta(\sigma) = \Gamma_{i_1}(X) + \ldots + \Gamma_{i_k}(X)$, for all type symbols $\sigma \notin \Delta_1 \cup \cdots \cup \Delta_n$, and $\Delta(\sigma) = \Delta_i(\sigma)$, otherwise.

Definition 8. Let Γ_i be contexts, and Δ_i be disjoint sets of type definitions defining the type symbols in Γ_i, respectively. Let V be the set of variables that occur in more than one context.
$\otimes((\Gamma_1, \ldots, \Gamma_n), (\Delta_1, \ldots, \Delta_n)) = (\Gamma, \Delta, Eq)$, where:
$\Gamma(X) = \sigma\prime$, where $\sigma\prime$ is a fresh type symbol, for all $X \in V$, and $\Gamma(X) = \Gamma_i(X)$, for all $X \notin V \wedge X \in domain(\Gamma_i)$;
$\Delta(\sigma) = \alpha$, where α is a fresh type variable, for all type symbols $\sigma \notin \Delta_1 \cup \cdots \cup \Delta_n$, and $\Delta(\sigma) = \Delta_i(\sigma)$, otherwise;
$Eq = \{\alpha = \Delta_i(\Gamma_i(X)), \ldots, \alpha = \Delta_j(\Gamma_j(X))\}$, for all fresh α, such that $(\sigma\prime = \alpha) \in \Delta$, $\Gamma(X) = \sigma\prime$, and $X \in domain(\Gamma_i) \wedge \cdots \wedge X \in domain(\Gamma_j)$.

Let P be a term, an atom, a query, a sequence of queries, or a clause. $generate(P)$ is a function that outputs a tuple of the form $(\tau, \Gamma, Eq, Ineq, \Delta)$, where τ is a type, Γ is an context for variables, Eq is a set of equality constraints, $Ineq$ is a set of subtyping constraints, and Δ is a set of type definitions. The function $generate$, which generates the initial type constraints, is defined case by case from the program syntax. Its definition follows:

$generate(P) =$

- $generate(X) = (\alpha, \{X : \sigma\}, \emptyset, \emptyset, \{\sigma = \alpha\})$, X is a variable, where α is a fresh type variable and σ is a fresh type symbol.
- $generate(c) = (basetype(c), \emptyset, \emptyset, \emptyset, \emptyset)$, c is a constant.
- $generate(f(t_1, \ldots, t_n)) = (basetype(f)(\tau_1, \ldots, \tau_n), \Gamma, Eq, \emptyset, \Delta)$, f is a function symbol,
  where $generate(t_i) = (\tau_i, \Gamma_i, Eq_i, \emptyset, \Delta_i)$,
  $(\Gamma, \Delta, Eq\prime) = \otimes((\Gamma_1, \ldots, \Gamma_n), (\Delta_1, \ldots, \Delta_n))$, and
  $Eq = Eq_1 \cup \ldots \cup Eq_n \cup Eq\prime$.
- $generate(t_1 = t_2) = (bool, \Gamma, Eq, \emptyset, \Delta)$
  where $generate(ti) = (\tau_i, \Gamma_i, Eq_i, \emptyset, \Delta_i)$,
  $(\Gamma, \Delta, Eq\prime) = \otimes((\Gamma_1, \Gamma_2), (\Delta_1, \Delta_2))$, and
  $Eq = Eq_1 \cup Eq_2 \cup \{\tau_1 = \tau_2\} \cup Eq\prime$.
- $generate(p(X_1, \ldots, X_n)) = (bool, (\{X_1 : \sigma_1, \ldots, X_n : \sigma_n\}, \emptyset, \{\sigma_1 \leq \tau_1, \ldots, \sigma_n \leq \tau_n\}, \Delta\prime)$, p is a predicate symbol,
  where $generate(p(Y_1, \ldots, Y_n) : -body) = (bool, \Gamma, Eq, Ineq, \Delta)$,
  $\{Y_1 : \tau_1, \ldots Y_n : \tau_n\} \in \Gamma$
  $\Delta\prime = \Delta \cup \{\sigma_i = \alpha_i\}$, and σ_i and α_i are all fresh.
- $generate(c_1, \ldots, c_n) = (bool, \Gamma, Eq, Ineq_1 \cup \ldots \cup Ineq_n, \Delta)$, a query,
  where $generate(c_i) = (bool, \Gamma_i, Eq_i, Ineq_i, \Delta_i)$,
  $(\Gamma, \Delta, Eq\prime) = \otimes((\Gamma_1, \ldots, \Gamma_n), (\Delta_1, \ldots, \Delta_n))$, and
  $Eq = Eq_1 \cup \ldots \cup Eq_n \cup Eq\prime$.

- $generate(b_1; \ldots; b_n) = (bool, \Gamma, Eq_1 \cup \ldots \cup Eq_n, Ineq_1 \cup \ldots \cup Ineq_n, \Delta)$,
  where $generate(c_i) = (bool, \Gamma_i, Eq_i, Ineq_i, \Delta_i)$, and
  $(\Gamma, \Delta) = \oplus((\Gamma_1, \ldots, \Gamma_n), (\Delta_1, \ldots, \Delta_n))$.
- $generate(p(X_1, \ldots, X_n) : -body.) = (bool, \Gamma, Eq, Ineq, \Delta)$, a non-recursive clause,
  where $generate(body) = (bool, \Gamma, Eq, Ineq, \Delta)$.
- $generate(p(X_1, \ldots, X_n) : -body) = (bool, \Gamma, Eq, Ineq\prime, \Delta)$, a recursive clause,
  where $generate(p(X_1, \ldots, X_n) : -body\prime) = (bool, \Gamma, Eq, Ineq, \Delta)$, such that
  $body\prime$ is $body$ after removing all recursive calls,
  and $Ineq\prime = Ineq \cup \{\overrightarrow{\sigma_1} \leq \overrightarrow{\tau}, \ldots, \overrightarrow{\sigma_k} \leq \overrightarrow{\tau}, \overrightarrow{\tau} \leq \overrightarrow{\sigma_1}, \ldots, \overrightarrow{\tau} \leq \overrightarrow{\sigma_k}\}$, such that
  τ are the types for the variables in the head of the clause in Γ and σ_i are the types for the variables in each recursive call.

Example 7. Consider the following predicate:

```
list(X) :- X = []; X = [Y|YS], list(Ys).
```

the output of applying the generate function to the predicate is:
$generate(list(X) : -X = [\,]; X = [Y|Ys], list(Ys)) = \{bool, \{X : \sigma_1, Y : \sigma_2, Ys : \sigma_3\}, \{\alpha = [\,], \beta = [\delta \mid \epsilon]\}, \{\sigma_3 \leq \sigma_1, \sigma_1 \leq \sigma_3\}, \{\sigma_1 = \alpha + \beta, \sigma_2 = \delta, \sigma_3 = \epsilon\}\}$.

The set $\{\sigma_3 \leq \sigma_1, \sigma_1 \leq \sigma_3\}$ comes from the recursive call to the predicate, while $\alpha = [\,]$ comes from $X = [\,]$, and $\beta = [\delta \mid \epsilon]$ comes from $X = [Y|Ys]$. The definition $\sigma_1 = \alpha + \beta$ comes from the application of the $\oplus$ operation.

5.3   Constraint Solving

Let Eq be a set of equality constraints, $Ineq$ be a set of subtyping constraints, and Δ a set of type definitions. Function $solve(Eq, Ineq, \Delta)$ is a rewriting algorithm that solves the constraints, outputting a pair of a substitution and a new set of type definitions. Note that the rewriting rules in the following definitions of the solver algorithm are assumed to be ordered.

Definition 9. *A set of equality constraints is in* solved form *if:*

- *all constraints are of the form $\alpha_i = \tau_i$;*
- *there are no two constraints with the same α_i on the left hand side;*
- *no type variables on the left-hand side of the equations occurs on the right-hand side of equations.*

A set of equality constraints in normal form can be interpreted as a substitution, where each constraint $\alpha_i = \tau_i$ corresponds to a substitution for the type variable α_i, $[\alpha_i \mapsto \tau_i]$.

A *configuration* is either the term *fail* (representing failure), a pair of a substitution and a set of type definitions (representing the end of the algorithm), or a triple of a set of equality constraints Eq, a set of subtyping constraints $Ineq$, and a set of type definitions Δ. The following rewriting algorithm consists of the transformation rules on configurations.

$solve(Eq, Ineq, \Delta) =$

1. $(\{\tau = \tau\} \cup Eq, Ineq, \Delta) \rightarrow (Eq, Ineq, \Delta)$
2. $(\{\alpha = \tau\} \cup Eq, Ineq, \Delta) \rightarrow (\{\alpha = \tau\} \cup Eq[\alpha \mapsto \tau], Ineq[\alpha \mapsto \tau], \Delta[\alpha \mapsto \tau])$, if type variable α occurs in Eq, $Ineq$, or Δ
3. $(\{\tau = \alpha\} \cup Eq, Ineq, \Delta) \rightarrow (\{\alpha = \tau\} \cup Eq, Ineq, \Delta)$, where α is a type variable and τ is not a type variable
4. $(\{f(\tau_1, \ldots, \tau_n) = f(\tau\prime_1, \ldots, \tau\prime_n)\} \cup Eq, Ineq, \Delta \rightarrow (\{\tau_1 = \tau\prime_1, \ldots, \tau_n = \tau\prime_n\} \cup Eq, Ineq, \Delta$
5. $(\{f(\tau_1, \ldots, \tau_n) = g(\tau\prime_1, \ldots, \tau\prime_m)\} \cup Eq, Ineq, \Delta) \rightarrow fail$
6. $(Eq, \{\tau \leq \tau\} \cup Ineq, \Delta) \rightarrow (Eq, Ineq, \Delta)$
7. $(Eq, \{f(\tau_1, \ldots, \tau_n) \leq f(\tau\prime_1, \ldots, \tau\prime_n)\} \cup Ineq, \Delta) \rightarrow (Eq, \{\tau_1 \leq \tau\prime_1, \ldots \tau_n \leq \tau\prime_n\} \cup Ineq, \Delta)$
8. $(Eq, \{\alpha \leq \tau_1, \ldots, \alpha \leq \tau_n\} \cup Ineq, \Delta) \rightarrow (Eq \cup Eq\prime, \{\alpha \leq \tau\} \cup Ineq, \Delta\prime)$, where α is a type variable, $n \geq 2$, and $intersect(\tau_1, \ldots, \tau_n, \Delta, I) = (\tau, Eq\prime, \Delta\prime)$
9. $(Eq, \{\alpha \leq \tau\} \cup Ineq, \Delta) \rightarrow (Eq \cup \{\alpha = \tau\}, Ineq, \Delta)$, where α is a type variable and no other constraints exist with α on the left-hand side
10. $(Eq, \{\tau_1 + \ldots + \tau_n \leq \tau\} \cup Ineq, \Delta) \rightarrow (Eq, \{\tau_1 \leq \tau, \ldots, \tau_n \leq \tau\} \cup Ineq, \Delta)$
11. $(Eq, \{\sigma \leq \tau\} \cup Ineq, \Delta) \rightarrow (Eq, Ineq, \Delta)$, if (σ, τ) are on the store of pairs of types that have already been compared
12. $(Eq, \{\sigma \leq \tau\} \cup Ineq, \Delta) \rightarrow (Eq, \{Rhs_\sigma \leq \tau\} \cup Ineq, \Delta)$, where σ is a type symbol, and $\sigma = Rhs_\sigma \in \Delta$. Also add (σ, τ) to the store of pairs of types that have been compared
13. $(Eq, \{\tau_1 \leq \alpha, \ldots \tau_n \leq \alpha\} \cup Ineq, \Delta) \rightarrow (Eq \cup \{\alpha = \tau_1 + \ldots + \tau_n\}, Ineq, \Delta)$
14. $(Eq, \{\tau \leq \tau_1 + \ldots + \tau_n\} \cup Ineq, \Delta) \rightarrow (Eq, \{\tau \leq \tau_i\} \cup Ineq, \Delta)$, where τ_i is one of the summands
15. $(Eq, \{\tau \leq \sigma\} \cup Ineq, \Delta) \rightarrow (Eq, Ineq, \Delta)$, if (σ, τ) are on the store of pairs of types that have already been compared
16. $(Eq, \{\tau \leq \sigma\} \cup Ineq, \Delta) \rightarrow (Eq, \{\tau \leq Rhs_\sigma\} \cup Ineq, \Delta)$, where σ is a type symbol, and $\sigma = Rhs_\sigma \in \Delta$. Also add (σ, τ) to the store of pairs of types that have been compared
17. $(Eq, \emptyset, \Delta) \rightarrow (Eq, \Delta\prime)$
18. otherwise $\rightarrow$ fail.

Note that an occur check is required in steps 2, 9, and 13. This rewriting algorithm is based on the one described in [Mah88] for equality constraints, and an original one for the subtyping constraints. We will now show an example of the execution of the algorithm on the output of the constraint generation algorithm, showed in Example 7.

Example 8. Following Example 7, applying *solve* to the tuple $(Eq, Ineq, \Delta)$, corresponding to $(\{X : \sigma_1, Y : \sigma_2, Ys : \sigma_3\}, \{\alpha = [\,], \beta = [\delta \mid \epsilon]\}, \{\sigma_3 \leq \sigma_1, \sigma_1 \leq \sigma_3\}, \{\sigma_1 - \alpha + \beta, \sigma_2 = \delta, \sigma_3 = \epsilon\})$:
$(\{\alpha = [\,], \beta = [\delta \mid \epsilon]\}, \{\sigma_3 \leq \sigma_1, \sigma_1 \leq \sigma_3\}, \{\sigma_1 = \alpha + \beta, \sigma_2 = \delta, \sigma_3 = \epsilon\}) \rightarrow_2$
$(\{\alpha = [\,], \beta = [\delta \mid \epsilon]\}, \{\sigma_3 \leq \sigma_1, \sigma_1 \leq \sigma_3\}, \{\sigma_1 = [\,] + \beta, \sigma_2 = \delta, \sigma_3 = \epsilon\}) \rightarrow_2$

$$(\{\alpha = [\,], \beta = [\delta \mid \epsilon]\}, \{\sigma_3 \le \sigma_1, \sigma_1 \le \sigma_3\}, \{\sigma_1 = [\,] + [\delta \mid \epsilon], \sigma_2 = \delta, \sigma_3 = \epsilon\}) \rightarrow_{12}$$
$$(\{\alpha = [\,], \beta = [\delta \mid \epsilon]\}, \{\epsilon \le \sigma_1, \sigma_1 \le \sigma_3\}, \{\sigma_1 = [\,] + [\delta \mid \epsilon], \sigma_2 = \delta, \sigma_3 = \epsilon\}) \rightarrow_9$$
$$(\{\alpha = [\,], \beta = [\delta \mid \epsilon], \epsilon = \sigma_1\}, \{\sigma_1 \le \sigma_3\}, \{\sigma_1 = [\,] + [\delta \mid \epsilon], \sigma_2 = \delta, \sigma_3 = \epsilon\}) \rightarrow_2$$
$$(\{\alpha = [\,], \beta = [\delta \mid \sigma_1], \epsilon = \sigma_1\}, \{\sigma_1 \le \sigma_3\}, \{\sigma_1 = [\,] + [\delta \mid \sigma_1], \sigma_2 = \delta, \sigma_3 = \sigma_1\}) \rightarrow_s$$
$$(\{\alpha = [\,], \beta = [\delta \mid \sigma_1], \epsilon = \sigma_1\}, \{\sigma_1 \le \sigma_1\}, \{\sigma_1 = [\,] + [\delta \mid \sigma_1], \sigma_2 = \delta\}) \rightarrow_6$$
$$(\{\alpha = [\,], \beta = [\delta \mid \sigma_1], \epsilon = \sigma_1\}, \emptyset, \{\sigma_1 = [\,] + [\delta \mid \sigma_1], \sigma_2 = \delta\})$$

Note that the resulting set of constraints only contains constraints in solved form, that can be seen as a substitution. Step $\rightarrow_s$, stands for the following simplification step: if two type definitions are equal, we delete one of them and replace every occurrence of the type symbol by the other. Therefore, the resulting context Γ is $\{X : \sigma_1, Y : \sigma_2, Ys : \sigma_1\}$.

Type intersection is calculated as follows, $intersect(\tau_1, \tau_2, \Delta, I) = (\tau, Eq\prime, \Delta\prime)$, where:

- if both τ_1 and τ_2 are type variables, then $\tau = \tau_2, \Delta\prime = \Delta, Eq\prime = \{\tau_1 = \tau_2\}$.
- if $\tau_1 = \tau_2$, then $\tau = \tau_1, \Delta\prime = \Delta, Eq\prime = \emptyset$.
- if $(\tau_1, \tau_2, \tau_3) \in I$, then $\tau = \tau_3, \Delta\prime = \Delta, Eq\prime = \emptyset$.
- if τ_1 is a type variable, then $\tau = \tau_2, \Delta\prime = \Delta, Eq\prime = \emptyset$.
- if τ_2 is a type variable, then $\tau = \tau_1, \Delta\prime = \Delta, Eq\prime = \emptyset$.
- if $\tau_1 = \sigma_1, \tau_2 = \sigma_2$, and $(\bar{\tau}, Eq, \Delta_2) = cpi(\bar{\tau}_1, \bar{\tau}_2, \Delta, I \cup \{(\tau_1, \tau_2, \tau_3)\})$, then $\tau = \tau_3, \Delta\prime = \Delta_2 \cup \{\tau_3 = \bar{\tau}\}, Eq\prime = Eq$, where $\sigma_1 = \bar{\tau}_1, \sigma_2 = \bar{\tau}_2 \in \Delta$ and τ_3 is fresh.
- if $\tau_1 = \sigma_1, \tau_2 = f(t_1, \ldots, t_n)$, and $(\bar{\tau}, Eq, \Delta_2) = cpi(\bar{\tau}, \tau_2, \Delta, I \cup \{(\tau_1, \tau_2, \tau_3)\})$, then $\tau = \tau_3, \Delta\prime = \Delta \cup \{\tau_3 = \bar{\tau}\}, Eq\prime = Eq$, where $\sigma_1 = \bar{\tau}_1 \in \Delta$ and τ_3 is fresh. Same for $\tau_2 = \sigma_1$ and $\tau_1 = f(t_1, \ldots, t_n)$.
- if $\tau_1 = f(\tau_1, \ldots, \tau_n), \tau_2 = f(\tau\prime_1, \ldots, \tau\prime_n)$, then $\forall i.1 \le i \le n, (\tau\prime\prime_i, Eq_i, \Delta_i) = intersect(\tau_i, \tau\prime_i, \Delta, I), \tau = f(\tau\prime\prime_1, \ldots, \tau\prime\prime_n), \Delta\prime = \Delta_1 \cup \ldots \cup \Delta_n, Eq\prime = Eq_1 \cup \ldots \cup Eq_n$.
- otherwise fail.

$cpi(\bar{\tau}_1, \bar{\tau}_2, \Delta, I)$ is a function that applies $intersect(\tau, \tau\prime, \Delta, I)$ to every pair of types $\tau, \tau\prime$, such that $\tau \in \bar{\tau}_1$ and $\tau\prime \in \bar{\tau}_2$, and gathers all results as the output.

This intersection algorithm is based on the one presented in [Zob87], with a few minor changes. The difference is that our types can be type variables, which could not happen in Zobel's algorithm, since intersection was only calculated between ground types. To deal with this extension, in our algorithm type variables are treated as Zobel's *any* type, except when both types are type variables, in which case we also unify them. Termination and correctness of type intersection for a tuple distributive version of Zobel's algorithm was proved previously in [Lu01] and replacing the *any* type with type variables maintains the same properties, because our use of type intersection considers types where type variables occur only once, thus they can be safely replaced by Zobel's *any* type. Note that we deal with type variables which occur more than once but with calls to type unification.

5.4 Decidability

The next theorem shows that both the equality constraint and subtyping constraint solvers terminate at every input set of constraints.

Theorem 1 (Termination). *solve always terminates, and when solve terminates, it either fails or the output is a pair of a substitution and a new set of type definitions.*

The proof for this theorem follows a usual termination proof approach, where we show that a carefully chosen metric decreases at every step.

To guarantee that the output set of equality constraints is in normal form, in order to be interpreted as a substitution, we also prove the lemma below.

Lemma 1. *If $solve(Eq, Ineq, \Delta) \to^* (S, \Delta\prime)$, then S is in normal form.*

5.5 Soundness

Here we prove that the type inference algorithm is sound, in the sense that inferred types are derivable in the type system, which defines well-typed programs. For this we need the following auxiliary definitions and lemmas which are used in the proofs of the main theorems.

The following lemmas state properties of the constraint satisfaction relation $\models$, subtyping, and the type intersection operation.

Lemma 2. *If we have S such that $S \models C \cup C\prime$, then $S \models C$ and $S \models C\prime$.*

Lemma 3. *If $S \models Eq$ such that $(\Gamma, \Delta, Eq) = \otimes((\Gamma_1, \ldots, \Gamma_n), (\Delta_1, \ldots, \Delta_n))$, and $\forall i.\Gamma_i, S(\Delta_i) \vdash M_i : S(\tau_i)$ then $\forall i.\Gamma, S(\Delta) \vdash M_i : S(\tau_i)$.*

Lemma 4. *If we know for all $i = 1, \ldots, n$ that $\Gamma_i, S(\Delta_i) \vdash b_i : bool$ and we know $(\Gamma, \Delta) = \otimes((\Gamma_1, \ldots, \Gamma_n), (\Delta_1, \ldots, \Delta_n))$, then $\Gamma, S(\Delta) \vdash b_i : bool$.*

Lemma 5. *Let $\tau_1, \ldots, \tau_n, \tau$ be types such that $\forall i.\tau_i \sqsubseteq \tau$. Then $\tau_1 + \ldots + \tau_n \sqsubseteq \tau$.*

Lemma 6. *Let $\tau_1, \ldots, \tau_n, \tau$ be types such that $\exists i.\tau \sqsubseteq \tau_i$. Then $\tau \sqsubseteq \tau_1 + \ldots + \tau_n$.*

Lemma 7. *If $intersect(\tau_1, \tau_2, I, \Delta) = (\tau, Eq, \Delta\prime)$, then $\tau \sqsubseteq \tau_1$, and $\tau \sqsubseteq \tau_2$.*

Proposition 1. *If Eq is a set of equality constraints in normal form, then $Eq \models Eq$.*

Now we have a theorem for the soundness of constraint generation which states that if one applies a substitution which satisfies the generated constraints to the type obtained by the constraint generation function, we get a well-typed program.

Theorem 2 (Soundness of Constraint Generation). *For a program, query, or term P, if $generate(P) = (\tau, \Gamma, Eq, Ineq, \Delta)$, then for any $S \models Eq, Ineq$, we have $\Gamma, S(\Delta) \vdash P : S(\tau)$.*

We also proved the soundness of constraint solving, which basically shows that the solved form returned by our constraint solver for a set of constrains C satisfies C.

Theorem 3 (Soundness of Constraint Solving). *Let Eq be a set of equality constraints, Ineq a set of subtyping constraints, and Δ a set of type definitions. If $solve(Eq, Ineq, \Delta) \rightarrow^* (S, \Delta\prime)$ then $S \models Eq, Ineq$.*

Finally, using the last two theorems we prove the soundness of the type inference algorithm. The soundness theorem states that if one applies the substitution corresponding to the solved form returned by the solver to the type obtained by the constraint generation function, we get a well-typed program.

Theorem 4 (Soundness of Type Inference). *Given P, if $generate(P) = (\tau, \Gamma, Eq, Ineq, \Delta)$ and $solve(Eq, Ineq, \Delta) \rightarrow^* (S, \Delta\prime)$, then $\Gamma, S(\Delta\prime) \vdash P : S(\tau)$.*

6   Related Work

Types have been used before in Prolog systems: relevant works on type systems and type inference in logic programming include types used in the logic programming systems CIAO Prolog [SG95, VB02], SWI and Yap [SCWD08]. CIAO uses types as approximations of the success set, while we use types as filters to the program semantics. There is an option where the programmer gives the types for the programs in the form of assertions, which is recommended in [PCPH08]. The well-typings given in [SBG08], also have the property that they never fail, in the sense that every program has a typing, which is not the case in our algorithm, which will fail for some predicates. The previous system of Yap only type checked predicate clauses with respect to programmer-supplied type signatures. Here we define a new type inference algorithm for pure Prolog, which is able to infer data types.

In several other previous works types approximated the success set of a predicate [Zob87, DZ92, YFS92, BJ88]. This sometimes led to overly broad types, because the way logic programs are written can be very general and accept more than what was initially intended. These approaches were different from ours in the sense that in our work types can filter the success set of a predicate, whenever the programmer chooses to do so, using the closure operation, or data type declarations.

A different approach relied on ideas coming from functional programming languages [MO84, LR91, HL94, SCWD08]. Other examples of the influence of functional languages on types for logic programming are the type systems used in several functional logic programming languages [Han13, SHC96]. Along this line of research, a rather influential type system for logic programs was Mycroft and O'Keefe type system [MO84], which was later reconstructed by Lakshman and Reddy [LR91]. This system had types declared for the constants, function symbols and predicate symbols used in a program. Key differences from our work are: 1) in previous works each clause of a predicate must have the same type.

We lift this limitation extending the type language with sums of types, where the type of a predicate is the sum of the types of its clauses; 2) although we may use type declarations, they are optional and we can use a closure operation to infer datatype declarations from untyped programs.

Set constraints have also been used by many authors to infer types for logic programming languages [HJ92, GdW94, TTD97, CP98, DMP00, DMP02]. Although these approaches differ from ours since they follow the line of conservative approximations to the success set, we were inspired from general techniques from this area to define our type constraint solvers.

7   Final Remarks

In this paper, we present a sound type inference algorithm for pure Prolog. Inferred types are semantic approximations by default, but the user may tune the algorithm, quite easily, to automatically infer types which correspond to the usual data types used in the program. Moreover, the algorithm may also be tuned to use predefined (optional) data type declarations to improve the output types. We proved the soundness of the algorithm, but completeness (meaning that the inferred types are a finite representation of *all* types which make the program well-typed) is an open problem for now. We strongly suspect that the algorithm is complete without closure, but could not prove it yet. On the implementation side we are now extending YAP^T to deal with full Prolog to be able to apply it to more elaborated programs. This includes built-ins and mutually recursive predicates. For this, we will have predefined rules for every built-in predicate and we are also extending the algorithm to generate constraints not for single predicates, but for each strongly connected component on the dependency graph of the program.

References

[BFC19] Barbosa, J., Florido, M., Costa, V.S.: A three-valued semantics for typed logic programming. In: Proceedings 35th International Conference on Logic Programming (Technical Communications), ICLP 2019 Technical Communications, Las Cruces, NM, USA, 20–25 September 2019. EPTCS, vol. 306, pp. 36–51 (2019)

[BFSC17] Barbosa, J., Florido, M., Costa, V.S.: Closed types for logic programming. In: 25th International Workshop on Functional and Logic Programming (WFLP 2017) (2017)

[BG92] Barbuti, R., Giacobazzi, R.: A bottom-up polymorphic type inference in logic programming. Sci. Comput. Program. **19**(3), 281–313 (1992)

[BJ88] Bruynooghe, M., Janssens, G.: An instance of abstract interpretation integrating type and mode inferencing. In: 1988 Fifth International Conference and Symposium, Washington, pp. 669–683 (1988)

[CP98] Charatonik, W., Podelski, A.: Directional type inference for logic programs. In: Levi, G. (ed.) SAS 1998. LNCS, vol. 1503, pp. 278–294. Springer, Heidelberg (1998). https://doi.org/10.1007/3-540-49727-7_17

[Dam84] Damas, L.: Type assignment in programming languages. Ph.D. thesis, University of Edinburgh, UK (1984)

[DMP00] Drabent, W., Małuszyński, J., Pietrzak, P.: Locating type errors in untyped CLP programs. In: Deransart, P., Hermenegildo, M.V., Małuszynski, J. (eds.) Analysis and Visualization Tools for Constraint Programming. LNCS, vol. 1870, pp. 121–150. Springer, Heidelberg (2000). https://doi.org/10.1007/10722311_5

[DMP02] Drabent, W., Małuszyński, J., Pietrzak, P.: Using parametric set constraints for locating errors in CLP programs. Theory Pract. Logic Program. 2(4–5), 549–610 (2002)

[DZ92] Dart, P.W., Zobel, J.: A regular type language for logic programs. In: Pfenning, F. (ed.) Types in Logic Programming, pp. 157–187. The MIT Press (1992)

[FD92] Florido, M., Damas, L.: Types as theories. In: Proceedings of post-conference workshop on Proofs and Types, Joint International Conference and Symposium on Logic Programming (1992)

[FSVY91] Frühwirth, T.W., Shapiro, E.Y., Vardi, M.Y., Yardeni, E.: Logic programs as types for logic programs. In: 1991 Proceedings of the Sixth Annual Symposium on Logic in Computer Science (LICS 1991), Netherlands, pp. 300–309 (1991)

[GdW94] Gallagher, J.P., de Waal, D.A.: Fast and precise regular approximations of logic programs. In: 1994 Logic Programming, International Conference on Logic Programming, Italy, pp. 599–613 (1994)

[Han89] Hanus, M.: Polymorphic high-order programming in prolog. In: Levi, G., Martelli, M. (eds.) Logic Programming, Proceedings of the Sixth International Conference, Lisbon, Portugal, 19–23 June 1989, pp. 382–397. MIT Press (1989)

[Han13] Hanus, M.: Functional logic programming: from theory to curry. In: Voronkov, A., Weidenbach, C. (eds.) Programming Logics. LNCS, vol. 7797, pp. 123–168. Springer, Heidelberg (2013). https://doi.org/10.1007/978-3-642-37651-1_6

[Hen93] Henglein, F.: Type inference with polymorphic recursion. ACM Trans. Program. Lang. Syst. 15(2), 253–289 (1993)

[HJ92] Heintze, N., Jaffar, J.: Semantic types for logic programs. In: Pfenning, F. (ed.) Types in Logic Programming, pp. 141–155. The MIT Press (1992)

[HL94] Hill, P.M., Lloyd, J.W.: The Gödel Programming Language. MIT Press, Cambridge (1994)

[LR91] Lakshman, T.L., Reddy, U.S.: Typed Prolog: a semantic reconstruction of the Mycroft-O'Keefe type system. In Logic Programming, Proceedings of the 1991 International Symposium, San Diego, California, USA (1991)

[Lu01] Lunjin, L.: On Dart-Zobel algorithm for testing regular type inclusion. SIGPLAN Not. 36(9), 81–85 (2001)

[Mah88] Maher, M.: Complete axiomatizations of the algebras of finite, rational and infinite trees. In: Proceedings Third Annual Symposium on Logic in Computer Science, Los Alamitos, CA, USA, pp. 348–357. IEEE Computer Society, July 1988

[Mis84] Mishra, P.: Towards a theory of types in Prolog. In: Proceedings of the 1984 International Symposium on Logic Programming, Atlantic City, New Jersey, USA, 6–9 February 1984, pp. 289–298. IEEE-CS (1984)

[MO84] Mycroft, A., O'Keefe, R.A.: A polymorphic type system for Prolog. Artif. Intell. 23(3), 295–307 (1984)

[Nai92] Naish, L.: Types and the intended meaning of logic programs. In: Pfenning, F. (ed.) Types in Logic Programming, pp. 189–216. The MIT Press (1992)

[PCPH08] Pietrzak, P., Correas, J., Puebla, G., Hermenegildo, M.V.: A practical type analysis for verification of modular Prolog programs. In: Proceedings of the ACM SIGPLAN Symposium on Partial Evaluation and Semantics-Based Program Manipulation, pp. 61–70, January 2008

[PR89] Pyo, C., Reddy, U.S.: Inference of polymorphic types for logic programs. In: 1989 Proceedings of the North American Conference on Logic Programming, USA, 2 Volumes, pp. 1115–1132 (1989)

[SBG08] Schrijvers, T., Bruynooghe, M., Gallagher, J.P.: From monomorphic to polymorphic well-typings and beyond. In: Hanus, M. (ed.) LOPSTR 2008. LNCS, vol. 5438, pp. 152–167. Springer, Heidelberg (2009). https://doi.org/10.1007/978-3-642-00515-2_11

[SCWD08] Schrijvers, T., Santos Costa, V., Wielemaker, J., Demoen, B.: Towards typed Prolog. In: Garcia de la Banda, M., Pontelli, E. (eds.) ICLP 2008. LNCS, vol. 5366, pp. 693–697. Springer, Heidelberg (2008). https://doi.org/10.1007/978-3-540-89982-2_59

[SG95] Sağlam, H., Gallagher, J.P.: Approximating constraint logic programs using polymorphic types and regular descriptions. In: Hermenegildo, M., Swierstra, S.D. (eds.) Programming Languages: Implementations, Logics and Programs, pp. 461–462. Springer, Heidelberg (1995)

[SHC96] Somogyi, Z., Henderson, F., Conway, T.C.: The execution algorithm of Mercury, an efficient purely declarative logic programming language. J. Log. Program. 29(1–3), 17–64 (1996)

[TTD97] Talbot, J.M., Tison, S., Devienne, P.: Set-based analysis for logic programming and tree automata. In: Van Hentenryck, P. (ed.) SAS 1997. LNCS, vol. 1302, pp. 127–140. Springer, Heidelberg (1997). https://doi.org/10.1007/BFb0032738

[Ull88] Ullman, J.D.: Principles of Database and Knowledge-Base Systems, Computer Science Press Inc. (1988)

[VB02] Vaucheret, C., Bueno, F.: More precise yet efficient type inference for logic programs. In: Hermenegildo, M.V., Puebla, G. (eds.) SAS 2002. LNCS, vol. 2477, pp. 102–116. Springer, Heidelberg (2002). https://doi.org/10.1007/3-540-45789-5_10

[VR90] Van Roy, P.L.: Can logic programming execute as fast as imperative programming? Ph.D. thesis, EECS Department, University of California, Berkeley, November 1990

[YFS92] Yardeni, E., Frühwirth, T.W., Shapiro, E.: Polymorphically typed logic programs. In: Pfenning, F. (ed.) Types in Logic Programming, pp. 63–90. The MIT Press (1992)

[Zob87] Zobel, J.: Derivation of polymorphic types for Prolog programs. In: 1987 Proceedings of the Fourth International Conference on Logic Programming, Melbourne (1987)

Automating the Functional Correspondence Between Higher-Order Evaluators and Abstract Machines

Maciej Buszka[ID] and Dariusz Biernacki[✉][ID]

Faculty of Mathematics and Computer Science, University of Wrocław,
Wrocław, Poland
{maciej.buszka,dabi}@cs.uni.wroc.pl

Abstract. The functional correspondence is a manual derivation technique transforming higher-order evaluators into the semantically equivalent abstract machines. The transformation consists of two well-known program transformations: translation to continuation-passing style that uncovers the control flow of the evaluator and Reynolds's defunctionalization that generates a first-order transition function. Ever since the transformation was first described by Danvy et al. it has found numerous applications in connecting known evaluators and abstract machines, but also in discovering new abstract machines for a variety of λ-calculi as well as for logic-programming, imperative and object-oriented languages.

We present an algorithm that automates the functional correspondence. The algorithm accepts an evaluator written in a dedicated minimal functional meta-language and it first transforms it to administrative normal form, which facilitates program analysis, before performing selective translation to continuation-passing style, and selective defunctionalization. The two selective transformations are driven by a control-flow analysis that is computed by an abstract interpreter obtained using the abstracting abstract machines methodology, which makes it possible to transform only the desired parts of the evaluator. The article is accompanied by an implementation of the algorithm in the form of a command-line tool that allows for automatic transformation of an evaluator embedded in a Racket source file and gives fine-grained control over the resulting machine.

Keywords: Evaluator · Abstract machine · Continuation-passing style · Defunctionalization

1 Introduction

When it comes to defining or prototyping a programming language one traditionally provides an interpreter for the language in question (the *object*-language) written in another language (the *meta*-language) [19,31]. These definitional interpreters can be placed on a spectrum from most abstract to most explicit.

© Springer Nature Switzerland AG 2022
E. De Angelis and W. Vanhoof (Eds.): LOPSTR 2021, LNCS 13290, pp. 38–59, 2022.
https://doi.org/10.1007/978-3-030-98869-2_3

At the abstract end lie the concise meta-circular interpreters which use meta-language constructs to interpret the same constructs in the object-language (e.g., using anonymous functions to model functional values, using conditionals for *if* expressions, etc.). In the middle one might place various evaluators with some constructs interpreted by simpler language features (e.g., with environments represented as lists or dictionaries instead of functions), but still relying on the evaluation order of the meta-language. The explicit end is occupied by first-order machine-like interpreters which use an encoding of a stack for handling control-flow of the object-language.

When it comes to modelling an implementation of a programming language, and a functional one in particular, one traditionally constructs an abstract machine, i.e., a first-order tail-recursive transition system for program execution. Starting with Landin's SECD machine [25] for λ-calculus, many abstract machines have been proposed for various evaluation strategies and with differing assumptions on capabilities of the runtime (e.g., substitution vs environments). Notable work includes: Krivine's machine [24] for call-by-name reduction, Felleisen and Friedman's CEK machine [17] and Crégut's machine [13] for normalization of λ-terms in normal order. Manual construction of an abstract machine for a given evaluation discipline can be challenging and it requires a proof of equivalence w.r.t. the higher-level semantics, therefore methods for deriving the machines from natural or reduction semantics have been developed [2,10,15,20,32]. However, one of the most fruitful and accessible abstract machine derivation methods was developed in the realm of interpreters and program transformations by Danvy et al. who introduced a functional correspondence between higher-order evaluators and abstract machines [4] – the topic of the present work.

The functional correspondence is a realization that Reynolds's [31] transformation to continuation-passing style[1] and defunctionalization, which allow one to transform higher-order, meta-circular, compositional definitional interpreters into first-order, tail-recursive ones, can be seen as a general method of actually transforming an encoding of a denotational or natural semantics into an encoding of an equivalent abstract machine. The technique has proven to be indispensable for deriving a correct-by-construction abstract machine given an evaluator in a diverse set of languages and calculi including normal and applicative order λ-calculus evaluation [4] and normalization [8], call-by-need strategy [5] and *Haskell*'s STG language [29], logic engine [11], delimited control [9], computational effects [6], object-oriented calculi [14] and *Coq*'s tactic language [23]. Despite these successes and its mechanical nature, the functional correspondence has not yet been transformed into a working tool which would perform the derivation automatically.

The goal of this work is to give an algorithmic presentation of the functional correspondence that has been implemented by the first author as a semantics transformer. In particular, we describe the steps required to successfully convert

---

[1] The transformation used by Reynolds was later formalized by Plotkin as call-by-value CPS translation [30].

the human-aided derivation method into a computer algorithm for transforming evaluators into a representation of an abstract machine. Our approach hinges on control-flow analysis as the basis for both selective continuation-passing style transformation and partial defunctionalization, and, unlike most of the works treating such transformations [7, 27], we do not rely on a type system. In order to obtain correct, useful and computable analysis we employ the abstracting abstract machines methodology (AAM) [22] which allows for deriving the analysis from an abstract machine for the meta-language. This derivation proved very capable in handling the non-trivial meta-language containing records, anonymous functions and pattern matching. The resulting analysis enables automatic transformation of user specified parts of the interpreter as opposed to whole-program-only transformations. The transformation, therefore, consists of: (1) transformation to administrative normal form (ANF) [18] that facilitates the subsequent steps, (2) control-flow analysis using the AAM technique and selective (based on the analysis) CPS transformation that makes the control flow in the evaluator explicit and idependent from the meta-language, (3) control-flow analysis once more and selective (again, based on the analysis) defunctionalization that replaces selected function spaces with their first-order representations (e.g., closures and stacks), and (4) let inlining that cleans up after the transformation.

The algorithm has been implemented in the *Haskell* programming language giving raise to a tool—semt—performing the transformation. The tool accepts evaluators embedded in Racket source files. Full Racket language is available for testing the evaluators. We tested the tool on multiple interpreters for a diverse set of programming language calculi. It is available at:

https://bitbucket.org/pl-uwr/semantic-transformer

The rest of this article is structured as follows: In Sect. 2, we introduce the *Interpreter Definition Language* which is the meta-language accepted by the transformer and will be used in example evaluators throughout the paper. In Sect. 3, we present the algorithmic characterization of the functional correspondence. In Sect. 4, we briefly discuss the performance of the tool on a selection of case studies. In Sect. 5, we point at future avenues for improvement and conclude. In Appendix A, we illustrate the functional correspondence with a minimal example, for the readers unfamiliar with the CPS transformation and/or defunctionalization. Appendix B contains an extended example—a transformation of a normalization-by-evaluation function for λ-calculus into the corresponding abstract machine.

2 Interpreters and the Meta-language

The *Interpreter Definition Language* or *IDL* is the meta-language used by semt – a semantic transformer that we have developed. It is a purely functional, higher-order, dynamically typed language with strict evaluation order. It features named records and pattern matching which allow for convenient modelling of abstract

```
(def-data Term
  String
  {Abs String Term}
  {App Term Term})

(def init (x) (error "empty environment"))

(def extend (env y v)
  (fun (x) (if (eq? x y) v (env x))))

(def eval (env term)
  (match term
    ([String x] (env x))
    ({Abs x body} (fun (v) (eval (extend env x v) body)))
    ({App fn arg} ((eval env fn) (eval env arg)))))

(def main ([Term term]) (eval init term))
```

Fig. 1. A meta-circular interpreter for λ-calculus

$$x, y, z, f \in Var \qquad r \in StructName \quad s \in String \quad b \in Int \cup Boolean \cup String$$
$$Tp \ni tp ::= \textbf{String} \mid \textbf{Integer} \mid \textbf{Boolean}$$
$$Pattern \ni p ::= x \mid b \mid \_ \mid \{r \ p \ldots\} \mid [tp \ x]$$
$$Term \ni t ::= x \mid b \mid (\textbf{fun} \ (x \ldots) \ t) \mid (t \ t \ldots) \mid \{r \ t \ldots\}$$
$$\mid (\textbf{let} \ p \ t \ t) \mid (\textbf{match} \ t \ (p \ t) \ldots) \mid (\textbf{error} \ s)$$

Fig. 2. Abstract syntax of the *IDL* terms

syntax of the object-language as well as base types of integers, booleans and strings. The concrete syntax is in fully parenthesized form and the programs can be embedded in a Racket source file using a provided library with syntax definitions.

As shown in Fig. 1 a typical interpreter definition consists of several top-level function definitions which may be mutually recursive. The def-data form introduces a datatype definition. In our case it defines a type Term for terms of λ-calculus. It is a union of three types: Strings representing variables of λ-calculus; records with label Abs and two fields of types String and Term representing abstractions; and records labeled App which contain two Terms and represent applications. A datatype definition may refer to itself, other previously defined datatypes and records, the base types of String, Integer and Boolean or a placeholder type Any. The main function is treated as an entry point for the evaluator and must have its arguments annotated with their type.

The match expression matches an expression against a list of patterns. Patterns may be variables (which will be bound to the value being matched), wildcards _, base type patterns, e.g., [String x] or record patterns, such as {Abs x body}. The fun form introduces anonymous function, error "..."

stops execution and signals the error. Finally, application of a function is written
as in Racket, i.e., as a list of expressions (e.g., (eval init term)). The evaluator in Fig. 1 takes advantage of the functional representation of environments
(init and extend) and it structurally recursively interprets λ-terms (eval).
The evaluation strategy for the object-language is in this case inherited from
the meta-language, and, therefore, call by value (we assumed *IDL* strict) [31].

The abstract syntax of the *IDL* terms is presented in Fig. 2. The meta-
variables x, y, z denote variables; r denotes structure (aka record) names; s is
used to denote string literals and b is used for all literal values – strings, integers
and booleans. The meta-variable tp is used in pattern matches which check
whether a value is one of the primitive types. The patterns are referred to with
variable p and may be a variable, a literal value, a wildcard, a record pattern
or a type test. Terms are denoted with variable t and are either a variable, a
literal value, an anonymous function, an application, a record constructor, a let
binding (which may destructure bound term with a pattern), a pattern match
or an error expression.

3   Transformation

The transformation described in this section consists of three main stages: translation to administrative normal form, selective translation to continuation-passing style, and selective defunctionalization. After defunctionalization the program is in the desired form of an abstract machine. The last step taken by
the transformer is inlining of administrative let-bindings introduced by previous
steps in order to obtain more readable results. In the remainder of this section
we will describe the three main stages of the transformation and the algorithm
used to compute the control-flow analysis.

3.1   Administrative Normal Form

The administrative normal form (ANF) [18] is an intermediate representation for
functional languages in which all intermediate results are let-bound to names.
This shape greatly simplifies later transformations as programs do not have
complicated sub-expressions. From the operational point of view, the only place
where a continuation is grown when evaluating program in ANF is a let-binding.
This property ensures that a program in ANF is also much easier to evaluate
using an abstract machine which will be taken advantage of in Sect. 3.2. The
abstract syntax of terms in ANF and an algorithm for transforming *IDL* programs into such form is presented in Fig. 3. The terms are partitioned into
three levels: variables, commands and expressions. Commands c extend variables
with values – base literals, record constructors (with variables as sub-terms) and
abstractions (whose bodies are in ANF); and with redexes like applications of
variables and match expressions (which match on a variable and have branches
in ANF). Expressions e in ANF have the shape of a possibly empty sequence of
let-bindings ending with either an error term or a command.

$$Com \ni c \quad ::= x \mid b \mid (\texttt{fun } (x \ldots) \ e) \mid (x \ x \ldots)$$
$$\mid \{r \ x \ldots\} \mid (\texttt{match } x \ (p \ e) \ldots)$$
$$Anf \ni e \quad ::= c \mid (\texttt{let } p \ c \ e) \mid (\texttt{error } s)$$

$$[\![\cdot]\!] \cdot \ : Term \times (Com \to Anf) \to Anf$$
$$[\![x]\!] \ k = k \, x$$
$$[\![b]\!] \ k = k \, b$$
$$[\![(\texttt{fun } (x \ldots) \ e)]\!] \ k = k \, (\texttt{fun } (x \ldots) \ [\![e]\!] \, id)$$
$$[\![(e_f \ e_{arg} \ldots)]\!] \ k = [\![e_f]\!] \, [\lambda x_f . \, [\![e_{arg} \ldots]\!]_s \, \lambda(x_{arg} \ldots).k \, (x_f \ x_{arg} \ldots)]_a$$
$$[\![(\texttt{let } p \ e_1 \ e_2)]\!] \ k = [\![e_1]\!] \, \lambda c_1.(\texttt{let } p \ c_1 \ [\![e_2]\!] \, k)$$
$$[\![\{r \ e \ldots\}]\!] \ k = [\![e \ldots]\!]_s \, \lambda(x \ldots).k \, \{r \ x \ldots\}$$
$$[\![(\texttt{match } e \ (p \ e_b))]\!] \ k = [\![e]\!] \, [\lambda x.k \, (\texttt{match } x \ (p \ [\![e_b]\!] \, id)]_a$$
$$[\![(\texttt{error } s)]\!] \ \_ = (\texttt{error } s)$$

$$[\cdot]_a \cdot \ : (Var \to Anf) \to Com \to Anf$$
$$[k]_a \ x = k \, x$$
$$[k]_a \ c = (\texttt{let } x \ c \ (k \, x))$$

$$[\![\cdot]\!]_s \cdot \ : Term^* \times (Var^* \to Anf) \to Anf$$
$$[\![e \ldots]\!]_s \ k = go(e \ldots, \epsilon, k)$$
$$go(\epsilon, x \ldots, k) \ = k \, (x \ldots)$$
$$go(e \, e_r \ldots, x_{acc} \ldots, k) \ = [\![e]\!] \, [\lambda x. go(e_r \ldots, x_{acc} \ldots x, k)]_a$$

Fig. 3. ANF transformation for *IDL*

The $[\![\cdot]\!]\cdot$ function, written in CPS[2], is the main transformation function. Its arguments are a term to be transformed and a meta-language continuation which will be called to obtain the term for the rest of the transformed input. This function decomposes the term according to the (informal) evaluation rules and uses two helper functions. Function $[\cdot]_a$ transforms a continuation expecting a variable (which are created when transforming commands) into one accepting any command by let-binding the passed argument c when necessary. Function $[\![\cdot]\!]_s\cdot$ sequences computation of multiple expressions by creating a chain of let-bindings (using $[\cdot]_a$) and then calling the continuation with created variables.

3.2 Control-Flow Analysis

The analysis most relevant to the task of deriving abstract machines from interpreters is the control-flow analysis. Its objective is to find for each expression in a program an over-approximation of a set of functions it may evaluate to [28]. This information can be used in two places: when determining whether a function and applications should be CPS transformed and for checking which functions an expression in operator position may evaluate to. There are a couple of different approaches to performing this analysis available in the literature: abstract interpretation [28], (annotated) type systems [28] and abstract abstract

---

[2] See Appendix A of [18].

$$\nu \in VAddr \ \kappa \in KAddr \quad l \in Label \quad \sigma \in Store$$
$$\delta \in PrimOp \subseteq Val^* \to Val$$
$$\rho \in Env = Var \to VAddr$$
$$Val \ni v ::= b \mid \delta \mid \{r\ \nu \ldots\} \mid \langle \rho, x \ldots, e \rangle \mid (\texttt{def}\ x\ (x \ldots)\ e)$$
$$Cont \ni k ::= \langle \rho, p, e, \kappa \rangle \mid \langle \rangle$$
$$PartialConf \ni \gamma ::= \langle \rho, e, \kappa \rangle_e \mid \langle \nu, \kappa \rangle_c$$
$$Conf \ni \varsigma ::= \langle \sigma, \gamma \rangle$$

$$\langle \sigma, \langle \rho, x, \kappa \rangle_e \rangle \Rightarrow \langle copy_v(\rho(x), l, \sigma), \langle \rho(x), \kappa \rangle_c \rangle$$
$$\langle \sigma, \langle \rho, b^l, \kappa \rangle_e \rangle \Rightarrow \langle \sigma', \langle \nu, \kappa \rangle_c \rangle$$
$$\text{where } \langle \sigma', \nu \rangle = alloc_v(b, l, \sigma)$$
$$\langle \sigma, \langle \rho, \{r\ x \ldots\}^l, \kappa \rangle_e \rangle \Rightarrow \langle \sigma', \langle \nu, \kappa \rangle_c \rangle$$
$$\text{where } \langle \sigma', \nu \rangle = alloc_v(\{r\ \rho(x) \ldots\}, l, \sigma)$$
$$\langle \sigma, \langle \rho, (\texttt{fun}\ (x \ldots)e)^l, \kappa \rangle_e \rangle \Rightarrow \langle \sigma', \langle \nu, \kappa \rangle_c \rangle$$
$$\text{where } \langle \sigma', \nu \rangle = alloc_v(\langle \rho, x \ldots, e \rangle, l, \sigma)$$
$$\langle \sigma, \langle \rho, (\texttt{let}\ p\ c^l\ e), \kappa \rangle_e \rangle \Rightarrow \langle \sigma', \langle \rho, c, \kappa' \rangle_e \rangle$$
$$\text{where } \langle \sigma', \kappa' \rangle = alloc_k(\langle \rho, p, e, \kappa \rangle, l, \sigma)$$
$$\langle \sigma, \langle \rho, (x\ y \ldots), \kappa \rangle_e \rangle \Rightarrow apply(\sigma, \rho(x), \rho(y) \ldots, l)$$
$$\langle \sigma, \langle \rho, (\texttt{match}\ x\ (p\ e) \ldots), \kappa \rangle_e \rangle \Rightarrow match(\sigma, \rho, \rho(x), \langle p, e \rangle \ldots)$$
$$\langle \sigma, \langle \nu, \kappa \rangle_c \rangle \Rightarrow match(\sigma, \rho, \nu, \kappa', \langle p, e \rangle))$$
$$\text{where } \langle \rho, p, e, \kappa' \rangle = deref_k(\sigma, \kappa)$$

$$apply(\sigma, \nu, \nu' \ldots, \kappa, l) = \begin{cases} \langle \sigma, \langle \rho[(x \mapsto \nu') \ldots], e, \kappa \rangle_e \rangle \\ \quad \text{when } deref_v(\sigma, \nu) = \langle \rho, x \ldots, e \rangle \\ \langle \sigma, \langle \rho_0[(x \mapsto \nu') \ldots], e, \kappa \rangle_e \rangle \\ \quad \text{when } deref_v(\sigma, \nu) = (\texttt{def}\ y\ (x \ldots)\ e) \\ \langle \sigma', \langle \nu'', \kappa \rangle_c \rangle \\ \quad \text{when } deref_v(\sigma, \nu) = \delta \\ \quad \text{and } \langle \sigma', \nu'' \rangle = alloc_v(\delta(\sigma(\nu') \ldots), l, \sigma) \end{cases}$$
$$match(\sigma, \rho, \nu, \kappa, \langle p, e \rangle \ldots) = \langle \sigma, \langle \rho', e', \kappa \rangle_e \rangle \text{ where } \rho' \text{ is the environment}$$
$$\text{for the first matching branch with body } e'$$

Fig. 4. A template abstract machine for *IDL* terms in ANF

machines [22]. We chose to employ the last approach as it allows for derivation of the control-flow analysis from an abstract machine for *IDL*. The derivation technique guarantees correctness of the resulting interpreter and hence provides high confidence in the actual implementation of the machine. We next present the template for acquiring both concrete and abstract versions of the abstract machine for *IDL*. The former machine defines the semantics of *IDL*; the latter computes the CFA.

A Machine Template. We will begin with a template of a machine for *IDL* terms in A-normal form, presented in Fig. 4. It is a CEK-style machine modified to explicitly allocate memory for values and continuations in an abstract store. The template is parameterized by: implementation of the store σ along with five operations: $alloc_v$, $alloc_k$, $deref_v$, $deref_k$ and $copy_v$; interpretation of primitive operations δ and implementation of *match* function which interprets pattern matching. The store maps value addresses ν to values v and continuation addresses κ to continuations k. The environment maps program variables to value locations. The values on which the machine operates are the following: base values b, primitive operations δ, records with addresses as fields, closures and top-level functions. Thanks to terms being in A-normal form, there are only two kinds of continuations which form a stack. The stack frames $\langle \rho, p, e, \kappa \rangle$ are introduced by let-bindings. They hold an environment ρ, a pattern p to use for destructuring a value, the body e of a let expression and a pointer to the next continuation κ. The bottom of the stack is marked by the empty continuation $\langle \rangle$. We assume that every term has a unique label l which will be used in the abstract version of the machine to implement store addresses.

The machine configurations are pairs of a store σ and a partial configuration γ. This split of configuration into two parts will prove beneficial when we instantiate the template to obtain an abstract interpreter. There are two classes of partial configurations. An evaluation configuration contains an environment ρ, an expression e and a continuation pointer κ. A continuation configuration holds an address ν of a value that has been computed so far and a pointer κ to a resumption which should be applied next.

The first case of the transition relation $\Rightarrow$ looks up a pointer for the variable x in the environment ρ and switches to continuation mode. It modifies the store via *copy* function which ensures that every occurrence of a variable has a corresponding binding in the store. The next three cases deal with values by *alloc*ating them in the store and switching to continuation mode. When the machine encounters a let-binding it allocates a continuation for the body e of the expression and proceeds to evaluate the bound command c with the new pointer κ'. In case of applications and match expressions the resulting configuration is decided using auxiliary functions *apply* and *match*, respectively. Finally, in continuation mode, the machine may only transition if the continuation loaded from the address κ is a frame. In such a case the machine matches the stored pattern against the value pointed-to by ν. Otherwise κ points to a $\langle \rangle$ instead and the machine has reached the final state. The auxiliary function *apply* checks what kind of function is referenced by ν and proceeds accordingly.

A Concrete Abstract Machine. The machine template can now be instantiated with a store, a *match* implementation which finds the first matching branch and interpretation for primitive operations in order to obtain a concrete abstract machine. By choosing *Store* to be a mapping with infinite domain we can ensure that *alloc* can always return a fresh address. In this setting the store-allocated continuations are just an implementation of a stack. The extra layer of indirection introduced by storing values in a store can also be disregarded as the machine operates on persistent values. Therefore, the resulting machine, which we omit, corresponds to a CEK-style abstract machine which is a canonical formulation for call-by-value functional calculi [16].

$$VAddr = KAddr = Label$$
$$\widetilde{Val} \ni v ::= tp \mid \widetilde{\delta} \mid \{r\, \nu \ldots\} \mid \langle \rho, x \ldots, e \rangle \mid (\text{def } x\ (x \ldots)\ e)$$
$$\sigma \in Store = (VAddr \rightarrow \mathbb{P}(\widetilde{Val})) \times (KAddr \rightarrow \mathbb{P}(Cont))$$
$$alloc_v(v, l, \langle \sigma_v, \sigma_k \rangle) = \langle \langle \sigma_v[l \mapsto \sigma_v(l) \cup \{v\}], \sigma_k \rangle, l \rangle$$
$$alloc_k(v, l, \langle \sigma_v, \sigma_k \rangle) = \langle \langle \sigma_v, \sigma_k[l \mapsto \sigma_k(l) \cup \{k\}] \rangle, l \rangle$$
$$copy_v(\nu, l, \langle \sigma_v, \sigma_k \rangle) = \langle \sigma_v[l \mapsto \sigma_v(l) \cup \sigma_v(\nu)], \sigma_k \rangle$$
$$deref_v(l, \langle \sigma_v, \sigma_k \rangle) = \sigma_v$$
$$\tilde{\varsigma} \in \widetilde{Conf} = Store \times \mathbb{P}(PartialConf)$$

$$\langle \sigma, C \rangle \Rightarrow_a \langle \sigma' \sqcup \sigma, C \cup C' \rangle$$
$$\text{where } \sigma' = \bigsqcup \{\sigma' \mid \exists \gamma \in C.\, \langle \sigma, \gamma \rangle \Rightarrow \langle \sigma', \gamma' \rangle\}$$
$$\text{and } C' = \{\gamma' \mid \exists \gamma \in C.\, \langle \sigma, \gamma \rangle \Rightarrow \langle \sigma', \gamma' \rangle\}$$

Fig. 5. An abstract abstract machine for *IDL*

An Abstract Abstract Machine. Let us now turn to a different instantiation of the template. Figure 5 shows the missing pieces of an abstract abstract machine for *IDL*. The abstract values use base type names *tp* to represent any value of that type, abstract versions of primitive operations, records, closures and top-level functions. The interpretation of primitive operations must approximate their concrete counterparts.

The store is represented as a pair of finite mappings from labels to sets of abstract values and continuations, respectively. This bounding of store domain and range ensures that the state-space of the machine becomes finite and therefore can be used for computing an analysis. To retain soundness w.r.t. the concrete abstract machine the store must map a single address to multiple values to account for address reuse. This style of abstraction is classical [28] and fairly straightforward [22]. When instantiated with this store, the transition relation $\Rightarrow$ becomes nondeterministic as pointer *deref*erencing nondeterministically returns one of the values available in the store. Additionally the implementation of the *match* function is also nondeterministic in the choice of the branch to match against.

This machine is not yet suitable for computing the analysis as the state space is still too large since every machine configuration has its own copy of the store. To circumvent this problem a standard technique of widening [28] can be employed. In particular, following [22], we use a global store. The abstract configuration $\tilde{\varsigma}$ is a pair of a store and a set of partial configurations. The abstract transition $\Rightarrow_a$ performs one step of computation using $\Rightarrow$ on the global store σ paired with every partial configuration γ. The resulting stores σ' are merged together and with the original store to create a new, extended global store. The partial configurations C' are added to the initial set of configurations C. The transition relation $\Rightarrow_a$ is deterministic so it can be treated as a function. This function is monotone on a finite lattice and therefore is amenable to fixed-point iteration.

$$[\![x]\!]_c\, k = (k\ x)$$
$$[\![b]\!]_c\, k = (\text{let}\ x\ b\ (k\ x))$$
$$[\![\{r\ x\ldots\}]\!]_c\, k = (\text{let}\ y\ \{r\ x\ldots\}\ (k\ y))$$
$$[\![(\text{fun}\ \#\text{:atomic}\ (x\ldots)e)]\!]_c\, k = (\text{let}\ y\ (\text{fun}\ (x\ldots)\ [\![e]\!]_d)\ (k\ y))$$
$$[\![(\text{fun}\ (x\ldots)e)]\!]_c\, k = (\text{let}\ y\ (\text{fun}\ (x\ldots k')\ [\![e]\!]_c k')\ (k\ y))$$
$$[\![(f^l\ x\ldots)]\!]_c\, k = \begin{cases} (f\ x\ldots\ k) & \text{when}\ noneA(l) \\ (\text{let}\ y\ (f\ x\ldots)\ (k\ y)) & \text{when}\ allA(l) \end{cases}$$
$$[\![(\text{match}\ x\ (p\ e)\ldots)]\!]_c\, k = (\text{match}\ x\ (p\ [\![e]\!]_c k)\ldots)$$
$$[\![(\text{let}\ p\ c\ e)]\!]_c\, k = \begin{cases} (\text{let}\ p\ [\![c]\!]_d\ [\![e]\!]_c k) & \text{when}\ trivial(c) \\ (\text{let}\ k'\ (\text{fun}\ (y)\ (\text{let}\ p\ y\ [\![e]\!]_c k))\ [\![c]\!]_c k') \end{cases}$$
$$[\![(\text{error}\ s)]\!]_c\, k = (\text{error}\ s)$$

Fig. 6. A translation for CPS terms

Computing the Analysis. With the abstract transition function in hand we can now specify the algorithm for obtaining the analysis. To start the abstract interpreter we must provide it with an initial configuration: a store, an environment, a term and a continuation pointer. The store will be assembled from datatype and structure definitions of the program as well as base types. The initial term is the body of the main function of the interpreter and the environment is the global environment extended with main's parameters bound to pointers to datatypes in the above-built store. The initial continuation is of course $\langle\rangle$ and the pointer is the label of the body of the main function. The analysis is computed by performing fixed-point iteration of $\Rightarrow_a$. The resulting store will contain a set of functions to which every variable (the only allowed term) in function position may evaluate (ensured by the use of $copy_v$ function). This result will be used in Sects. 3.3 and 3.4.

3.3 Selective CPS Transformation

In this section we formulate an algorithm for selectively transforming the program into continuation-passing style. All functions (both anonymous and top-level) marked #:atomic by the user will be kept in direct style. The main function is implicitly marked as atomic since its interface should be preserved as it is an entry point of the interpreter. Primitive operations are treated as atomic at call-site. Atomic functions may call non-atomic ones by providing the called function an identity continuation. The algorithm uses the results of the control-flow analysis to determine atomicity of functions to which a variable labeled l in function position may evaluate. If all functions are atomic then $allA(l)$ holds; if none of them are atomic then $noneA(l)$ holds. When both atomic and non-atomic functions may be called the algorithm cannot proceed and signals an error in the source program.

The algorithm consists of two mutually recursive transformations. The first, $[\![e]\!]_c k$ in Fig. 6 transforms a term e into CPS. Its second parameter is a program variable k which will bind the continuation at runtime. The second, $[\![e]\!]_d$ in Fig. 7 transforms a term e which should be kept in direct style.

$$[\![x]\!]_d = x$$
$$[\![b]\!]_d = b$$
$$[\![\{r\ x \ldots\}]\!]_d = \{r\ x \ldots\}$$
$$[\![(\texttt{fun}\ \texttt{\#:atomic}\ (x \ldots) e)]\!]_d = (\texttt{fun}\ (x \ldots)\ [\![e]\!]_d)$$
$$[\![(\texttt{fun}\ (x \ldots) e)]\!]_d = (\texttt{fun}\ (x \ldots k')\ [\![e]\!]_c\ k')$$
$$[\![(f^l\ x \ldots)]\!]_d = \begin{cases} (f\ x \ldots) & \text{when } allA(l) \\ (\texttt{let}\ k\ (\texttt{fun}\ (y)\ y)\ (f\ x \ldots\ k)) & \text{when } noneA(l) \end{cases}$$
$$[\![(\texttt{match}\ x\ (p\ e) \ldots)]\!]_d = (\texttt{match}\ x\ (p\ [\![e]\!]_d) \ldots)$$
$$[\![(\texttt{let}\ p\ (f^l\ y \ldots)\ e)]\!]_d = \begin{matrix} (\texttt{let}\ k\ (\texttt{fun}\ (z)\ z) \\ (\texttt{let}\ p\ (f\ y \ldots\ k)\ [\![e]\!]_d)) \end{matrix} \quad \text{when } noneA(l)$$
$$[\![(\texttt{let}\ p\ c\ e)]\!]_d = (\texttt{let}\ p\ [\![c]\!]_d\ [\![e]\!]_d)$$
$$[\![(\texttt{error}\ s)]\!]_d = (\texttt{error}\ s)$$

Fig. 7. A translation for terms which should be left in direct style

The first five clauses of the CPS translation deal with values. When a variable is encountered it may be immediately returned by applying a continuation. In other cases the value must be let-bound in order to preserve the A-normal form of the term and then the continuation is applied to the introduced variable. The body e of an anonymous function is translated using $[\![e]\!]_d$ when the function is marked atomic. When the function is not atomic a new variable k' is appended to its parameter list and its body is translated using $[\![e]\!]_c k'$. The form of an application depends on the atomicity of functions which may be applied. When none of them is atomic the continuation k is passed to the function. When all of them are atomic the result of the call is let-bound and returned by applying the continuation k. Match expression is transformed by recursing on its branches. Since the continuation is always a program variable no code gets duplicated. When transforming a let expression the algorithm checks whether the bound command c is *trivial* – meaning it will call only atomic functions when evaluated If it is, then it can remain in direct style $[\![c]\!]_d$, no new continuation has to be introduced and the body can be transformed by $[\![e]\!]_c k$. If the command is non-trivial then a new continuation is created and bound to k'. This continuation uses a fresh variable y as its parameter. Its body is the let-expression binding y instead of command c and with body e transformed with the input continuation k. The bound command c is transformed with the newly introduced continuation k'. Finally, the translation of **error** throws out the continuation.

The transformation for terms which should be kept in direct style begins similarly to the CPS one – with five clauses for values. In case of an application the algorithm considers two possibilities: when all functions are atomic the call remains in direct style, when none of them are atomic a new identity continuation k is constructed and is passed to the called function. A match expression is again transformed recursively. A let binding of a call to a CPS function gets special treatment to preserve A-normal form by chaining allocation of identity continuation with the call. In other cases a let binding is transformed recursively. An **error** expression is left untouched.

```
(def eval (env term k)
  (match term
    ([String x] (k (env x)))
    ({Abs x body}
      (k (fun (v k') (eval (extend env x v) body k'))))
    ({App fn arg}
      (eval env fn
        (fun (fn') (eval env arg (fun (v) (fn' v k))))))))

(def main ([Term term]) (eval init term (fun (x) x)))
```

Fig. 8. An interpreter for λ-calculus in CPS

Each top-level function definition in a program is transformed in the same fashion as anonymous functions. After the transformation the program is still in ANF and can be again analyzed by the abstract abstract machine of the previous section. CPS-transforming the direct-style interpreter of Fig. 1 yields an interpreter in CPS shown in Fig. 8 (after let-inlining for readability), where we assume that the operations on environments were marked as atomic and therefore have not changed.

3.4 Selective Defunctionalization

The second step of the functional correspondence and the last stage of the transformation is selective defunctionalization. The goal is to defunctionalize function spaces deemed interesting by the author of the program. To this end top-level and anonymous functions may be annotated with #:no-defun to skip defunctionalization of function spaces they belong to. In the algorithm of Fig. 9 the predicate *defun* specifies whether a function should be transformed. Predicates *primOp* and *topLevel* specify whether a variable refers to (taking into account the scoping rules) primitive operation or top-level function, respectively. There are three cases to consider when transforming an application. If the variable in operator position refers to top-level function or primitive operation it can be left as is. Otherwise we can utilize the results of control-flow analysis to obtain the set of functions which may be applied. When all of them should be defunctionalized (*allDefun*) then a call to the generated apply function is introduced, when none of them should (*noneDefun*) then the application is left as is. If the requirements are mixed then an error in the source program is signaled. To transform an abstraction, its free variables ($fvs(l)$) are collected into a record. The apply functions are generated using *mkApply* as specified in Fig. 10 where the $fn \ldots$ is a list of functions which may be applied. After the transformation the program is no longer in A-normal form since variables referencing top-level functions may have been transformed into records. However it does not pose a problem since the majority of work has already been done and the last step – let-inlining does not require the program to be in ANF. Defunctionalizing the CPS interpreter

$$[\![x]\!] = \begin{cases} \{\texttt{Prim}_x\} & \text{when } primOp(x) \\ \{\texttt{Top}_x\} & \text{when } topLevel(x) \wedge defun(x) \\ x & \text{otherwise} \end{cases}$$

$$[\![b]\!] = b$$
$$[\![\{\texttt{r } x \ldots\}]\!] = \{\texttt{r } [\![x]\!] \ldots\}$$

$$[\![(\texttt{fun } (x \ldots)e)^l]\!] = \begin{cases} \{\texttt{Fun}_l \ fvs(l)\} & \text{when } defun(l) \\ (\texttt{fun } (x \ldots) \ [\![e]\!]) & \text{otherwise} \end{cases}$$

$$\left[\!\left[(f^{l'} \ x \ldots)^l\right]\!\right] = \begin{cases} (f \ [\![x]\!] \ldots) & \text{when } primOp(f) \vee topLevel(f) \\ (\texttt{apply}_l \ f \ [\![x]\!] \ldots) & \text{else when } allDefun(l') \\ (f \ [\![x]\!] \ldots) & \text{when } noneDefun(l') \end{cases}$$

$$[\![(\texttt{match } x \ (p \ e) \ldots)]\!] = (\texttt{match } x \ (p \ [\![e]\!]) \ldots)$$
$$[\![(\texttt{let } p \ c \ e)]\!] = (\texttt{let } p \ [\![c]\!] \ [\![e]\!])$$
$$[\![(\texttt{error } s)]\!] = (\texttt{error } s)$$

Fig. 9. Selective defunctionalization algorithm for *IDL*

$$mkBranch(x \ldots, \qquad\qquad \delta) = (\{\texttt{Prim}_\delta\} \ (\delta \ x \ldots))$$
$$mkBranch(x \ldots, (\texttt{def } f \ (y \ldots) \ e)) = (\{\texttt{Top}_f\} \ (f \ x \ldots))$$
$$mkBranch(x \ldots, \quad (\texttt{fun } (y \ldots) \ e)^l) = (\{\texttt{Fun}_l \ fvs(l)\} \ [\![e]\!] \ [y \mapsto x])$$

$$mkApply(l, fn \ldots) = \begin{array}{l} (\texttt{def } \texttt{apply}_l \ (f \ x \ldots) \\ \quad (\texttt{match } f \\ \qquad mkBranch(x \ldots, fn) \ldots)) \end{array}$$

Fig. 10. Top-level apply function generation

of Fig. 8 and performing let-inlining yields an encoding of the CEK abstract machine shown in Fig. 11 (again, the environment is left intact).

4   Case Studies

We studied the efficacy of the algorithm and the implementation on a number of programming language calculi. Figure 12 shows a summary of interpreters on which we tested the transformer. The first group of interpreters is denotational (mostly meta-circular) in style and covers various extensions of the base λ-calculus with call-by-value evaluation order. The additions we tested include: integers with addition, recursive let-bindings, delimited control operators – *shift* and *reset* with CPS interpreter based on [9] and exceptions in two styles: monadic with exceptions as values (functions return either value or an exception) and in CPS with success and error continuations. The last interpreter for call-by-value in Fig. 12 is a normalization function based on normalization by evaluation technique transcribed from [1]. We find this result particularly satisfactory, since it leads to a non-trivial and previously unpublished abstract machine – we give more details in Appendix B. The next three interpreters correspond to big-step operational semantics for call-by-name λ-calculus, call-by-need (call-by-name with memoization) and a simple imperative language, respectively.

```
(def-data Cont
  {Halt}
  {App1 arg env cont}
  {App2 fn cont})

(def-struct {Closure body env x})

(def eval (env term cont)
  (match term
    ([String x] (continue cont (env x)))
    ({Abs x body} (continue cont {Closure body env x}))
    ({App fn arg} (eval env fn {App1 arg env cont}))))

(def apply (fn v cont)
  (let {Fun body env x} fn)
    (eval (extend env x v) body cont))

(def continue (cont val)
  (match cont
    ({Halt} val))
    ({App1 arg env cont} (eval env arg {App2 val cont}))
    ({App2 fn cont} (apply fn val cont)))

(def main ([Term term]) (eval {Init} term {Halt}))
```

Fig. 11. An encoding of the CEK machine for λ-calculus

Transformation of call-by-value and call-by-need λ-calculus yielded machines very similar to the CEK and Krivine machines, respectively. We were also able to replicate the machines previously obtained via manual application of the functional correspondence [4, 9, 11]. The biggest differences were due to introduction of administrative transitions in handling of applications. This property hints at a potential for improvement by introducing an inlining step to the transformation. An interesting feature of the transformation is the ability to select which parts of the interpreter should be transformed and which should be considered atomic. These choices are reflected in the resulting machine, e.g., by transforming an environment look up in call-by-need interpreter we obtain a Krivine machine which has the search for a value in the environment embedded in its transition rules, while marking it atomic gives us a more abstract formulation from [4]. Another consequence of this feature is that one can work with interpreters already in CPS and essentially skip directly to defunctionalization (as tested on micro-Prolog interpreter of [11]).

Language	Interpreter style	Lang. Features	Result
call-by-value λ-calculus	denotational	·	CEK machine
	denotational	integers with add	CEK with add
	denotational, recursion via environment	integers, recursive let-bindings	similar to Reynolds's first-order interpreter
	denotational with conts.	shift and reset	two layers of conts.
	denotational, monadic	exceptions with handlers	explicit stack unwinding
	denotational, CPS		pointer to exception handler
	normalization by evaluation	·	strong CEK machine
call-by-name λ-calculus	big-step	·	Krivine machine
call-by-need λ-calculus	big-step (state passing)	memoization	lazy Krivine machine
simple imperative	big-step (state passing)	conditionals, while, assignment	
micro-Prolog	CPS	backtracking, cut operator	logic engine

Fig. 12. Summary of tested interpreters

5 Conclusion

In this article we described an algorithm, based on the functional correspondence [4], that allows for automatic derivation of an abstract machine given an interpreter which typically corresponds to denotational or natural semantics, allowing the user for fine-grained control over the shape of the resulting machine. In order to enable the transformation we derived a control-flow analysis for *IDL* using the abstracting abstract machines methodology. We implemented the algorithm in the *Haskell* programming language and used this tool to transform a selection of interpreters. To the best of our knowledge this is the first, reasonably generic, implementation of the functional correspondence.

The correctness of the tool relies on the correctness of each of the program transformations involved in the derivation that are classic and in some form have been proven correct in the literature [7,26,27,30], as well as on the correctness of the control-flow analysis we take advantage of. An extensive number of experiments we have carried out indicates that the tool indeed is robust.

In order to improve the capabilities of semt as a practical tool for semantics engineering, the future work could include extending the set of primitive operations and adding the ability to import arbitrary Racket functions and provide their abstract specification. The tool could also be extended to accommodate other output formats such as LaTeX figures or low level *C* code [19].

Another avenue for improvement lies in extensions of the meta-language capabilities. Investigation of additions such as control operators, nondeterministic choice and concurrency could yield many opportunities for diversifying the set of interpreters (and languages) that may be encoded in the *IDL*. In particular control operators could allow for expressing the interpreter for a language with delimited control (or algebraic effects [12,21]) in direct style.

Acknowledgements. This article is based on the MSc thesis by the first author, written under the supervision of the second author at the Institute of Computer Science, University of Wrocław.

The project is co-financed by the Polish National Agency for Academic Exchange (PHC Polonium PPN/BFR/2020/1/00001), and by the National Science Centre of Poland, under grant no. 2019/33/B/ST6/00289.

We thank Tomasz Drab and Alan Schmitt for their encouraging interest in this project. We are also grateful to Maciej Piróg for his valuable comments on an earlier version and to the anonymous reviewers for their help in improving the presentation of this work.

A   A Primer on the Functional Correspondence

In this section we present a simple illustrative example for the reader unfamiliar with CPS transformations and/or defunctionalization applied in program development. We use *IDL* as our meta-language, and we perform the two transformations by hand, without using our tool automating the functional correspondence.

In this example, our object-language is the built-in data type of integers, and the interpreter we are going to transform interprets a given natural number as its factorial (the negative integers are arbitrarily mapped to 1):

```
(def factorial (n)
  (match (< 0 n)
    (#t (* n (factorial (- n 1))))
    (#f 1)))

(def main ([Integer n]) (factorial n))
```

The familiar `factorial` function is written in direct style, with no explicit mention of the return stack and with a nested recursive call. The `main` function is the entry point for the computation.

Let us CPS transform `factorial`. To this end, we introduce a functional parameter `cont` – a continuation – that represents the rest of the computation before `factorial` returns a value to `main`. Returning a value from the function is expressed by passing it to the continuation (`(cont 1)`). The nested recursive function call becomes a tail call by passing the function a continuation (`fun (var) (cont (* n var))`). The initial continuation is the identity function – once `factorial` completes, it returns the final result. Here is the CPS version of the program:

```
(def factorial (n cont)
  (match (< 0 n)
    (#t (factorial (- n 1)
                    (fun (var) (cont (* n var)))))
    (#f (cont 1)))))

(def main ([Integer n]) (factorial n (fun (x) x)))
```

Next, we defunctionalize the continuations. Defunctionalization consists in replacing a function space with a first-order data type and a function interpreting the constructors of this data type. Each constructor represents a function introduction in the defunctionalized function space; the arguments of the constructor are the values of the free variables of the corresponding function.

In our case there are two constructors, one for the continuation in the recursive call that should remember the values of the variables cont and n (call it Cont), and a 0-argument one for the initial continuation (call it Halt). We then introduce the continue function that interprets the constructors accordingly and we replace calls to continuations with calls to this function. The resulting first-order program reads as follows:

```
(def-struct {Cont cont n})
(def-struct {Halt })

(def continue (fn var)
  (match fn
    ({Cont cont n} (continue cont (* n var)))
    ({Halt } var)))

(def factorial (n cont)
  (match (< 0 n)
    (#t (factorial (- n 1) {Cont cont n}))
    (#f (continue cont 1)))))

(def main ([Integer n]) (factorial n {Halt}))
```

What we have obtained is a functional encoding of an abstract machine. The machine operates in two modes: factorial and continue. The mutually tail-recursive calls model machine transitions. The data type of the defunctionalized conitnuation, isomorphic with a list of integers, represents the stack of the machine. The machine did not have to be invented, but instead it was mechanically derived. This is a very simple example of the general phenomenon known as the functional correspondence that applies to evaluators of virtually arbitrary complexity.

B   Normalization by Evaluation for λ-calculus

In this section we present a more involved case study: deriving a previously unknown abstract machine from a normalization function for λ-calculus. The

```
1   (def-data Term
2     {Var Integer}
3     {App Term Term}
4     {Abs Term})
5
6   (def-struct {Level Integer})
7   (def-struct {Fun Any})
8
9   (def cons #:atomic (val env)
10    (fun #:atomic #:no-defun (n)
11      (match n
12        (0 val)
13        (_ (env (- n 1))))))
14
15  (def reify (ceil val)
16    (match val
17      ({Fun f}
18       {Abs (reify (+ ceil 1) (f {Level ceil}))})
19      ({Level k} {Var (- ceil (+ k 1))})
20      ({App f arg} {App (reify ceil f) (reify ceil arg)})))
21
22  (def apply (f arg)
23    (match f
24      ({Fun f} (f arg))
25      (_ {App f arg})))
26
27  (def eval (expr env)
28    (match expr
29      ({Var n} (env n))
30      ({App f arg} (apply (eval f env) (eval arg env)))
31      ({Abs body} {Fun (fun #:name Closure (x)
32                         (eval body (cons x env)))})))
33
34  (def run (term)
35    (reify 0
36      (eval term (fun #:atomic #:no-defun (x)
37                    (error "empty env")))))
```

Fig. 13. A normalization function for call-by-value λ-calculus

normalization function is shown in Fig. 13. It is based on the technique called normalization by evaluation, and this particular definition has been adapted from [1]. The main idea is to use standard evaluator for call-by-value λ-calculus to evaluate terms to values and then reify them back into terms.

The terms use de Bruijn indices to represent bound variables. Since normalization requires reduction under binders the evaluator must work with open terms. We use de Bruijn levels (Level) to model variables in open terms. The eval function as usual transforms a term in a given environment into a value

```
1   (def reify (ceil val cont)
2     (match val
3       ({Fun f} (apply1 f {Level ceil} {Fun1 cont (+ ceil 1)}))
4       ({Level k} (continue1 cont {Var (- ceil (+ k 1))}))
5       ({App f arg} (reify ceil f {App1 arg ceil cont}))))
6
7   (def apply (f arg cont1)
8     (match f
9       ({Fun f} (apply1 f arg cont1))
10      (_ (continue cont1 {App f arg}))))
11
12  (def eval (expr env cont2)
13    (match expr
14      ({Var n} (continue cont2 (env n)))
15      ({App f arg} (eval f env {App3 arg cont2 env}))
16      ({Abs body} (continue cont2 {Fun {Closure body env}}))))
17
18  ;; evaluation
19  (def continue (fn2 var13)
20    (match fn2
21      ({Fun1 cont var3} (reify var3 var13 {Fun2 cont}))
22      ({App4 cont2 var12} (apply var12 var13 cont2))
23      ({App3 arg cont2 env} (eval arg env {App4 cont2 var13}))
24      ({Cont cont4 var16} (reify var16 var13 cont4))))
25
26  (def run (term cont4)
27    (eval term (fun (x) (error "empty env")) {Cont cont4 0}))
28
29  (def apply1 (fn x cont3)
30    (match fn ({Closure body env}
31              (eval body (cons x env) cont3))))
32
33  ;; reification
34  (def continue1 (fn1 var11)
35    (match fn1
36      ({Fun2 cont} (continue1 cont {Abs var11}))
37      ({App2 cont var10} (continue1 cont {App var10 var11}))))
```

Fig. 14. A strong call-by-value machine for λ-calculus

which is represented as a function wrapped in a Fun record. The values also include Levels and Terms which are introduced by the reify function. The apply function handles both the standard case of applying a functional value (case Fun) and the non-standard one which occurs during reification of the value and amounts to emitting the syntax node for application. The reification function (reify) turns a value back into a term. When its argument is a Fun it applies the function f to a Level representing unknown variable. When reified, a Level is turned back into de Bruijn index. Lastly, reification of an (syntactic) application proceeds recursively. The main function first evaluates a term in an empty environment and then reifies it back into its normal form. As usual, we keep the environment implementation unchanged during the transformation and we annotate the functional values to be named `Closure`.

The transformed normalization function is presented in Fig. 14. We notice that the machine has two classes of continuations. The first set (handled by `continue1`) is responsible for the control-flow of reification procedure. The second set (handled by `continue`) is responsible for the control-flow of evaluation and for switching to reification mode. We observe that the stack used by the machine consists of a prefix of only evaluation frames and a suffix of only reification frames. The machine switches between evaluation and reification in three places. In line 3 reification of a closure requires evaluation of its body therefore machine uses `apply1` to evaluate the closure with a `Level` as an argument. The switch in other direction is due to evaluation finishing: in line 32 a closure's body has been evaluated and has to be reified and then enclosed in an `Abs` (enforced by the `Fun2` frame); in line 35 the initial term has been reduced and the value can be reified.

The machine we obtained, to our knowledge, has not been described in the literature. It is somewhat similar to the one mechanically obtained by Ager et al. [3] who also used the functional correspondence to derive the machine. Their machine uses meta-language with mutable state in order to generate fresh identifiers for variables in open terms instead of de Bruijn levels and it operates on compiled rather than source terms. The machine we obtained using `semt` is as legible as the one derived manuallly.

References

1. Abel, A.: Normalization by evaluation: dependent types and impredicativity. Habilitation thesis, LMU (2013)
2. Ager, M.S.: From natural semantics to abstract machines. In: Etalle, S. (ed.) LOPSTR 2004. LNCS, vol. 3573, pp. 245–261. Springer, Heidelberg (2005). https://doi.org/10.1007/11506676_16
3. Ager, M.S., Biernacki, D., Danvy, O., Midtgaard, J.: From interpreter to compiler and virtual machine: a functional derivation. BRICS Rep. Ser. **10**(14) (2003)
4. Ager, M.S., Biernacki, D., Danvy, O., Midtgaard, J.: A functional correspondence between evaluators and abstract machines. In: Proceedings of the 5th International ACM SIGPLAN Conference on Principles and Practice of Declarative Programming, 27–29 August 2003, Uppsala, Sweden, pp. 8–19. ACM (2003). https://doi.org/10.1145/888251.888254
5. Ager, M.S., Danvy, O., Midtgaard, J.: A functional correspondence between call-by-need evaluators and lazy abstract machines. Inf. Process. Lett. **90**(5), 223–232 (2004). https://doi.org/10.1016/j.ipl.2004.02.012
6. Ager, M.S., Danvy, O., Midtgaard, J.: A functional correspondence between monadic evaluators and abstract machines for languages with computational effects. Theor. Comput. Sci. **342**(1), 149–172 (2005). https://doi.org/10.1016/j.tcs.2005.06.008

7. Banerjee, A., Heintze, N., Riecke, J.G.: Design and correctness of program transformations based on control-flow analysis. In: Kobayashi, N., Pierce, B.C. (eds.)
TACS 2001. LNCS, vol. 2215, pp. 420–447. Springer, Heidelberg (2001). https://
doi.org/10.1007/3-540-45500-0_21
8. Biernacka, M., Biernacki, D., Charatonik, W., Drab, T.: An abstract machine for
strong call by value. In: Oliveira, B.C.S. (ed.) APLAS 2020. LNCS, vol. 12470, pp.
147–166. Springer, Cham (2020). https://doi.org/10.1007/978-3-030-64437-6_8
9. Biernacka, M., Biernacki, D., Danvy, O.: An operational foundation for delimited continuations in the CPS hierarchy. Log. Methods Comput. Sci. 1(2) (2005).
https://doi.org/10.2168/LMCS-1(2:5)2005
10. Biernacka, M., Charatonik, W., Zielinska, K.: Generalized refocusing: from hybrid
strategies to abstract machines. In: Miller, D. (ed.) 2nd International Conference on
Formal Structures for Computation and Deduction, FSCD 2017, 3–9 September
2017, Oxford, UK. LIPIcs, vol. 84, pp. 10:1–10:17. Schloss Dagstuhl - Leibniz-
Zentrum für Informatik (2017). https://doi.org/10.4230/LIPIcs.FSCD.2017.10
11. Biernacki, D., Danvy, O.: From interpreter to logic engine by defunctionalization.
In: Bruynooghe, M. (ed.) LOPSTR 2003. LNCS, vol. 3018, pp. 143–159. Springer,
Heidelberg (2004). https://doi.org/10.1007/978-3-540-25938-1_13
12. Biernacki, D., Piróg, M., Polesiuk, P., Sieczkowski, F.: Abstracting algebraic effects.
Proc. ACM Program. Lang. 3(POPL), 6:1–6:28 (2019). https://doi.org/10.1145/
3290319
13. Crégut, P.: An abstract machine for lambda-terms normalization. In: Proceedings
of the 1990 ACM Conference on LISP and Functional Programming, LFP 1990,
Nice, France, 27–29 June 1990, pp. 333–340. ACM (1990). https://doi.org/10.1145/
91556.91681
14. Danvy, O., Johannsen, J.: Inter-deriving semantic artifacts for object-oriented programming. J. Comput. Syst. Sci. 76(5), 302–323 (2010). https://doi.org/10.1016/
j.jcss.2009.10.004
15. Danvy, O., Nielsen, L.R.: Refocusing in reduction semantics. BRICS Rep. Ser.
11(26) (2004)
16. Felleisen, M., Findler, R.B., Flatt, M.: Semantics Engineering with PLT Redex.
MIT Press, Cambridge (2009)
17. Felleisen, M., Friedman, D.P.: Control operators, the SECD-machine, and the λ-
calculus. In: Wirsing, M. (ed.) Formal Description of Programming Concepts - III:
Proceedings of the IFIP TC 2/WG 2.2 Working Conference on Formal Description
of Programming Concepts - III, Ebberup, Denmark, 25–28 August 1986, pp. 193–
222. North-Holland (1987)
18. Flanagan, C., Sabry, A., Duba, B.F., Felleisen, M.: The essence of compiling with
continuations. In: Cartwright, R. (ed.) Proceedings of the ACM SIGPLAN'93
Conference on Programming Language Design and Implementation (PLDI), Albu-
querque, New Mexico, USA, 23–25 June 1993, pp. 237–247. ACM (1993). https://
doi.org/10.1145/155090.155113
19. Friedman, D.P., Wand, M.: Essentials of Programming Languages, 3rd edn. MIT
Press, Cambridge (2008)
20. Hannan, J., Miller, D.: From operational semantics to abstract machines.
Math. Struct. Comput. Sci. 2(4), 415–459 (1992). https://doi.org/10.1017/
S0960129500001559
21. Hillerström, D., Lindley, S.: Liberating effects with rows and handlers. In: Chap-
man, J., Swierstra, W. (eds.) Proceedings of the 1st International Workshop on
Type-Driven Development, TyDe@ICFP 2016, Nara, Japan, 18 September 2016,
pp. 15–27. ACM (2016). https://doi.org/10.1145/2976022.2976033

22. Horn, D.V., Might, M.: Abstracting abstract machines. In: Hudak, P., Weirich, S. (eds.) Proceeding of the 15th ACM SIGPLAN International Conference on Functional Programming, ICFP 2010, Baltimore, Maryland, USA, 27–29 September 2010, pp. 51–62. ACM (2010). https://doi.org/10.1145/1863543.1863553
23. Jedynak, W., Biernacka, M., Biernacki, D.: An operational foundation for the tactic language of Coq. In: Peña, R., Schrijvers, T. (eds.) 15th International Symposium on Principles and Practice of Declarative Programming, PPDP 2013, Madrid, Spain, 16–18 September 2013, pp. 25–36. ACM (2013). https://doi.org/10.1145/2505879.2505890
24. Krivine, J.: A call-by-name lambda-calculus machine. High. Order Symb. Comput. **20**(3), 199–207 (2007). https://doi.org/10.1007/s10990-007-9018-9
25. Landin, P.J.: The mechanical evaluation of expressions. Comput. J. **6**(4), 308–320 (1964). https://doi.org/10.1093/comjnl/6.4.308
26. Nielsen, L.: A denotational investigation of defunctionalization. BRICS Rep. Ser. **7** (2010). https://doi.org/10.7146/brics.v7i47.20214
27. Nielsen, L.R.: A selective CPS transformation. In: Brookes, S.D., Mislove, M.W. (eds.) Seventeenth Conference on the Mathematical Foundations of Programming Semantics, MFPS 2001, Aarhus, Denmark, 23–26 May 2001. Electronic Notes in Theoretical Computer Science, vol. 45, pp. 311–331. Elsevier (2001). https://doi.org/10.1016/S1571-0661(04)80969-1
28. Nielson, F., Nielson, H.R., Hankin, C.: Principles of Program Analysis. Springer, Heidelberg (1999). https://doi.org/10.1007/978-3-662-03811-6
29. Piróg, M., Biernacki, D.: A systematic derivation of the STG machine verified in Coq. In: Gibbons, J. (ed.) Proceedings of the 3rd ACM SIGPLAN Symposium on Haskell, Haskell 2010, Baltimore, MD, USA, 30 September 2010, pp. 25–36. ACM (2010). https://doi.org/10.1145/1863523.1863528
30. Plotkin, G.D.: Call-by-name, call-by-value and the lambda-calculus. Theor. Comput. Sci. **1**(2), 125–159 (1975). https://doi.org/10.1016/0304-3975(75)90017-1
31. Reynolds, J.C.: Definitional interpreters for higher-order programming languages. High. Order Symb. Comput. **11**(4), 363–397 (1998). https://doi.org/10.1023/A:1010027404223
32. Sieczkowski, F., Biernacka, M., Biernacki, D.: Automating derivations of abstract machines from reduction semantics: - a generic formalization of refocusing in Coq. In: Hage, J., Morazán, M.T. (eds.) IFL 2010. LNCS, vol. 6647, pp. 72–88. Springer, Heidelberg (2011). https://doi.org/10.1007/978-3-642-24276-2_5

S-Semantics–an Example

Włodzimierz Drabent[1,2]([envelope]) [iD]

[1] Institute of Computer Science, Polish Academy of Sciences,
ul. Jana Kazimierza 5, 01-248 Warszawa, Poland
[2] Department of Computer and Information Science, Linköping University,
581 83 Linköping, Sweden
drabent@ipipan.waw.pl
https://home.ipipan.waw.pl/w.drabent/

Abstract. The s-semantics makes it possible to explicitly deal with variables in program answers. So it seems suitable for programs using nonground data structures, like open lists. However it is difficult to find published examples of using the s-semantics to reason about particular programs.

Here we apply s-semantics to prove correctness and completeness of Frühwirth's n queens program. This is compared with a proof, published elsewhere, based on the standard semantics and Herbrand interpretations.

Keywords: Logic programming · s-semantics · Program correctness · Program completeness · Declarative programming · Specification

1 Introduction

The s-semantics for definite logic programs [FLPM89, BGLM94, Bos09] deals explicitly with variables in program answers. So such semantics may seem suitable for reasoning about programs which use nonground data structures, like open lists. This paper applies the s-semantics to establish correctness and completeness of the n queen program of Frühwirth [Frü91]. The program uses open lists with possibly nonground members. Due to the importance of nonground data structures for the program, it may even seem that the standard semantics is not sufficient here. This is not the case, another paper [Dra21] presents correctness and completeness proofs for the program, based on Herbrand interpretations and the standard semantics. So those proofs can be compared with the ones presented here. Maybe surprisingly, it turns out that the standard semantics is preferable, as it leads to substantially simpler specifications and proofs. It should be added that many ideas from the former paper [Dra21] are used here.

It is difficult to find applications of s-semantics to reasoning about particular programs. (The author is not aware of any.) Thus the proofs presented here provide a, hopefully useful, example.

© Springer Nature Switzerland AG 2022
E. De Angelis and W. Vanhoof (Eds.): LOPSTR 2021, LNCS 13290, pp. 60–74, 2022.
https://doi.org/10.1007/978-3-030-98869-2_4

The paper is organized as follows. This introduction is concluded with pre-liminaries. The next two sections present, respectively, the s-semantics (together with sufficient conditions for correctness and completeness) and the n queens program. Section 4 discusses correctness of the program, first constructing a specification for correctness, then presenting a correctness proof. Section 5 discusses completeness in a similar way. The next section contains some comments, and compares the presented proofs with those based on the standard semantics. The last section summarizes the paper.

Preliminaries. This paper considers definite clause logic programs. It uses the standard notation and terminology, following [Apt97]. So we deal with queries (conjunctions of atoms) instead of goals. We assume a fixed alphabet (of predicate and function symbols, and variables). The set of variables will be denoted by Var, the set of terms (over the alphabet) by TU, and the set of atoms by TB; $\mathbb{N}$ stands for the set of natural numbers. Given a program P, a query Q such that $P \models Q$ is called an *answer* (or correct answer) of P. We will use answers, to avoid dealing with computed (or correct) answer substitutions. (In [Apt97], answers are called correct instances of queries.) By a *computed* (or SLD-computed) *answer* Q' for a query Q we mean an answer obtained by means of SLD-resolution (so Q' is a computed instance [Apt97] of Q, in other words $Q' = Q\theta$ for a computed answer substitution θ). By the *relation* defined by a predicate p in P we mean $\{\, t \in TU^n \mid P \models p(t)\,\}$.

An expression (term, atom, sequence of terms, etc.) is *linear* if no variable occurs in it twice. Expressions $E_1, \ldots, E_n$ $(n > 0)$ are *variable disjoint* if for each $0 < i < j \leq n$ no variable occurs in both E_i and E_j. As in Prolog, each occurrence of _ in an expression denotes a distinct variable.

We use the standard list notation of Prolog. An *open list* (a *list*) of length $n \geq 0$ is a term $[t_1, \ldots, t_n|v] \in TU$ where $v \in Var$ (resp. $[t_1, \ldots, t_n] \in TU$); v is the *open list variable* of $[t_1, \ldots, t_n|v]$. The term t_i $(0 < i \leq n)$ is called the i-th *member* of the (open) list. For $n = 0$, $[t_1, \ldots, t_n|t]$ stands for t. So an empty open list (i.e. of length 0) is a variable. The tail of a list l will be denoted by $tl(l)$, so $tl([t|u]) = u$. By the tail of an empty open list, $tl(\_)$ we mean a new variable, distinct from any other variable in the context.

2   S-semantics

The s-semantics [FLPM89] was introduced to capture the phenomenon that logically equivalent programs may have distinct sets of computed answers for a given query. Consider an example [DM87, DM88] of two programs

$$p(f(X)). \qquad\qquad p(f(X)).$$
$$p(f(a)).$$

They are logically equivalent, have the same set of logical consequences (thus the same set of answers), and have the same least Herbrand model (for any alphabet containing p, f, a). However for a query $p(Y)$, the SLD-resolution produces two answers for the first program, while only one answer is produced for the second one. (The answer $p(f(a))$ is not produced)[1].

The s-semantics captures such differences by describing the answers produced for most general atomic queries.

Definition 1 (S-semantics). Let P be a program. Its s-semantics is given by the set

$$
\mathcal{O}(P) = \left\{ A \in \mathcal{TB} \;\middle|\; \begin{array}{l} A \text{ is an SLD-computed answer} \\ \text{for a query } p(V_1, \dots, V_n), \text{where} \\ p \text{ is a predicate symbol of arity } n, \\ \text{and } V_1, \dots, V_n \text{ are distinct variables} \end{array} \right\}.
$$

In other words, $A = p(V_1, \dots, V_n)\theta$ where θ is an SLD-computed answer substitution for query $p(V_1, \dots, V_n)$.

We use here a slight simplification of the original s-semantics. There, the members of $\mathcal{O}(P)$ are not atoms but equivalence classes of atoms under the equivalence relation $\approx$ of variable renaming.[2] Obviously, the set of ground instances of $\mathcal{O}(P)$ is the least Herbrand model of P. This is a main property of the s-semantics:

Lemma 2. Let P be a program. A query $Q = B_1, \dots, B_n$ has an SLD-computed answer Q' iff there exist $A_1, \dots, A_n \in \mathcal{O}(P)$ such that

the $n + 1$ expressions $Q, A_1, \dots, A_n$ are variable disjoint,

$Q' = Q\gamma$ for an mgu γ of Q and $A_1, \dots, A_n$.

The s-semantics is the $\subseteq$-least fixed point of a specific immediate consequence operator.

Definition 3. The s-semantics **immediate consequence operator** for a program P is the function $\mathbf{T}_P^\pi \colon 2^{\mathcal{TB}} \to 2^{\mathcal{TB}}$ defined by

$$
\mathbf{T}_P^\pi(I) = \left\{ H\theta \;\middle|\; \begin{array}{l} \theta \text{ is an mgu of } (B_1, \dots, B_n) \text{ and } (A_1, \dots, A_n) \text{ for} \\ \text{some } n \geq 0, \ (H \leftarrow B_1, \dots, B_n) \in P, \ A_1, \dots, A_n \in I \\ \text{such that } A_1, \dots, A_n, (H \leftarrow B_1, \dots, B_n) \text{ are variable} \\ \text{disjoint} \end{array} \right\}.
$$

---

[1] The observation (that logically equivalent programs may have distinct sets of computed answers for the same query) is sometimes [BGLM94, p. 151] [Bos09, p. 4695] incorrectly attributed to [FLPM89]. However, it was previously presented in Pisa [DM87]. The author is not aware of any earlier appearance of such observation.

[2] Both versions are equivalent. Let $\mathcal{O}'(P)$ be the original s-semantics of P. Then $\mathcal{O}(P) = \bigcup \mathcal{O}'(P)$, and $\mathcal{O}'(P)$ is the quotient set $\mathcal{O}(P)/_\approx$ of $\mathcal{O}(P)$ w.r.t. $\approx$.

In the definition and in Lemma 2 it is important that $n + 1$ expressions are pairwise variable disjoint.[3] Also, note that an mgu of two ground expressions is any renaming substitution. So $\mathbf{T}_P^\pi(I)$ includes all unit clauses of P.

For any $I \subseteq \mathcal{TB}$, $\mathbf{T}_P^\pi(I)$ is closed under variable renaming (as for any renaming γ, if θ is an mgu of B and A then $\theta\gamma$ is an mgu of B and A too [Apt97, Lemma 2.23]). The operator is continuous in the lattice $(2^{\mathcal{TB}}, \subseteq)$, its least fixed point is $(\mathbf{T}_P^\pi)^\omega(\emptyset)$, and we have

$$\mathcal{O}(P) = (\mathbf{T}_P^\pi)^\omega(\emptyset).$$

By a **specification** (for s-semantics) we mean a set $S \subseteq \mathcal{TB}$, a program P is **correct** w.r.t. S when $\mathcal{O}(P) \subseteq S$. Here are sufficient conditions for correctness.

Theorem 4 (Correctness). Let P be a program and $S \subseteq \mathcal{TB}$.
  If $\mathbf{T}_P^\pi(S) \subseteq S$ then $\mathcal{O}(P) \subseteq S$.
  If $\mathbf{T}_{\{C\}}^\pi(S) \subseteq S$ for each clause $C \in P$ then $\mathcal{O}(P) \subseteq S$.

PROOF. The least fixed point $\mathcal{O}(P)$ of $\mathbf{T}_P^\pi$ is the least $I \subseteq \mathcal{TB}$ such that $\mathbf{T}_P^\pi(I) \subseteq I$. The premises of both implications are equivalent, as $\mathbf{T}_P^\pi(I) = \bigcup_{C \in P} \mathbf{T}_{\{C\}}^\pi(I)$. □

The notion of correctness in logic programming differs from that in imperative and functional programming. Due to the nondeterministic nature of logic programming, it is not sufficient that a program is correct; e.g. the empty program is correct w.r.t. any specification. We also need that the program produces the required answers; we are interested in program completeness. A program p is **complete** w.r.t. a specification S when $S \subseteq \mathcal{O}(P)$.

To deal with completeness, let us introduce an auxiliary notion. By a **level mapping** we mean a function $|\ |: S \to \mathbb{N}$ assigning natural numbers to atoms from a set $S \in \mathcal{TB}$, such that if $A, A' \in \mathcal{TB}$ are variants then $|A| = |A'|$. (Note that usually one considers level mappings defined on ground atoms [Apt97]).

Theorem 5 (Completeness). Let P be a finite program and $S \subseteq \mathcal{TB}$. Assume that there exists a level mapping $|\ |: S \to \mathbb{N}$ such that for each $A \in S$
  $A \in \mathbf{T}_C^\pi(\{A_1, \ldots, A_n\})$ for some clause $C \in P$ and some variable disjoint
  $A_1, \ldots, A_n \in S$ such that $|A| > |A_i|$ for $i = 1, \ldots, n$.
Then $S \subseteq \mathcal{O}(P)$.

It is sufficient to consider only n that is the number of body atoms in C. As S may be not closed under renaming, it is sometimes useful to generalize condition "$A_1, \ldots, A_n \in S$" to "$A_1, \ldots, A_n$ are variants of some atoms from S".

---

[3] The wording used in [FLPM89, BGLM94, Bos09] may be incorrectly understood as requiring that $(H \leftarrow B_1, \ldots, B_n)$ is variable disjoint with $(A_1, \ldots, A_n)$. Cf. e.g. "[atoms] are renamed apart w.r.t. the clause" in the definition of $\mathbf{T}_P^\pi$ in [Bos09, p. 4696]. For instance, such reading would lead to incorrect conclusion that $P(Z, Z) \in (\mathbf{T}_P^\pi)^2(\emptyset) = \mathcal{O}(P)$ for a program $P = \{p(X, Y) \leftarrow q(X), q(Y).\ q(V).\}$ (by taking $A_1 = A_2 = q(V)$).

PROOF (of the more general version of Theorem 5). By induction on i we show that $S_i = \{A \in S \mid |A| < i\} \subseteq (\mathbf{T}_P^\pi)^i(\emptyset)$.

For $i = 0$ the thesis holds vacuously. Assume that it holds for some $i \in \mathbb{N}$ and consider an $A \in S_{i+1}$. For some clause $C \in P$ we have $A \in \mathbf{T}_C^\pi(\{A_1, \ldots, A_n\})$, where for $k = 1, \ldots, n$ atom A_k is a variant of some $A_k' \in S$ and $i+1 > |A| > |A_k| = |A_k'|$. Hence $A_k' \in S_i$ and, by the inductive assumption, $A_k', A_k \in (\mathbf{T}_P^\pi)^i(\emptyset)$. As $A \in \mathbf{T}_C^\pi(\{A_1, \ldots, A_n\})$, we have $A \in (\mathbf{T}_P^\pi)^{j+1}(\emptyset)$.   □

The sufficient conditions for correctness and completeness of Theorems 4, 5 are similar to those related to the standard semantics [Cla79, DM93], (see [Dra16] for comments and references).

3   The n Queens Program

Thom Frühwirth presented a short, elegant and efficient Prolog program for the n-queens problem [Frü91]. However the program may be seen as rather tricky and one may be not convinced about its correctness. We apply the s-semantics to prove its correctness and completeness. This section, based on a former paper [Dra21], presents the program and introduces some notions used later in the specifications and proofs.

The problem is to place n queens on an $n \times n$ chessboard, so that no two queens are placed on the same row, column, or diagonal. The main idea of the program is to describe the placement of the queens by a data structure in which it is impossible that two queens violate the restriction (there are some exceptions, this will be clear later on). In this way all the constraints of the problem are treated implicitly and efficiently. Here is the program, in its simplest version not using Prolog arithmetic, with predicate names abbreviated (qu for queensp, gl for gen_listp, pq for place_queen, and pqs for place_queensp).

$$qu(N, Qs) \leftarrow gl(N, Qs), pqs(N, Qs, \_, \_).$$
$$gl(0, []).$$
$$gl(s(N), [\_|L]) \leftarrow gl(N, L).$$
$$pqs(0, \_, \_, \_). \tag{1}$$
$$pqs(s(I), Cs, Us, [\_|Ds]) \leftarrow pqs(I, Cs, [\_|Us], Ds), \tag{2}$$
$$pq(s(I), Cs, Us, Ds).$$

% $pq(Queen, Column, Updiagonal, Downdiagonal)$ places a single queen
$$pq(I, [I|\_], [I|\_], [I|\_]). \tag{3}$$
$$pq(I, [\_|Cs], [\_|Us], [\_|Ds]) \leftarrow pq(I, Cs, Us, Ds). \tag{4}$$

Its main predicate qu provides solutions to the problem, in an answer $qu(n, qs)$, n is a number and qs encodes a solution as a list of length n. The interesting part of the program consists of clauses (1),...,(4). So this fragment is our program of interest, it will be called NQUEENS.

Solutions to the n queens problem are provided by the answers of program NQUEENS of the form $pqs(n, qs, t_1, t_2)$, where $n > 0$ and qs is a list of length n.

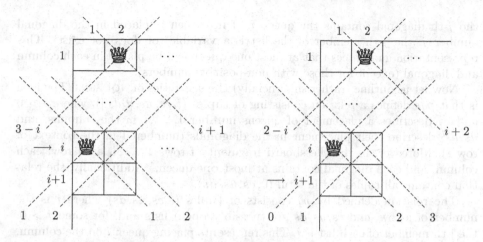

Fig. 1. [Dra21] Numbering of rows and columns. Numbering of up ($\nearrow$) diagonals and down ($\searrow$) diagonals in the context of row i (left), and $i + 1$ (right).

The board with two queens is represented in the context of row i as follows: the columns by $[i, 1| \ldots]$, the up diagonals by $[i| \ldots]$, the down diagonals by $[i, \ldots, 1| \ldots]$ (where 1 is the member number $i + 1$). Diagonals with non-positive numbers are not represented. In the context of row $i + 1$, the down diagonals are represented by $[t, i, \ldots, 1| \ldots]$ (where 1 is the member number $i + 2$, and t is arbitrary).

(The remaining arguments may be understood as internal data.) So an initial query $pqs(n, qs_0, \_, \_)$, where qs_0 is a list of n distinct variables can be used to obtain the solutions.

To understand a logic program from a declarative point of view we need to understand the relations defined by the predicates of the program. This can be done abstracting from any operational semantics. Such possibility is an advantage of declarative programming, and of logic programming in particular. We first explain the relations informally and then construct a formal specification. We begin with discussing the data of the program.

The natural numbers are represented by terms in a standard way, a number n as $s^n(0)$. Assume that columns and rows of the chessboard are numbered from the left/top. Each queen is identified by its row number. The chessboard is represented as a (possibly) open list, with number i appearing as the j-th member when the queen (of row) i is in column j. Empty column j is represented as a variable being the j-th member (or the length of the list being $< j$).

An up (respectively down) diagonal consists of the fields with the same sum (difference) of the row and column number. Diagonals intersecting a given row are numbered from the left (Fig. 1). In contrast to the numbering of rows and columns, this numbering is not fixed. It depends on the context, namely on which row we focus. Diagonal j includes the j-th field of the row. Thus, in the context of row number i, its queen i is in the column and in the up and down diagonals of the same number. The up (the same for down) diagonals are represented by an open list of numbers, a number i as the j-th member of the list means that the j-th diagonal contains the queen i. If no queen is placed in the diagonal number j, the j-th member of the list is a variable (or does not exist). This representation guarantees that at most one queen can be placed in each column and diagonal (except for those with non-positive numbers).

Now let us outline (rather superficially) the semantics of NQUEENS. The idea is that pqs defines a relation consisting of tuples $(i, cs, us, [t|ds'])$, where $i > 0$ and cs describes a placement of queens number $1, \ldots, i$ in the columns, and us, ds' describe their placement in the diagonals (numbered in the context of row i). Moreover, in the chessboard fragment of rows $1, \ldots, i$, each row, each column, and each diagonal contains at most one queen.[4] Additionally, the relation contains all tuples of the form $(0, cs, us, ds)$.

The relation defined by pq consists of tuples (i, cs, us, ds) where i is the number of a row, and cs, us, ds are (possibly open) lists and, for some $j > 0$, the j-th member of each list is i. This represents placing queen i on the column, up-diagonal and down-diagonal of the same number j.

4 Correctness of NQUEENS

4.1 Specification for Correctness

For discussing program correctness it is reasonable to use a specification which is a suitable superset of the actual semantics $\mathcal{O}(\text{NQUEENS})$ of the program. The specification should imply the program properties of interest. (More precisely, correctness w.r.t. the specification should imply them). Also, it is useful when a specification neglects unnecessary details of the semantics of the program. This may make simpler both the specification and the correctness proof.

Our specification for pq is

$$S_{pq} = \{\, pq(v, [c_1, \ldots, c_k, v|c_0], [u_1, \ldots, u_k, v|u_0], [d_1, \ldots, d_k, v|d_0]) \in \mathcal{TB} \mid$$
$$k \geq 0, \; v, c_0, \ldots, c_k, u_0, \ldots, u_k, d_0, \ldots, d_k \text{ are distinct variables}\,\}$$

Here all the variables occurring in the three open lists are distinct, except for v, which occurs in the three lists at position $k + 1$, to represent the same queen in the column, up diagonal, and down diagonal number $k + 1$.

For a formal specification of pqs, let us introduce some auxiliary notions. Assume that a queen $j \in \mathbb{N} \setminus \{0\}$ (i.e. the queen of row j) is placed in column k (i.e. j is the k-th member of a possibly open list cs representing columns). Then, in the context of row i (say $i \geq j$), the queen j is on the up diagonal with number $k + j - i$; we say $k + j - i$ is the **up diagonal number** of queen j in cs w.r.t. i [Dra21]. Similarly, $k + i - j$ is the **down diagonal number** of queen j (in cs w.r.t. i), as this is the number of its down diagonal in the context of row i. Consider, for instance, the queen $i - 3$ placed in column 2. Then its up (down) diagonal number w.r.t. i is, respectively, -1 and 5.

---

[4] Notice that the last statement follows from the previous one, but only for the diagonals represented by us, ds' (i.e. those with positive numbers w.r.t. row i).

Writing that some queens have distinct up (or down) diagonal numbers, we will usually skip "w.r.t. i", as the numbers are distinct w.r.t. any $i \in \mathbb{N}$.

We say that a term $t \in \mathcal{TU}$ is a **g.v.d.** (ground-or-variable open list with distinct members) if t

> is linear,
> is an open list with distinct members,
> and each its member is ground or is a variable.

Note that unification of two (unifiable) variable disjoint g.v.d.'s which do not have a common ground member results in a g.v.d..

We say that an open list cs *represents a correct placement* up to row m (in short: is **correct** up to m) when $0 \le m$ and

> cs is a g.v.d.,
> the ground members of cs are $1, \dots, m$,
> their up diagonal numbers in cs are distinct,
> their down diagonal numbers in cs are distinct,

We have to take care that the placement of the queens on the diagonals is properly reflected in the open lists us, ds representing the diagonals. Actually, we do not need to specify that us, ds are open lists. Let us generalize the notion of list membership: A term s is the k-**th member** of a term t if t is of the form $t = [t_1, \dots, t_{k-1}, s | t_0]$ (where $0 < k$). We say that a pair of terms (us, ds) is **correct** (represents a correct placement) up to m w.r.t. a row $i \in \mathbb{N}$ and an (open) list cs when

> for each $j \in \{1, \dots, m\}$,
> j is a member of cs, and
> if the up (down) diagonal number of j in cs w.r.t. i is $l > 0$
> then the l-th member of us (respectively ds) is j.

This notion will be used when $m \le i$, so $l > 0$ holds for each down diagonal number l. Note that

$$\begin{aligned} &\text{if } (us, ds) \text{ is correct up to } m \text{ w.r.t. } i \text{ and } cs \text{ (where } m \le i) \\ &\text{then } (tl(us), [\_|ds]) \text{ is correct up to } m \text{ w.r.t. } i+1 \text{ and } cs \end{aligned} \qquad (5)$$

(as the up diagonal number l w.r.t. i means the up diagonal number $l - 1$ w.r.t. $i + 1$, for the down diagonal number l this is $l + 1$).

Now the specification for pqs is $S_{pqs} = S_{pqs1} \cup S_{pqs2}$ where

$$S_{pqs1} = \left\{ pqs(i, cs, us, [\_|ds]) \;\middle|\; \begin{array}{l} i > 0, \; cs \text{ is correct up to } i, \\ (us, ds) \text{ is correct up to } i \text{ w.r.t. } i \text{ and } cs, \\ \text{terms } cs, us, ds \text{ are variable disjoint.} \end{array} \right\}$$

$$S_{pqs2} = \left\{ pqs(0, cs, us, ds) \mid cs, us, ds \text{ are distinct variables} \right\}$$

and the whole specification for NQUEENS is[5]

$$S = S_{pq} \cup S_{pqs}.$$

For a specification to be useful, it should imply the program property of interest. (Each program is correct w.r.t. $\mathcal{TB}$, but this implies nothing.) Indeed, any answer for a query $Q = pqs(n, qs_0, \_, \_)$ is a result $A\theta$ of unification of Q and an atom $A \in \mathcal{O}(\text{NQUEENS})$. If qs_0 is a list of length n and NQUEENS is correct w.r.t. S (thus $A \in S$) then the second argument of the answer, $qs_0\theta$, is a solution to the n queens problem.[6]

Note that the specification is approximate (formally, that it is a proper super-set of the s-semantics of NQUEENS). For instance it allows multiple occurrences of an element in us or ds (in S_{pqs1}), and does not require that us, cs are open lists. Note also that S is closed under renaming.

4.2   Correctness Proof for NQUEENS

The proof of correctness of NQUEENS w.r.t. S is based on Theorem 4. The proof for the unary clauses

$$pq(I, [I|\_], [I|\_], [I|\_]).$$
$$pqs(0, \_, \_, \_).$$

is immediate, as both are members of S (and hence any their variants are).

Consider clause (4):

$$pq(I, [\_|Cs], [\_|Us], [\_|Ds]) \leftarrow pq(I, Cs, Us, Ds).$$

It is easy to check that unifying the body of (4) with any atom from S (thus from S_{pq}) and applying the mgu to the head of (4) results in an atom from S_{pq}, provided that the clause and the atom are variable disjoint. Hence $\mathbf{T}^\pi_{\{(4)\}}(S) \subseteq S_{pq} \subseteq S$.

The nontrivial part of the proof is to show that $\mathbf{T}^\pi_{\{(2)\}}(S) \subseteq S$. Remember that clause (2) is

$$pqs(s(I), Cs, Us, [\_|Ds]) \leftarrow pqs(I, Cs, [\_|Us], Ds),\, pq(s(I), Cs, Us, Ds).$$

---

[5] As a specification for the whole original program one can use $S \cup S_{gl} \cup S_{qu}$, where

$$S_{gl} = \Big\{ gl(i, [v_1, \dots, v_i]) \mid i \geq 0,\ v_1, \dots, v_i \text{ are distinct variables} \Big\},$$

$$S_{qu} = \left\{ qu(i, cs) \;\middle|\; \begin{array}{l} i \geq 0, cs \text{ is a list of length } i, \\ \text{its members are } 1, \dots, i, \\ \text{their up (down) diagonal numbers are distinct} \end{array} \right\}.$$

[6] Detailed justification: As $A \in S_{pqs}$, $A = pqs(n, cs, us, [\_|ds])$ where cs is correct up to n, and thus the ground members of cs are $1, \dots, n$. Hence they are members of $qs_0\theta = cs\theta$. So $qs_0\theta$ is a permutation of $[1, \dots, n]$, as the length of list qs_0 is n. The up (down) diagonal numbers of $1, \dots, n$ in $qs_0\theta$ are those in cs, thus distinct.

Let H stand for the head of the clause, and B_1, B_2 for its body atoms. To find $\mathbf{T}^\pi_{\{(2)\}}(S)$ consider the unification of B_1, B_2 with a pair of atoms

$$A_1 = pqs(i, cs_1, us_1, ds_1) \in S_{pqs} \quad \text{and} \quad A_2 = pq(v, cs_2, us_2, ds_2) \in S_{pq}.$$

(where A_1, A_2, $(H \leftarrow B_1, B_2)$ are variable disjoint and $i \geq 0$). Note that if $i > 0$ then us_1 is of the form $[t|t']$, as there are i distinct up diagonal numbers (in cs_1 w.r.t. i) and each is $\geq 2-i$, hence some of them must be positive.

We have to show that if (B_1, B_2) and (A_1, A_2) are unifiable then applying the mgu to H results in a member of S. So assume they are unifiable. It is sufficient to consider a single mgu of (B_1, B_2) and (A_1, A_2) (as S is closed under renaming).

We perform the unification in two steps, first unifying $(B_1, s(I))$ and (A_1, v), then the remaining arguments of B_2 and A_2. (Formally, Lemma 2.24 of [Apt97] is applied here). For $i > 0$ the first step produces $\varphi = \{I/i, Cs/cs_1, \_/h, Us/\mathrm{tl}(us_1), Ds/ds_1, v/s(i)\}$ (where h is the head of us_1). For $i = 0$ we obtain $\varphi = \{I/0, Cs/cs_1, us_1/[\_|Us], Ds/ds_1, v/s(0)\}$.

We show that pair $(Us, Ds)\varphi$ is correct up to i w.r.t. $i+1$ and $Cs\varphi = cs_1$. This holds vacuously for $i = 0$; for $i > 0$ it follows by (5) as $(us_1, \mathrm{tl}(ds_1))$ is correct up to i w.r.t. i and $(Us, Ds)\varphi = (\mathrm{tl}(us_1), ds_1)$. Hence for any substitution ψ

$$(Us, Ds)\varphi\psi \text{ is correct up to } i \text{ w.r.t. } i+1 \text{ and } Cs\varphi\psi. \tag{6}$$

In the second step, the remaining three arguments of $B_2\varphi$ are to be unified with those of $A_2\varphi$, this means obtaining an mgu ψ for $(Cs, Us, Ds)\varphi$ and $(cs_2, us_2, ds_2) = ([c_1, \ldots, c_k, s(i)|c_0], [u_1, \ldots, u_k, s(i)|u_0], [d_1, \ldots, d_k, s(i)|d_0])$, where $k \geq 0$, and $c_0, \ldots, c_k, u_0, \ldots, u_k, d_0, \ldots, d_k$ are distinct variables. This gives $\varphi\psi$ as an mgu of B_1, B_2 with A_1, A_2. As the terms $Cs\varphi, Us\varphi, Ds\varphi, cs_2, us_2, ds_2$ are variable disjoint, unifier ψ can be represented as a union of three mgu's

$$\psi = \psi_c \cup \psi_u \cup \psi_d, \quad \text{where}$$
$$\psi_c \text{ is an mgu of } Cs\varphi \text{ and } cs_2,$$
$$\psi_u \text{ is an mgu of } Us\varphi \text{ and } us_2,$$
$$\psi_d \text{ is an mgu of } Ds\varphi \text{ and } ds_2,$$
$$Cs\varphi\psi = Cs\varphi\psi_c, \quad Us\varphi\psi = Us\varphi\psi_u, \quad Ds\varphi\psi = Ds\varphi\psi_d,$$

and ψ_c, ψ_u, ψ_d are variable disjoint. Hence $Cs\varphi\psi$, $Us\varphi\psi$ and $Ds\varphi\psi$ are variable disjoint.

Note that $Cs\varphi\psi$ is a g.v.d. (as the result of unification of two variable disjoint g.v.d.'s with disjoint sets of ground members), and its ground members are $1, \ldots, s(i)$.

In the rest of this proof we consider diagonal numbers in $Cs\varphi\psi$ w.r.t. $i + 1$.

To show that $Cs\varphi\psi = cs_1\psi$ is correct up to $i+1$, it remains to show that for $i > 0$ the up (respectively down) diagonal numbers of $s(0), \ldots, s(i)$ are distinct. The up (resp. down) diagonal number for $s(i)$ is $k + 1$, and the $k+1$-th element of Us (resp. Ds) is $s(i)$. So by (6) no up (down) diagonal number of $s(0), \ldots, i$

is $k+1$. Moreover the up (down) diagonal numbers of $s(0), \ldots, i$ are distinct (as $Cs\varphi$ is correct up to i).

To show that $(Us, Ds)\varphi\psi$ is correct up to $i+1$ w.r.t. $i+1$ and $Cs\varphi\psi$, it remains to show that for each each $j \in \{s(0), \ldots, s(i)\}$ the condition on the up (down) diagonal numbers from the definition holds. For $j \le i$ this follows from (6). For $j = s(i)$ this holds, as $s(i)$ is the $k+1$-th member of $Cs\varphi\psi$, $Us\varphi\psi$, and $Ds\varphi\psi$, and this $k+1$ is its up (and down) diagonal number.

Now applying the mgu to the head H of the clause results in $H\varphi\psi = pqs(s(i), Cs\varphi\psi, Us\varphi\psi, [\_|Ds\varphi\psi])$. From what was shown above, by the definition of S_{pqs1}, it follows that $H\varphi\psi \in S$. We showed that $\mathbf{T}^{\pi}_{\{(2)\}}(S) \subseteq S$. This completes the correctness proof.

5   Completeness

5.1   Specification for Completeness

Obviously, program NQUEENS is not complete w.r.t. specification S. To construct a specification for completeness for NQUEENS, we need to describe (a set of) atoms from S_{pqs} which actually are answers of the program.

We first introduce some auxiliary notions. Let us say that a g.v.d. $s = [t_1, \ldots, t_n|v]$ is **short** if t_n is a ground term, or $n = 0$. Consider the short g.v.d. s and a $k \in \{1, \ldots, n\}$ such that t_k is ground and $t_{k+1}, \ldots, t_{n-1}$ are variables; if all $t_1, \ldots, t_{n-1}$ are variables then let $k = 0$. Now the g.v.d. s **with t_n removed** is $s' = [t_1, \ldots, t_k|v]$. For an $i \in \{1, \ldots, n-1\}$, the g.v.d. s **with a ground t_i removed** is obtained from s by replacing t_i by a new variable. Note that in both cases a short g.v.d. with a ground member removed is a short g.v.d.

Now this is our specification for pqs for completeness:

$$
S^0_{pqs} = \left\{ pqs(i, cs, us, [\_|ds]) \;\middle|\; \begin{array}{l} i > 0, \quad cs \text{ is correct up to } i, \\ (us, ds) \text{ is correct up to } i \text{ w.r.t. } i \text{ and } cs, \\ \text{terms } cs, us, ds \text{ are variable disjoint}, \\ cs, us, ds \text{ are short g.v.d.'s,} \\ \text{if } j \text{ is a ground member of } us \text{ or } ds \\ \text{then } j \in \{1, \ldots, i\}, \\ \text{if } j \text{ is a ground member of } us \text{ then its} \\ \text{up diagonal number in } cs \text{ w.r.t. } i \text{ is } > 0 \end{array} \right\}.
$$

So here we require us and ds to have only such ground members that are necessary for correctness of (us, ds). Note that $S^0_{pqs} \subseteq S_{pqs}$.

Such specification makes sense, as its atoms describe all the solutions to the i queens problems. So completeness of NQUEENS (w.r.t. S^0_{pqs}) implies that each solution is contained in an answer to the initial query considered previously.

We are interested in completeness of NQUEENS w.r.t. S^0_{pqs}. However this cannot be proved using Theorem 5. We need to strengthen the specification, to describe requirements on pq and on the answers for pqs with the first argument 0. Fortunately, relevant fragments of the specification for correctness can be reused here. Our specification for completeness of NQUEENS is

$$S^0 = S^0_{pqs} \cup S_{pqs2} \cup S_{pq}.$$

Note that this is a proper subset of the specification S for correctness.

5.2 Completeness Proof

Now we apply Theorem 5 to prove completeness of the program, i.e. that $S^0 \subseteq \mathcal{O}(\text{NQUEENS})$. Let us define, similarly to [Dra21], a level mapping $|\ |\colon S^0 \to \mathbb{N}$ by

$$|\,pqs(i, cs, us, ds)\,| = |i| + |cs|,$$
$$|\,pq(i, cs, us, ds)\,| = |cs|,$$

where

$$|\,[h|t]\,| = 1 + |t|,$$
$$|\,s(t)\,| = 1 + |t|,$$
$$|\,f(t_1, \ldots, t_n)\,| = 0,$$
$$|v| = 0,$$

where $i, cs, us, ds, h, t, t_1, \ldots, t_n \in \mathcal{TU}$, $v \in \mathcal{V}ar$ and f is any n-ary function symbol ($n \geq 0$) distinct from s and from $[\ |\ ]$. Note that for an (open) list l, its length is $|l|$. Note also that if s' is a short g.v.d. s with a ground member removed then $|s'| \leq |s|$.

The atoms from S_{pqs2} and those of the form $pq(v, [v|_-], [v|_-], [v|_-]) \in S_{pq}$ are variants of unary clauses of NQUEENS, thus obviously they are in, respectively, $\mathbf{T}^\pi_{\{(1)\}}(\emptyset)$ and $\mathbf{T}^\pi_{\{(3)\}}(\emptyset)$.

The nontrivial part of the proof is to show that the sufficient condition from Theorem 5 holds for the elements of S^0_{pqs}.

Consider an atom $A = pqs(s(i), cs, us, [v|ds]) \in S^0_{pqs}$. Let j be the (both up and down) diagonal number of $s(i)$ in cs w.r.t. $s(i)$. So $s(i)$ is the j-th member of each short g.v.d.'s cs, us, ds. We find $A_1, A_2 \in S^0$ such that $A \in \mathbf{T}^\pi_{\{(2)\}}(\{A_1, A_2\})$, Remember that clause (2) is

$$pqs(s(I), Cs, Us, [\_|Ds]) \leftarrow pqs(I, Cs, [\_|Us], Ds), pq(s(I), Cs, Us, Ds).$$

Below we choose the variables in A_1, A_2 so that (2),A_1, A_2 are variable disjoint.

As A_2 we choose $A_2 = pq(v', cs'', us'', ds'') \in S_{pq}$, where $v' \in \mathcal{V}ar$ is the j-th member of each cs'', us'', ds''. For $i = 0$ we choose $A_1 = pqs(0, v_1, v_2, v_3) \in S_{pqs2}$. Let $\rho = \{v'/s(0)\}$. A most general unifier of A_1, A_2 and the body of clause (2) is $\theta = \rho \cup \{I/0, Cs/cs''\rho, Us/us''\rho, Ds/ds''\rho, \ldots\}$. Note that $cs''\rho, us''\rho, ds''\rho$ are short g.v.d.'s. Applying θ to the head of the clause results in $pqs(s(0), cs'', us'', [\_|ds''])\rho$. This is a variant of A. Thus $A \in \mathbf{T}^\pi_{\{(2)\}}(\{A_1, A_2\})$.

If $i > 0$ then as A_1 we choose $A_1 = pqs(i, cs', [t|us'], ds')$, where cs' (respectively us', ds') is cs (us, ds) with $s(i)$ removed, and t is as follows. If 1 is the up diagonal number in cs w.r.t. i of some $k \in \{s(0), \ldots, i\}$ then $t = k$. Otherwise t is a variable such that A_1 is linear.

Note that the diagonal numbers of $1, \ldots, i$ in cs are the same as those in cs'. So a pair of terms is correct up to i w.r.t. l and cs iff it is correct up to i w.r.t. l and cs' (for any $l \geq i$).

We first show that $A_1 \in S^0_{pqs}$. Note that cs', us', ds' are short g.v.d.'s. They are variable disjoint, as cs, us, ds are. Also, cs' is correct up to i (as cs is correct up to $s(i)$), and (us', ds') is correct up to i w.r.t. $s(i)$ and cs (as (us, ds) is, up to $s(i)$). Thus $([t|us'], \mathrm{tl}(ds'))$ is correct up to i w.r.t. i and cs'. A ground member m of $[t|us']$ or of $\mathrm{tl}(ds')$ is k or a member of us' or ds'. Hence $m \in \{1, \ldots, i\}$.

It remains to show that the diagonal numbers of the ground members of $[t|us']$ w.r.t. i are positive. In this paragraph we consider diagonal numbers and correctness w.r.t. cs', so we skip the phrases "in cs'", "w.r.t. cs'". Consider a ground member m of $[t|us']$. If $m = t$ then its up diagonal number w.r.t. i is 1. If m is a member of us' then $m \neq s(i)$ and m is a member of us. As us is the third argument of pqs in $A \in S^0_{pqs}$, $m \in \{1, \ldots, i\}$ and the up diagonal number of m w.r.t. $i+1$ is positive. Thus the up diagonal number of m w.r.t. i is > 1. This completes a proof that $A_1 \in S^0_{pqs}$.

Now we show that A_1, A_2 are unifiable with the body atoms B_1, B_2 of the clause (2) and the resulting mgu produces (a variant of) A. Similarly as in the previous proof, let us perform unification in two steps. An mgu of (A_1, v') and $(B_1, s(I))$ is $\varphi = \{I/i, Cs/cs', \_/t, Us/us', Ds/ds', v'/s(i)\}$. The rest of unification is unifying three variable disjoint short g.v.d.'s cs', us', ds' with three short g.v.d.'s $cs''\varphi, us''\varphi, ds''\varphi$, the latter are $cs''\{v'/s(i)\}$, $us''\{v'/s(i)\}$, $ds''\{v'/s(i)\}$ (as v' is the only variable from φ that occurs in cs'', us'', ds''). Remember that cs' is cs with its j-th member $s(i)$ removed, and $cs''\{v'/s(i)\}$ is a short g.v.d. with its j-th member $s(i)$, and this is the only nonground member of the g.v.d. Hence unifying cs' and $cs''\{v'/s(i)\}$ results in cs. The same holds for us' and ds'. Applying the resulting mgu of A_1, A_2 and B_1, B_2 to the head of the clause results in A.

This completes our proof that $A \in \mathbf{T}^{\pi}_{\{(2)\}}(\{A_1, A_2\})$, where $A_1, A_2 \in S^0$. Note now that $|A_2| = |cs''| = j$. For $i = 0$, $|A_1| = 0$; for $i > 0$ we have $|A_1| = i + |cs'| \leq i + |cs|$ (as cs' is the short g.v.d. cs with a ground member removed). Also, $|A| = i + 1 + |cs| \geq i + 1 + j$ (as the g.v.d. cs has at least j members). Hence $|A| > |A_1|$ and $|A| > |A_2|$. So we have shown that the sufficient condition for completeness from Theorem 5 holds for any $A \in S^0_{pqs}$.

It remains to show that the sufficient condition holds for any atom $B_k = pq(v, [c_1, \ldots, c_k, v|c_0], [u_1, \ldots, u_k, v|u_0], [d_1, \ldots, d_k, v|d_0]) \in S_{pq}$, where $k > 0$. Note that $|B_k| = k + 1$. We skip (simple) details of showing that $B_k \in \mathbf{T}^{\pi}_{\{(4)\}}(\{B'_{k-1}\})$ for some variant $B'_{k-1} \in S_{pq}$ of B_{k-1}. This completes the proof.

6 Comments

The correctness and completeness proofs presented here can be compared with those based on Herbrand interpretations and the standard semantics of definite logic programs [Dra21]. The specifications used there are Herbrand interpretations (sets of ground atoms) and program correctness means that the least

Herbrand model of the program is a subset of the specification. Similarly, completeness means that this model is a superset of the specification.

To deal with correctness of NQUEENS in the framework of the standard semantics, a difficulty had to be overcome: some answers of NQUEENS have instances which are in a sense wrong. For example, elements of S_{pqs1} have ground instances in which the same queen is placed in two columns. The main idea of solving the difficulty was to allow (i.e. to include in the specification) all ground atoms $pqs(i, cs, us, [t|ds])$ in which cs is not a list of distinct members. Thus the specification neglects the atoms with such cs and describes the other arguments of pqs only when cs "makes sense", i.e. is a list with distinct members [Dra21]. Such specification is not more complicated than the one used here.

The specification for completeness from Sect. 5 was difficult to construct and is substantially more complicated than that based on the standard semantics. This is mainly because each element of the specification has to be an exact answer for a most general query.

The reader may compare the proofs based on Herbrand interpretations with those presented here. The former turn out substantially simpler. Note that the presentation of the former proofs [Dra21] is more detailed than that of Sects. 4.2 and 5.2, where many details were skipped. For instance we have not proved that (under the given conditions) unification of two g.v.d.'s results in a g.v.d. Despite of this, the proofs of Sects. 4.2, 5.2 above are longer and seem more complicated.

The author began with a correctness proof based on the s-semantics, before it turned out that employing the standard semantics was preferable.

A well founded comparison of the volume of the two proofs could be obtained by formalizing the specifications and the proofs, using some proof assistant. This is however outside of the scope of this work.

Comparing two pairs of proofs may not be a convincing argument that s-semantics is less suitable for proving program correctness or completeness than the standard semantics. However an undeniable fact is that when dealing with the standard semantics one employs simpler mathematical objects. Basically, such specifications and proofs refer only to ground atoms, ground instances of atoms and clauses, sets of ground atoms, and inclusion of such sets. In the context of the s-semantics we additionally have to deal with arbitrary atoms, variables, substitutions, substitution composition, and unification. Reasoning about properties of substitutions and mgu's is known to be difficult and error prone. Formalizing the proofs dealing with the standard semantics should be simpler, at least due to no need of formally describing the definitions and basic properties of substitutions, unification etc.

The discussion of this section suggests that the standard semantics may be preferable to the s-semantics in reasoning about program correctness and completeness, even for programs that employ nonground data.

7 Summary

This paper presents correctness and completeness proofs (together with suitable specifications) of program NQUEENS. It is a definite clause program, working on non-ground terms. The specifications and proofs are based on the s-semantics [FLPM89,BGLM94,Bos09]. The employed approach is declarative; the specifications/proofs abstract from any operational semantics. Our specification is approximate, it consists of distinct specifications for correctness and completeness.

The proposed sufficient condition for completeness seems to be a contribution of this work. The employed simplification of the s-semantics may be of separate interest. The author is not aware of any published examples of applying the s-semantics to reasoning about properties of particular programs.

The program works on nonground data, and the s-semantics explicitly deals with variables in program answers. Thus the choice of this semantics seems reasonable. However comparison (Sect. 6) with analogical specifications and proofs [Dra21] based on the standard semantics and (ground) Herbrand interpretations shows that the latter are simpler.

References

[Apt97]   Apt, K.R.: From Logic Programming to Prolog. International Series in Computer Science. Prentice Hall Europe, Hemel Hempstead (1997)

[BGLM94]   Bossi, A., Gabbrielli, M., Levi, G., Martelli, M.: The s-semantics approach: theory and applications. J. Log. Program. **19/20**, 149–197 (1994). https://doi.org/10.1016/0743-1066(94)90026-4

[Bos09]   Bossi, A.: S-semantics for logic programming: a retrospective look. Theor. Comput. Sci. **410**(46), 4692–4703 (2009). https://doi.org/10.1016/j.tcs.2009.07.039

[Cla79]   Clark, K.L.: Predicate logic as computational formalism. Technical report 79/59, Imperial College, London, December 1979

[DM87]   Drabent, W., Małuszyński, J.: Inductive assertion method for logic programs. In: Ehrig, H., Kowalski, R., Levi, G., Montanari, U. (eds.) TAPSOFT 1987. LNCS, vol. 250, pp. 167–181. Springer, Heidelberg (1987). https://doi.org/10.1007/BFb0014980. Preliminary version of [DM88]

[DM88]   Drabent, W., Małuszyński, J.: Inductive assertion method for logic programs. Theoret. Comput. Sci. **59**, 133–155 (1988). https://doi.org/10.1016/S1571-0661(05)80659-0

[DM93]   Deransart, P., Małuszyński, J.: A Grammatical View of Logic Programming. The MIT Press, Cambridge (1993)

[Dra16]   Drabent, W.: Correctness and completeness of logic programs. ACM Trans. Comput. Log. **17**(3), 18:1–18:32 (2016). https://doi.org/10.1145/2898434

[Dra21]   Drabent, W.: On correctness and completeness of an n queens program. Theory Pract. Log. Program. **22**(1), 37–50 (2022). https://doi.org/10.1017/S1471068421000223

[FLPM89]   Falaschi, M., Levi, G., Palamidessi, C., Martelli, M.: Declarative modeling of the operational behavior of logic languages. Theor. Comput. Sci. **69**(3), 289–318 (1989). https://doi.org/10.1016/0304-3975(89)90070-4

[Frü91]   Frühwirth, T.: nqueens. A post in comp.lang.prolog (1991). 1991-03-08. Also in [SS94, Section 4.1, Exercise (v)]. https://groups.google.com/d/msg/comp.lang.prolog/qiyibDALhTE/uk6f6AQzOCAJ. Accessed 4 Mar 2022

[SS94]   Sterling, L., Shapiro, E.: The Art of Prolog, 2 edn. The MIT Press (1994). https://mitpress.mit.edu/books/art-prolog-second-edition

Disjunctive Delimited Control

Alexander Vandenbroucke[1] and Tom Schrijvers[2(✉)]

[1] Standard Chartered, London, UK
alexander.vandenbroucke@sc.com
[2] KU Leuven, Leuven, Belgium
tom.schrijvers@kuleuven.be

Abstract. Delimited control is a powerful mechanism for programming language extension which has been recently proposed for Prolog (and implemented in SWI-Prolog). By manipulating the control flow of a program from inside the language, it enables the implementation of powerful features, such as tabling, without modifying the internals of the Prolog engine. However, its current formulation is inadequate: it does not capture Prolog's unique non-deterministic nature which allows multiple ways to satisfy a goal.

This paper fully embraces Prolog's non-determinism with a novel interface for *disjunctive* delimited control, which gives the programmer not only control over the sequential (conjunctive) control flow, but also over the non-deterministic control flow. We provide a meta-interpreter that conservatively extends Prolog with delimited control and show that it enables a range of typical Prolog features and extensions, now at the library level: findall, cut, branch-and-bound optimisation, probabilistic programming, ...

Keywords: Delimited control · Disjunctions · Prolog ·
Meta-interpreter · Branch-and-bound

1 Introduction

Delimited control is a powerful programming language mechanism for control flow manipulation that was developed in the late '80s in the context of functional programming [2,5]. Schrijvers et al. [12] have recently ported this mechanism to Prolog.

Compared to both low-level abstract machine extensions and high-level global program transformations, delimited control is much more light-weight and robust for implementing new control-flow and dataflow features. Indeed, the Prolog port has enabled powerful applications in Prolog, such as high-level implementations of both tabling [3] and algebraic effects & handlers [8]. Yet, at the same time, there is much untapped potential, as the port fails to recognise the unique nature of Prolog when compared to functional and imperative languages that have previously adopted delimited control.

© Springer Nature Switzerland AG 2022
E. De Angelis and W. Vanhoof (Eds.): LOPSTR 2021, LNCS 13290, pp. 75–91, 2022.
https://doi.org/10.1007/978-3-030-98869-2_5

Indeed, computations in other languages have only one *continuation*, i.e., one way to proceed from the current point to a result. In contrast, at any point in a Prolog continuation, there may be multiple ways to proceed and obtain a result. More specifically, we can distinguish 1) the success or *conjunctive* continuation which proceeds with the current state of the continuation; and 2) the failure or *disjunctive* continuation which bundles the alternative ways to proceed, e.g., if the conjunctive continuation fails.

The original delimited control only accounts for one continuation, which Schrijvers et al. have unified with Prolog's conjunctive continuation. More specifically, for a given subcomputation, they allow to wrest the current conjunctive continuation from its track, and to resume it at leisure, however many times as desired. Yet, this entirely ignores the disjunctive continuation, which remains as and where it is.

In this work, we adapt delimited control to embrace the whole of Prolog and capture both the conjunctive and the disjunctive continuations. This makes it possible to manipulate Prolog's built-in search for custom search strategies and enables clean implementations of, e.g., `findall/3` and branch-and-bound. This new version of delimited control has an executable specification in the form of a meta-interpreter (Sect. 3), that can run both the above examples, amongst others. Appendices to this paper are available in the extended version [18].

2   Overview and Motivation

2.1   Background: Conjunctive Delimited Control

In earlier work, Schrijvers et al. [12] have introduced a Prolog-compatible interface for delimited control that consists of two predicates: `reset/3` and `shift/1`.

Motivation. While library developers and advanced users typically do not build in new language features in Prolog, they have traditionally been able to add various language extensions by means of Prolog's rich meta-programming and program transformation facilities. Examples are definite clause grammars (DCGs), extended DCGs [17], Ciao Prolog's structured state threading [7] and logical loops [11]. However, there are several important disadvantages to non-local program transformations for defining new language features: A transformation that combines features can be quite complex and is fragile under language evolution. Moreover, existing code bases typically need pervasive changes to, e.g., include DCGs.

Delimited continuations enable new language features at the program level rather than as program transformations. This makes features based on delimited continuations more light-weight and more robust with respect to changes, and it does not require pervasive changes to existing code.

Behavior. The precicate `reset(Goal,ShiftTerm,Cont)` executes `Goal`, and, 1. if `Goal` fails, `reset/3` also fails; 2. if `Goal` succeeds, then `reset/3` also succeeds and unifies `Cont` and `ShiftTerm` with 0; 3. if `Goal` calls `shift(Term)`, then the execution of Goal is suspended and reset/3 succeeds immediately, unifying ShiftTerm with Term and Cont with the remainder of Goal.

The shift/reset pair resembles the more familiar catch/throw predicates, with the following differences: shift/1 does not copy its argument (i.e., it does not refresh the variables), it does not delete choice points, and also communicates the remainder of Goal to reset/3.

Example 1. Consider Definite Clause Grammars (DCGs), a language extension to sequentially access the elements of an implicit list. It is conventionally defined by a program transformation that requires special syntax to mark DCG clauses H --> B and to mark non-DCG goals {G}. The delimited control approach requires neither. It introduces two new predicates: c(E) consumes the next element E in the implicit list, and phrase(G,Lin,Lout) runs goal G with implicit list Lin and returns unconsumed remainder Lout. For instance, the following predicate implements the grammar $(ab)^n$ and returns n.

```
ab(0).
ab(N) :- c(a), c(b), ab(M), N is M + 1.

?- phrase(ab(N),[a,b,a,b],[]).
N = 2.
```

The two DCG primitives are implemented as follows in terms of shift/1 and reset/3.

```
c(E) :- shift(c(E)).

phrase(Goal,Lin,Lout) :-
  reset(Goal,Cont,Term),
  ( Cont == 0 ->
      Lin = Lout
  ; Term = c(E) ->
      Lin = [E|Lmid],
      phrase(Cont,Lmid,Lout)
  ).
```

In words, phrase/3 executes the given goal within a reset/3 and analyzes the possible outcomes. If Cont == 0, this means the goal succeeds without consuming any input. Then the remainder Lout is equal to the input list Lin. Alternatively, the execution of the goal has been suspended midway by the invocation of a shift/1 because it wants to consume an element from the implicit list with c/1. In that case, Term has been instantiated with a request c(E) for an element E. This request is satisfied by instantiating E with the first element of Lin. Finally, the remainder of the suspended goal, Cont (the continuation), is resumed with the remainder of the list Lmid.

Other examples of language features implemented in terms of delimited control are co-routines, algebraic effects [8] and tabling [3].

Obliviousness to Disjunctions. This form of delimited control only captures the conjunctive continuation. For instance `reset((shift(a),G1),Term,Cont)` captures in `Cont` goal `G1` that appears in conjunction to `shift(a)`. In a low-level operational sense this corresponds to delimited control in other (imperative and functional) languages where the only possible continuation to capture is the computation that comes sequentially after the shift. Thus this approach is very useful for enabling conventional applications of delimited control in Prolog.

In functional and imperative languages delimited control can also be characterised at a more conceptual level as capturing the entire remainder of a computation. Indeed, in those languages the sequential continuation coincides with the entire remainder of a computation. Yet, the existing Prolog approach fails to capture the entire remainder of a goal, as it only captures the conjunctive continuation and ignores any disjunctions. This can be illustrated by the `reset((shift(a),G1;G2),Term,Cont)` which only captures the conjunctive continuation `G1` in `Cont` and not the disjunctive continuation `G2`. In other words, only the conjunctive part of the goal's remainder is captured.

This is a pity because disjunctions are a key feature of Prolog and many advanced manipulations of Prolog's control flow involve manipulating those disjunctions in one way or another.

2.2   Delimited Continuations with Disjunction

This paper presents an approach to delimited control for Prolog that is in line with the conceptual view that the whole remainder of a goal should be captured, including in particular the disjunctive continuation.

For this purpose we modify the `reset/3` interface, where depending on `Goal`, `reset(Pattern,Goal,Result)` has three possible outcomes:

1. If `Goal` fails, then the `reset` succeeds and unifies `Result` with `failure`. For instance,

```
?- reset(_,fail,Result).
Result = failure.
```

2. If `Goal` succeeds, then `Result` is unified with `success(PatternCopy, DisjCont)` and the `reset` succeeds. Here `DisjCont` is a goal that represents the disjunctive remainder of `Goal`. For instance,

```
?- reset(X,(X = a; X = b),Result).
X = a, Result = success(Y,Y = b).
```

Observe that, similar to `findall/3`, the logical variables in `DisjCont` have been renamed apart to avoid interference between the branches of the computation. To be able to identify any variables of interest after renaming, we provide `PatternCopy` as a likewise renamed-apart copy of `Pattern`.

3. If `Goal` calls `shift(Term)`, then the `reset` succeeds and `Result` is unified with `shift(Term,ConjCont,PatternCopy,DisjCont)`. This contains in
   addition to the disjunctive continuation also the conjunctive continuation.
   The latter is not renamed apart and can share variables with `Pattern` and
   `Term`. For instance,

```
?- reset(X,(shift(t),X = a; X = b),Result).
Result = shift(t,X = a, Y, Y = b).
```

Note that `reset(P,G,R)` always succeeds if R is unbound and never leaves choi-
cepoints.

Encoding. findall/3 Sect. 4 presents a few larger applications, but our encoding
of `findall/3` with disjunctive delimited control already gives some idea of the
expressive power:

```
findall(Pattern,Goal,List) :-
   reset(Pattern,Goal,Result),
   findall_result(Result,Pattern,List).

findall_result(failure,_,[]).
findall_result(success(PatternCopy,DisjCont),Pattern,List) :-
   List = [Pattern|Tail],
   findall(PatternCopy,DisjCont,Tail).
```

This encoding is structured around a `reset/3` call of the given `Goal` followed by
a case analysis of the result. Here we assume that `shift/1` is not called in `Goal`,
which is a reasonable assumption for plain `findall/3`.

Encoding. !/0 Our encoding of the `!/0` operator illustrates the use of `shift/1`:

```
cut :- shift(cut).

scope(Goal) :-
   copy_term(Goal,Copy),
   reset(Copy,Copy,Result),
   scope_result(Result,Goal,Copy).

scope_result(failure,_,_) :-
   fail.
scope_result(success(DisjCopy,DisjGoal),Goal,Copy) :-
   Goal = Copy.
scope_result(success(DisjCopy,DisjGoal),Goal,Copy) :-
   DisjCopy = Goal,
   scope(DisjGoal).
scope_result(shift(cut,ConjGoal,DisjCopy,DisjGoal),Goal,Copy) :-
   Copy = Goal,
   scope(ConjGoal).
```

The encoding provides `cut/0` as a substitute for `!/0`. Where the scope of regular cut is determined lexically, we use `scope/1` here to define it dynamically. For instance, we encode

<table>
<tr>
<td>

```
p(X,Y) :- q(X), !, r(Y).
p(4,2).
```

</td>
<td>as</td>
<td>

```
p(X,Y) :- scope(p_aux(X,Y)).
p_aux(X,Y) :- q(X), cut, r(Y).
p_aux(4,2).
```

</td>
</tr>
</table>

The logic of cut is captured in the definition of `scope/1`; all the `cut/0` predicate does is request the execution of a cut with `shift/1`.

In `scope/1`, the `Goal` is copied to avoid instantiation by any of the branches. The copied goal is executed inside a `reset/3` with the copied goal itself as the pattern. The `scope_result/3` predicate handles the result:

- `failure` propagates with `fail`;
- `success` creates a disjunction to either unify the initial goal with the now instantiated copy to propagate bindings, or to invoke the disjunctive continuation;
- `shift(cut)` discards the disjunctive continuation and proceeds with the conjunctive continuation only.

3   Meta-interpreter Semantics

We provide an accessible definition of disjunctive delimited control in the form of a meta-interpreter. Broadly speaking, it consists of two parts: the core interpreter, and a top level predicate to initialise the core and interpret the results.

3.1   Core Interpreter

Figure 1 defines the interpreter's core predicate, `eval(Conj, PatIn, Disj, PatOut, Result)`. It captures the behaviour of `reset(Pattern,Goal,Result)` where the goal is given in the form of a list of goals, `Conj`, together with the alternative branches, `Disj`. The latter is renamed apart from `Conj` to avoid conflicting instantiations.

The pattern that identifies the variables of interest (similar to `findall/3`) is present in three forms. Firstly, `PatIn` is an input argument that shares the variables of interest with `Conj` (but not with `Disj`). Secondly, `PatOut` outputs the instantiated pattern when the goal succeeds or suspends on a `shift/1`. Thirdly, the alternative branches `Disj` are of the form `alt(BranchPatIn,BranchGoal)` with their own copy of the pattern.

When the conjunction is empty (1–4), the output pattern is unified with the input pattern, and `success/2` is populated with the information from the alternative branches.

When the first conjunct is `true/0` (5–6), it is dropped and the meta-interpreter proceeds with the remainder of the conjunction. When it is a composite conjunction (`G1,G2`) (7–8), the individual components are added separately to the list of conjunctions.

When the first conjunct is `fail/0` (9–10), the meta-interpreter backtracks explicitly by means of auxiliary predicate `backtrack/3`.

```
backtrack(Disj,PatOut,Result) :-
    ( empty_alt(Disj) ->
      Result = failure
    ; Disj = alt(BranchPatIn,BranchGoal) ->
      empty_alt(EmptyDisj),
      eval([BranchGoal],BranchPatIn,EmptyDisj,PatOut,Result)
    ).

empty_alt(alt(_,fail)).
```

If there is no alternative branch, it sets the `Result` to `failure`. Otherwise, it resumes with the alternative branch. Note that by managing its own backtracking, `eval/5` is entirely deterministic with respect to the meta-level Prolog system.

```
1   eval([],PatIn,Disj,PatOut,Result) :- !,
2       PatOut = PatIn,
3       Disj  = alt(BranchPatIn,BranchGoal),
4       Result = success(BranchPatIn,BranchGoal).
5   eval([true|Conj],PatIn,Disj,PatOut,Result) :- !,
6       eval(Conj,PatIn,Disj,PatOut,Result).
7   eval([(G1,G2)|Conj],PatIn,Disj,PatOut,Result) :- !,
8       eval([G1,G2|Conj],PatIn,Disj,PatOut,Result).
9   eval([fail|_Conj],_,Disj,PatOut,Result) :- !,
10      backtrack(Disj,PatOut,Result).
11  eval([(G1;G2)|Conj],PatIn,Disj,PatOut,Result) :- !,
12      copy_term(alt(PatIn,conj([G2|Conj])),Branch),
13      disjoin(Branch,Disj,NewDisj),
14      eval([G1|Conj],PatIn,NewDisj,PatOut,Result).
15  eval([conj(Cs)|Conj],PatIn,Disj,PatOut,Result) :- !,
16      append(Cs,Conj,NewConj),
17      eval(NewConj,PatIn,Disj,PatOut,Result).
18  eval([shift(Term)|Conj],PatIn,Disj,PatOut,Result) :- !,
19      PatOut = PatIn,
20      Disj   = alt(BranchPatIn,Branch),
21      Result = shift(Term,conj(Conj),BranchPatIn,Branch).
22  eval([reset(RPattern,RGoal,RResult)|Conj],PatIn,Disj,PatOut,Result):- !,
23      copy_term(RPattern-RGoal,RPatIn-RGoalCopy),
24      empty_alt(RDisj),
25      eval([RGoalCopy],RPatIn,RDisj,RPatOut,RResultFresh),
26      eval([RPattern=RPatOut,RResult=RResultFresh|Conj]
27          ,PatIn,Disj,PatOut,Result).
28  eval([Call|Conj],PatIn,Disj,PatOut,Result) :- !,
29      findall(Call-Body,clause(Call,Body), Clauses),
30      ( Clauses = [] -> backtrack(Disj,PatOut,Result)
31      ; disjoin_clauses(Call,Clauses,ClausesDisj),
32        eval([ClausesDisj|Conj],PatIn,Disj,PatOut,Result)
33      ).
```

Fig. 1. Meta-interpreter core

When the first conjunct is a disjunction (G1;G2) (11–14), the meta-interpreter adds (a renamed apart copy of) (G2,Conj) to the alternative branches with disjoin/3 and proceeds with [G1|Conj].

```
disjoin(alt(_,fail),Disjunction,Disjunction) :- !.
disjoin(Disjunction,alt(_,fail),Disjunction) :- !.
disjoin(alt(P1,G1),alt(P2,G2),Disjunction) :-
    Disjunction = alt(P3, (P1 = P3, G1 ; P2 = P3, G2)).
```

Note that we have introduced a custom built-in conj(Conj) that turns a list of goals into an actual conjunction. It is handled (15–17) by prepending the goals to the current list of conjuncts, and never actually builds the explicit conjunction.

When the first goal is shift(Term) (18–21), this is handled similarly to an empty conjunction, except that the result is a shift/4 term which contains Term and the remainder of the conjunction in addition the branch information.

When the first goal is a reset(RPattern,RGoal,RResult) (22–27), the meta-interpreter sets up an isolated call to eval/5 for this goal. When the call returns, the meta-interpreter passes on the results and resumes the current conjunction Conj. Notice that we are careful that this does not result in meta-level failure by meta-interpreting the unification.

Finally, when the first goal is a call to a user-defined predicate (28–33), the meta-interpreter collects the bodies of the predicate's clauses whose head unifies with the call. If there are none, it backtracks explicitly. Otherwise, it builds an explicit disjunction with disjoin_clauses, which it pushes on the conjunction stack.

```
disjoin_clauses(_G,[],fail) :- !.
disjoin_clauses(G,[GC-Clause],(G=GC,Clause)) :- !.
disjoin_clauses(G,[GC-Clause|Clauses], ((G=GC,Clause) ; Disj)) :-
    disjoin_clauses(G,Clauses,Disj).
```

An example execution trace of the interpreter can be found in [18, Appendix C].

Toplevel. The toplevel(Goal)-predicate initialises the core interpreter with a conjunction containing only the given goal, the pattern and pattern copy set to (distinct) copies of the goal, and an empty disjunction. It interprets the result by non-deterministically producing all the answers to Goal and signalling an error for any unhandled shift/1.

```
toplevel(Goal) :-
    copy_term(Goal,GoalCopy),
    PatIn = GoalCopy,
    empty_alt(Disj),
    eval([GoalCopy],PatIn,Disj,PatOut,Result),
    ( Result = success(BranchPatIn,Branch) ->
        ( Goal = PatOut ; Goal = BranchPatIn, toplevel(Branch))
```

```
; Result = shift(_,_,_,_) ->
    write('toplevel: uncaught shift/1.\n'), fail
; Result = failure ->
    fail
).
```

4   Case Studies

To illustrate the usefulness and practicality of our approach, we present two case studies that use the new reset/3 and shift/1.

4.1   Branch-and-Bound: Nearest Neighbour Search

Branch-and-bound is a well-known general optimisation strategy, where the solutions in certain areas or branches of the search space are known to be bounded. Such branches can be pruned, when their bound does not improve upon a previously found solution, eliminating large swaths of the search space in a single stroke.

We provide an implementation of branch-and-bound (see Fig. 2) that is generic, i.e., it is not specialised for any application. In particular it is not specific to nearest neighbour search, the problem on which we demonstrate the branch-and-bound approach here.

```
bound(V) :- shift(V).

bb(Value,Data,Goal,Min) :-
    reset(Data,Goal,Result),
    bb_result(Result,Value,Data,Min).

bb_result(success(BranchCopy,Branch),Value,Data,Min) :-
  ( Data @< Value -> bb(Data,BranchCopy,Branch,Min)
  ; bb(Value,BranchCopy,Branch,Min)
  ).
bb_result(shift(ShiftTerm,Cont,BranchCopy,Branch),Value,Data,Min) :-
  ( ShiftTerm @< Value ->
    bb(Value,Data,(Cont ; (BranchCopy = Data,Branch)),Min)
  ; bb(Value,BranchCopy,Branch,Min)
  ).
bb_result(failure,Value,_Data,Min) :- Value = Min.
```

Fig. 2. Branch-and-Bound effect handler.

```
nn((X,Y),BSP,D-(NX,NY)) :-
    ( BSP = xsplit((SX,SY),Left,Right) ->
        DX is X - SX,
        branch((X,Y), (SX,SY), Left, Right, DX, D-(NX,NY))
    ; BSP = ysplit((SX,SY),Up,Down) ->
        DY is Y - SY,
        branch((X,Y), (SX,SY), Up, Down, DY, D-(NX,NY))
    ).
branch((X,Y), (SX,SY), BSP1, BSP2, D, Dist-(NX,NY)) :-
    ( D < 0 -> % Find out which partition contains (X,Y).
        TargetPart = BSP1, OtherPart = BSP2, BoundaryDistance is -D
    ;
        TargetPart = BSP2, OtherPart = BSP1, BoundaryDistance is D
    ),
    ( nn((X,Y), TargetPart, Dist-(NX,NY))
    ; Dist is (X - SX) * (X - SX) + (Y - SY) * (Y - SY),
      (NX,NY) = (SX,SY)
    ; bound(BoundaryDistance-nil),
      nn((X,Y), OtherPart,Dist-(NX,NY))
    ).
run_nn((X0,Y0),BSP,(NX,NY)) :-
    toplevel(bb(10-nil,D-(X,Y),nn((X0,Y0),BSP,D-(X,Y)),_-(NX,NY))).
```

Fig. 3. 2D nearest neighbour search with branch-and-bound.

The framework requires minimal instrumentation: it suffices to begin every prunable branch with bound(V), where V is a lower bound on the values in the branch.[1]

1. If the Goal succeeds normally (i.e., Result is success), then Data contains a new solution, which is only accepted if it is an improvement over the existing Value. The handler then tries the next Branch.
2. If the Goal calls bound(V), V is compared to the current best Value:
   - if it is less than the current value, then Cont could produce a solution that improves upon the current value, and thus must be explored. The alternative Branch is disjoined to Cont, and DataCopy is restored to Data (ensuring that a future reset/3 copies the right variables);
   - if it is larger than or equal to the current value, then Cont can be safely discarded.
3. Finally, if the goal fails entirely, Min is the current minimum Value.

Nearest Neighbour Search. The code in Fig. 3 shows how the branch and bound framework efficiently solves the problem of finding the point (in a given set) that is nearest to a given target point on the Euclidean plane.

---

[1] The framework searches for a minimal solution.

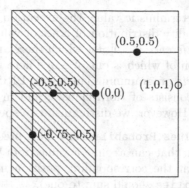

Fig. 4. Nearest-neighbour search using a BSP-tree

The run_nn/3 predicate takes a point (X,Y), a Binary Space Partitioning (BSP)-tree[2] that represents the set of points, and returns the point, nearest to (X,Y). The algorithm implemented by nn/3 recursively descends the BSP-tree. At each node it first tries the partition to which the target point belongs, then the point in the node, and finally the other partition. For this final step we can give an easy lower bound: any point in the other partition must be at least as far away as the (perpendicular) distance from the given point to the partition boundary.

As an example, we search for the point nearest to $(1, 0.1)$ in the set $\{(0.5, 0.5), (0, 0), (-0.5, 0), (-0.75, -0.5)\}$. Figure 4 shows a BSP-tree containing these points, the solid lines demarcate the partitions. The algorithm visits the points $(0.5, 0.5)$ and $(0, 0)$, in that order. The shaded area is never visited, since the distance from $(1, 0.1)$ to the vertical boundary through $(0, 0)$ is greater than the distance to $(0.5, 0.5)$ (1 and about 0.64). The corresponding call to run_nn/3 is:

```
?- BSP = xsplit((0,0),
            ysplit((-0.5,0),leaf,xsplit((-0.75,-0.5),leaf,leaf)),
            ysplit((0.5,0.5),leaf,leaf)),
    run_nn((1,0.1),BSP,(NX,NY)).
NX = NY, NY = 0.5.
```

4.2 Probabilistic Programming

Probabilistic programming languages (PPLs) are programming languages designed for probabilistic modelling. In a probabilistic model, components behave in a variety of ways—just like in a non-deterministic model—but do so with a certain probability.

---

[2] A BSP-tree is a tree that recursively partitions a set of points on the Euclidean plane, by picking points and alternately splitting the plane along the x- or y-coordinate of those point. Splitting along the x-coordinate produces an xsplit/3 node, along the y-coordinate produces a ysplit/3 node.

Instead of a single deterministic value, the execution of a probabilistic program results in a probability distribution of a set of values. This result is produced by probabilistic *inference* [6,19], for which there are many strategies and algorithms, the discussion of which is out of scope here. Here, we focus on one concrete probabilistic *logic* programming languages: PRISM [10].

A PRISM program consists of Horn clauses, and in fact, looks just like a regular Prolog program. However, we distinguish two special predicates:

- values_x(Switch,Values,Probabilities) This predicate defines a probabilistic switch Switch, that can assume a value from Values with the probability that is given at the corresponding position in Probabilities (the contents of Probabilities should sum to one).
- msw(Switch,Value) This predicate samples a value Value from a switch Switch. For instance, if the program contains a switch declared as values_x(coin, [h,t], [0.4,0.6]), then msw(coin,V) assigns h (for heads) to V with probability 0.4, and t (for tails) with probability 0.6. Remark that each distinct call to msw leads to a different sample from that switch. For instance, in the query msw(coin,X),msw(coin,Y), the outcome could be either (h,h),(t,t), (h,t) or (t,h).

Consider the following PRISM program, the running example for this section:

```
values_x(coin1,[h,t],[0.5,0.5]).
values_x(coin2,[h,t],[0.4,0.6]).
twoheads :- msw(coin1,h),msw(coin2,h).
onehead :- msw(coin1,V), (V = t, msw(coin2,h) ; V = h).
```

This example defines two predicates: twoheads which is true if both coins are heads, and onehead which is true if either coin is heads. However, note the special structure of onehead: PRISM requires the *exclusiveness condition*, that is, branches of a disjunction cannot be both satisfied at the same time. The simpler goal msw(coin1,heads) ; msw(coin2, heads) violates this assumption.

The code in Fig. 5 interprets this program. Line 1 defines msw/2 as a simple shift. Lines 6–9 install a reset/3 call over the goal, and analyse the result. The result is analysed in the remaining lines: A *failure* never succeeds, and thus has success probability 0.0 (line 9). Conversely, a successful computation has a success probability of 1.0 (line 10). Finally, the probability of a switch (lines 11–15) is the sum of the probability of the remainder of the program given each possible value of the switch multiplied with the probability of that value, and summed with the probability of the alternative branch.

The predicate msw_prob finds the joint probability of all choices. It iterates over the list of values, and sums the probability of their continuations.

```
msw_prob(_,_,[],[],Acc,Acc).
msw_prob(V,C,[Value|Values],[Prob|Probs],Acc,ProbOfMsw) :-
   prob((V = Value,C),ProbOut),
   msw_prob(V,C,Values,Probs,Prob*ProbOut + Acc,ProbOfMsw).
```

```
1   msw(Key,Value) :- shift(msw(Key,Value)).
2   prob(Goal) :-
3       prob(Goal,ProbOut),
4       write(Goal), write(': '), write(ProbOut), write('\n').
5   prob(Goal,ProbOut) :-
6       copy_term(Goal,GoalCopy),
7       reset(GoalCopy,GoalCopy,Result),
8       analyze_prob(GoalCopy,Result,ProbOut).
9   analyze_prob(_,failure,0.0).
10  analyze_prob(_,success(_,_),1.0).
11  analyze_prob(_,shift(msw(K,V),C,_,Branch),ProbOut) :-
12      values_x(K,Values,Probabilities),
13      msw_prob(V,C,Values,Probabilities,0.0,ProbOfMsw),
14      prob(Branch,BranchProb),
15      ProbOut is ProbOfMsw + BranchProb.
```

Fig. 5. An implementation of probabilistic programming with delimited control.

Now, we can compute the probabilities of the two predicates above:

```
?- toplevel(prob(twoheads)).
twoheads: 0.25
?- toplevel(prob(onehead)).
onehead: 0.75
```

In [18, Appendix B.3] we implement the semantics of a definite, non-looping fragment of ProbLog [6], another logic PPL, on top of the code in this section.

5   Properties of the Meta-interpreter

In this section we establish two important correctness properties of our meta-interpreter with respect to standard SLD resolution. Together these establish that disjunctive delimited control is a conservative extension. This means that programs that do not use the feature behave the same as before.

The proofs of these properties are in [18, Appendix A]. The first theorem establishes the soundness of the meta-interpreter, i.e., if a program (not containing shift/1 or reset/3) evaluates to success, then an SLD-derivation of the same answer must exist.

Theorem 1 (Soundness). *For all lists of goals* $[A_1, \ldots, A_n]$, *terms* $\alpha, \beta, \gamma, \nu$, *variables* P, R *conjunctions* $B_1, \ldots, B_m$; $C_1, \ldots, C_k$ *and substitutions* θ, *if*

$$? - eval([A_1, \ldots, A_n], \alpha, alt(\beta, (B_1, \ldots, B_m)), P, R).$$
$$P = \nu, R = success(\gamma, C_1, \ldots, C_k).$$

and the program contains neither `shift/1` *nor* `reset/3`, *then SLD-resolution*[3] *finds the following derivation:*

$$\leftarrow (A_1, \ldots, A_n, true); (\alpha = \beta, B_1, \ldots, B_m)$$

$$\vdots$$

$$\Box$$

(with solution θ s.t. $\alpha\theta = \nu$)

Conversely, we want to argue that the meta-interpreter is complete, i.e., if SLD-derivation finds a refutation, then meta-interpretation—provided that it terminates—must find the same answer eventually. The theorem is complicated somewhat by the fact that the first answer that the meta-interpreter arrives at might not be the desired one due to the order of the clauses in the program. To deal with this problem, we use the operator ?-$_p$, which is like ?-, but allows a different permutation of the program in every step.

Theorem 2 (Completeness). *For any goal $\leftarrow A_1, \ldots, A_n$, if it has solution θ, then*

$$\text{?-}_p\ eval([A_1, \ldots, A_n], \alpha, alt(\beta, (B_1, \ldots, B_m)), P, R).$$
$$P = success(\gamma, (C_1, \ldots, C_k)), R = \alpha\theta.$$

Together, these two theorems show that our meta-interpreter is a conservative extension of the conventional Prolog semantics.

6   Related Work

Conjunctive Delimited Control. Disjunctive delimited control is the culmination of a line of research on mechanisms to modify Prolog's control flow and search, which started with the hook-based approach of TOR [13] and was followed by the development of conjunctive delimited control for Prolog [12,14].

The listing below shows that disjunctive delimited control entirely subsumes conjunctive delimited control. The latter behaviour is recovered by disjoining the captured disjunctive branch. We believe that TOR is similarly superseded.

```
nd_reset(Goal,Ball,Cont) :-
  copy_term(Goal,GoalCopy),
  reset(GoalCopy,GoalCopy,R),
  ( R = failure -> fail
  ; R = success(BranchPattern,Branch) ->
    ( Goal = GoalCopy, Cont = 0
    ; Goal = BranchPattern, nd_reset(Branch,Ball,Cont))
  ; R = shift(X,C,BranchPattern,Branch) ->
    ( Goal = GoalCopy, Ball = X, Cont = C
    ; Goal = BranchPattern, nd_reset(Branch,Ball,Cont))
  ).
```

---

[3] Standard SLD-resolution, augmented with disjunctions and `conj/1` goals.

```
get(Interactor,Answer) :-
  get_engine(Interactor,Engine),        % get engine state
  run_engine(Engine,NewEngine,Answer),  % run up to the next answer
  update_engine(Interactor,NewEngine).  % store the new engine state
return(X) :- shift(return(X)).
run_engine(engine(Pattern,Goal),NewEngine,Answer) :-
  reset(Pattern,Goal,Result),
  run_engine_result(Pattern,NewEngine,Answer,Result).
run_engine_result(Pattern,NewEngine,Answer,failure) :-
  NewEngine = engine(Pattern,fail),
  Answer    = no.
run_engine_result(Pattern,NewEngine,Answer,success(BPattern,B)) :-
  NewEngine = engine(BPattern,B),
  Answer    = the(Pattern).
run_engine_result(Pattern,NewEngine,Answer,S) :-
  S = shift(return(X),C,BPattern,B)
  BPattern = Pattern,
  NewEngine = engine(Pattern,(C;B)),
  Answer    = the(X).
```

Fig. 6. Interoperable Engines in terms of delimited control.

Abdallah [1] presents a higher-level interface for (conjunctive) delimited control on top of that of Schrijvers et al. [12]. In particular, it features *prompts*, first conceived in a Haskell implementation by Dyvbig et al. [4], which allow shifts to dynamically specify up to what reset to capture the continuation. We believe that it is not difficult to add a similar prompt mechanism on top of our disjunctive version of delimited control.

Interoperable Engines. Tarau and Majumdar's Interoperable Engines [16] propose *engines* as a means for co-operative coroutines in Prolog. An engine is an independent instance of a Prolog interpreter that provides answers to the main interpreter on request.

The predicate new_engine(Pattern,Goal,Interactor) creates a new engine with answer pattern Pattern that will execute Goal and is identified by Interactor. The predicate get(Interactor,Answer) has an engine execute its goal until it produces an answer (either by proving the Goal, or explicitly with return/1). After this predicate returns, more answers can be requested, by calling get/2 again with the same engine identifier. The full interface also allows bi-directional communication between engines, but that is out of scope here.

Figure 6 shows that we can implement the get/2 engine interface in terms of delimited control (the full code is available in [18, Appendix B.2]). The opposite, implementing disjunctive delimited control with engines, seems impossible as engines do not provide explicit control over the disjunctive continuation. Indeed, get/2 can only follow Prolog's natural left-to-right control flow and thus we cannot, e.g., run the disjunctive continuation before the conjunctive continuation, which is trivial with disjunctive delimited control.

Tabling without Non-bactrackable Variables. Tabling [9,15] is a well-known technique that eliminates the sensitivity of SLD-resolution to clause and goal ordering, allowing a larger class of programs to terminate. As a bonus, it may improve the run-time performance (at the expense of increased memory consumption).

One way to implement tabling—with minimal engineering impact to the Prolog engine—is the tabling-as-a-library approach proposed by Desouter et al. [3]. This approach requires (global) mutable variables that are not erased by backtracking to store their data structures in a persistent manner. With the new `reset/3` predicate, this is no longer needed, as (non-backtracking) state can be implemented in directly with disjunctive delimited control.

7 Conclusion and Future Work

We have presented *disjunctive delimited control*, an extension to delimited control that takes Prolog's non-deterministic nature into account. This is a conservative extension that enables implementing disjunction-related language features and extensions as a library.

In future work, we plan to explore a WAM-level implementation of disjunctive delimited control, inspired by the stack freezing functionality of tabling engines, to gain access to the disjunctive continuations efficiently. Similarily, the use of `copy_term/2` necessitated by the current API has a detrimental impact on performance, which might be overcome by a sharing or shallow copying scheme.

Inspired by the impact of conjunctive delimited control, which has brought tabling to SWI-Prolog, we believe that further development of disjunctive delimited control is worthwhile. Indeed, it has the potential of bringing powerful disjunctive control abstractions like branch-and-bound search to a wider range of Prolog systems.

Acknowledgment. We are grateful to Paul Tarau and the anonymous LOPSTR 2021 reviewers for their helpful feedback. Part of this work was funded by FWO grant G0D1419N and by KU Leuven grant C14/20/079.

References

1. Abdallah, S.: More declarative tabling in Prolog using multi-prompt delimited control. CoRR abs/1708.07081 (2017)
2. Danvy, O., Filinski, A.: Abstracting control. In: Proceedings of the LFP 1990, pp. 151–160 (1990)
3. Desouter, B., van Dooren, M., Schrijvers, T.: Tabling as a library with delimited control. TPLP **15**(4–5), 419–433 (2015)
4. Dyvbig, R.K., Jones, S.P., Sabry, A.: A monadic framework for delimited continuations. Technical report 615, Computer Science Department Indiana University (2005)

5. Felleisen, M.: The theory and practice of first-class prompts. In: Proceedings of the POPL 1988, pp. 180–190 (1988)
6. Fierens, D., et al.: Inference and learning in probabilistic logic programs using weighted Boolean formulas. TPLP **15**(3), 358–401 (2015)
7. Ivanovic, D., Morales Caballero, J.F., Carro, M., Hermenegildo, M.: Towards structured state threading in Prolog. In: CICLOPS 2009 (2009)
8. Saleh, A.H., Schrijvers, T.: Efficient algebraic effect handlers for Prolog. TPLP **16**(5–6), 884–898 (2016)
9. Santos Costa, V., Rocha, R., Damas, L.: The YAP Prolog system. TPLP **12**(1–2), 5–34 (2012)
10. Sato, T.: Generative modeling by PRISM. In: Hill, P.M., Warren, D.S. (eds.) ICLP 2009. LNCS, vol. 5649, pp. 24–35. Springer, Heidelberg (2009). https://doi.org/10.1007/978-3-642-02846-5_4
11. Schimpf, J.: Logical loops. In: Stuckey, P.J. (ed.) ICLP 2002. LNCS, vol. 2401, pp. 224–238. Springer, Heidelberg (2002). https://doi.org/10.1007/3-540-45619-8_16
12. Schrijvers, T., Demoen, B., Desouter, B., Wielemaker, J.: Delimited continuations for Prolog. TPLP **13**(4–5), 533–546 (2013)
13. Schrijvers, T., Demoen, B., Triska, M., Desouter, B.: Tor: modular search with hookable disjunction. Sci. Comput. Program. **84**, 101–120 (2014)
14. Schrijvers, T., Wu, N., Desouter, B., Demoen, B.: Heuristics entwined with handlers combined: from functional specification to logic programming implementation. In: Proceedings of PPDP 2014, pp. 259–270. ACM (2014)
15. Swift, T., Warren, D.S.: XSB: extending Prolog with tabled logic programming. TPLP **12**(1–2), 157–187 (2012)
16. Tarau, P., Majumdar, A.: Interoperating logic engines. In: Gill, A., Swift, T. (eds.) PADL 2009. LNCS, vol. 5418, pp. 137–151. Springer, Heidelberg (2008). https://doi.org/10.1007/978-3-540-92995-6_10
17. Van Roy, P.: A useful extension to Prolog's definite clause grammar notation **24**(11), 132–134 (1989)
18. Vandenbroucke, A., Schrijvers, T.: Disjunctive delimited control. CoRR abs/2108.02972 (2021). https://arxiv.org/abs/2108.02972
19. Wood, F.D., van de Meent, J., Mansinghka, V.: A new approach to probabilistic programming inference. In: AISTATS. JMLR Workshop and Conference Proceedings, vol. 33, pp. 1024–1032. JMLR.org (2014)

Towards Substructural Property-Based Testing

Marco Mantovani and Alberto Momigliano[(✉)]

Dipartimento di Informatica, Università degli Studi di Milano, Milan, Italy
`momigliano@di.unimi.it`

Abstract. We propose to extend property-based testing to substructural logics to overcome the current lack of reasoning tools in the field. We take the first step by implementing a property-based testing system for specifications written in the linear logic programming language Lolli. We employ the foundational proof certificates architecture to model various data generation strategies. We validate our approach by encoding a model of a simple imperative programming language and its compilation and by testing its meta-theory via mutation analysis.

Keywords: Linear logic · Property-based testing · Focusing · Semantics of programming languages

1 Introduction

Since their inception in the late 80's, logical frameworks based on intuitionistic logic [43] have been successfully used to represent and animate deductive systems (*λProlog*) as well as to reason (*Twelf*) about them. The methodology of *higher-order abstract syntax* (HOAS) together with parametric-hypothetical judgments yields elegant encodings that lead to elegant proofs, since it delegates to the meta-logic the handling of many common notions, in particular the representation of *contexts*. For example, when modeling a typing system, we represent the typing context as a set of parametric (atomic) assumptions: this tends to simplify the meta-theory since properties such as weakening and context substitution come for free: in fact, they are inherited from the logical framework, and do not need to be proved on a case-by-case basis. For an early example, see the proof of subject reduction for MiniML in [35], which completely avoids the need to establish intermediate lemmas, as opposed to more standard and labor-intensive treatments [15].

However, this identification of meta and object level contexts turns out to be problematic in *state-passing* specifications. To fix ideas, consider specifying the operational semantics of an imperative programming language: evaluating

This work has been partially supported by the National Group of Computing Science (GNCS-INdAM) within the project "Estensioni del *Property-based Testing* di e con linguaggi di programmazione dichiarativa".

E. De Angelis and W. Vanhoof (Eds.): LOPSTR 2021, LNCS 13290, pp. 92–112, 2022.
https://doi.org/10.1007/978-3-030-98869-2_6

an assignment requires taking an input state, modifying it and finally returning it. A state (and related notions such as heaps, stacks, etc.) cannot be adequately encoded as a set of intuitionistic assumptions, since it is intrinsically ephemeral. The standard solution of reifing the state into a data structure, while doable, betrays the whole HOAS approach.

Luckily, linear logic can change the world [51]—Linear logic being of course the main example of *substructural* logics, i.e., those non-classical logics characterized by the absence of some structural rules [41]. Linearity provides a notion of context which has an immediate reading in terms of *resources*. A state can be seen as a set of linear assumptions and the linear connectives can be used to model in a declarative way reading and writing said state. In the early 90's this idea was taken up in linear logic programming and specification languages such as *Lolli* [22], *LLF* [7] and *Forum* [36].

In the ensuing years, given the richness of linear logic and the flexibility of the proof-theoretic foundations of logic programming [37], more sophisticated languages emerged, with additional features such as order (*Olli* [46]), subexponentials [40], bottom-up evaluation and concurrency (*Lollimon* [29], *Celf* [49]). Each extension required significant ingenuity, since it relied on the development of appropriate notions of canonical forms, resource management, unification etc. At the same time, tools for *reasoning* over such substructural specifications did not materialize. Meta-reasoning over a logical framework, in fact, asks for formulating appropriate meta-logics, which, again, is far from trivial, the more when the framework is substructural; in fact no implementation of the latter have appeared. The case for the concurrent logical framework CLF [8] is particularly striking, where, notwithstanding a wide and promising range of applications, the only meta-theoretic analysis available in *Celf* is checking that a program is well-moded. Compare this with the successful deployment of dedicated HOAS-based intuitionistic proof assistants such as *Beluga* [45] and *Abella* [1].

If linear verification is too hard, or just while we wait for the field to catch up, this paper suggests *validation* as a useful alternative, in particular in the form of *property-based testing* [24] (PBT). This is a lightweight validation technique whereby the user specifies executable properties that the code should satisfy and the system tries to refute them via automatic (typically random) data generation.

Previous work [4] gave a proof-theoretic reconstruction of PBT in terms of focusing and *foundational proof certificates* (FPC) [12], which, in theory, applies to all the languages mentioned above. The promise of the approach is that we can state and check properties in the very logic where we specify them, without resorting to a further meta-logic. Of course, validation falls rather short of verification, but as by now common in mainstream proof assistants, e.g., [5,42], we may resort to testing not only *in lieu of* proving, but *before* proving, so as to avoid pointless effort in trying to prove false theorems or true properties over bugged models.

In fact, the two-level architecture [19] underlying the *Abella* system and the *Hybrid* library [17] seems a good match for the combination of testing and proving over substructural specifications. In this architecture we keep the meta-logic fixed, while making substructural the specification logic. Indeed, some case studies have been already carried out, as we detail in Sect. 6.

In this paper we move the first steps in this programme implementing PBT for Lolli and evaluating its capability in catching bugs by applying it to a mid-size case study: we give a linear encoding of the static and dynamic semantic of an imperative programming language and its compilation into a stack machine and validate several properties, among which type preservation and soundness of compilation. We have tried to test properties in the way they would be stated and hopefully proved in a linear proof assistant based on the two-level architecture. That is, we are not arguing (yet) that linear PBT is "better" than traditional ones for state-passing specifications. Besides, in the case studies we have carried out so far, we generate only *persistent* data (expressions, programs) under a given linear context. Rather, we advocate the coupling of validation and (eventually) verification for those encoding where linearity makes a difference in terms of drastically simplifying the infrastructure needed to prove the main result: one of the original success stories of linear specifications, namely type preservation of MiniML with *references* [7,34], still stands and nicely extends the cited one for MiniML: linearly, the theorem can be proven from first principles, while with a standard encoding, for example the Coq formalization in *Software foundations*[1], one needs literally dozens of preliminary lemmas.

The rest of the paper is organized as follows: we start in the next Sect. 2 with a short example of model-based testing of a linear specification. Section 3 gives a short introduction to the proof-theory of intuitionistic linear logic programming, while Sect. 4 applies the notion of FPC to our reconstruction of PBT. Next (Sect. 5), we validate our approach with a case study concerning the meta-theory of a basic imperative language including an experimental evaluation (Sect. 5.2). We conclude in Sect. 6 with a short review of related and future work.

We assume in the following a passing familiarity with linear logic and with the proof-theoretic foundations of logic programming [37].

2   A Motivating Example

To preview our methodology, we present a self-contained example where we use PBT in the guise of *model-based* testing: we test an implementation against a *trusted* version. We choose as trusted model the linear encoding of the implicational fragment of the *contraction-free* calculus for propositional intuitionistic logic, popularized by Dyckhoff. Figure 1 lists the rules for the judgment $\Gamma \vdash C$, together with a Lolli implementation. Here, and in the following, we will use Lolli's concrete syntax, where the lollipop (in both directions) is linear implication, x is multiplicative conjunction (tensor), & is additive conjunction and erase its unit $\top$. The of-course modality is bang.

As shown originally in [22], we can encode provability with a predicate pv that uses a linear context of propositions hyp for assumptions, that is occurring

---

[1] https://softwarefoundations.cis.upenn.edu/plf-current/References.html.

$$\frac{\Gamma, A \vdash B}{\Gamma \vdash A \to B} \ R_{\to} \qquad \frac{}{\Gamma, A \vdash A} \ init$$

$$\frac{\Gamma, B, a \vdash C}{\Gamma, a \to B, a \vdash C} \ L_{\to}^a \qquad \frac{\Gamma, A_2 \to B \vdash A_1 \to A_2 \quad \Gamma, B \vdash C}{\Gamma, (A_1 \to A_2) \to B \vdash C} \ L_{\to}^i$$

. . . .

```
pv(imp(A,B)) o- (hyp(A) -o pv(B)).
pv(A) o- hyp(A) x erase.
pv(C) o- hyp(imp(A,B)) x bang(atom(A)) x hyp(A) x
        (hyp(B) -o hyp(A) -o pv(C)).
pv(C) o- hyp(imp(imp(A1,A2),B)) x
        (hyp(imp(A2,B) -o pv(imp(A1,A2))) &
        (hyp(B) -o pv(C))).
```

Fig. 1. Rules for contraction free LJF$_\to$ and their Lolli encoding

at the left of the turnstile; this is shown in the first clause encoding the implication right rule $R_\to$ via the embedded implication `hyp(A) -o pv(B)`. In the left rules, the premises are consumed by means of the tensor and new assumptions (re)asserted. The fact `atom(A)` lives on thanks to the bang, since it may need to be reused. Note how in the encoding of rule $L_\to^i$, the context Γ is duplicated through additive conjunction. The *init* rule disposes via `erase` of any remaining assumption since the object logic enjoys weakening. By construction, the above code is a decision procedure for LJF$_\to$.

Taking inspiration from Tarau's [50], we consider next an optimization where we factor the two left rules for implication in one:

```
... % similar to before
pvb(C) o- hypb(imp(A,B)) x pvbi(A,B) x
          (hypb(B) -o pvb(C)).

pvbi(imp(C,D),B) o- hypb(imp(D,B)) -o pvb(imp(C,D)).
pvbi(A,_)          o- hypb(A).
```

Does the optimization preserve provability? Formally, the conjecture is $\forall A: form. \ pv(A) \supset pvb(A)$. We could try to prove it, although, for the reasons alluded to in the introduction, it is not clear in which (formalized) meta-logic we would carry out such proof. Instead, it is simpler to test, that is to search for a counter-example. And the answer is no, the (encoding of the) optimization is faulty, as witnessed by the (pretty printed) counterexample `A => ((A => (A => B)) => B)`: this intuitionistic tautology fails to be provable in the purported optimization. We leave the fix to the reader.

3 A Primer on Linear Logic Programming

In this section we introduce some basic notions concerning the proof-theoretic foundations of intuitionistic linear logic programming. We follow quite closely

$$\frac{}{B \vdash B} \ \text{id} \qquad \frac{}{\Delta \vdash \top} \ \text{T-R}$$

$$\frac{\Delta, B_i \vdash C}{\Delta, B_1 \,\&\, B_2 \vdash C} \ \&\text{-L}_i \ (i = 1, 2) \qquad \frac{\Delta \vdash B \quad \Delta \vdash C}{\Delta \vdash B \,\&\, C} \ \&\text{-R}$$

$$\frac{\Delta, B_1, B_2 \vdash C}{\Delta, B_1 \otimes B_2 \vdash C} \ \otimes\text{-L}_i \qquad \frac{\Delta_1 \vdash B \quad \Delta_2 \vdash C}{\Delta_1, \Delta_2 \vdash B \otimes C} \ \otimes\text{-R}$$

$$\frac{\Delta_1 \vdash B \quad \Delta_2, C \vdash E}{\Delta_1, \Delta_2, B \multimap C \vdash E} \ \multimap\text{-L} \qquad \frac{\Delta, B \vdash C}{\Delta \vdash B \multimap C} \ \multimap\text{-R}$$

$$\frac{\Gamma, B \vdash C}{\Delta, !B \vdash C} \ !\text{-D} \qquad \frac{!\Delta \vdash B}{!\Delta \vdash !B} \ !\text{-R}$$

$$\frac{\Delta \vdash E}{\Delta, !B \vdash E} \ !\text{-W} \qquad \frac{\Delta, !B, !B \vdash C}{\Delta, !B \vdash C} \ !\text{-C}$$

$$\frac{\Delta, B[t/x] \vdash C}{\Delta, \forall x.B \vdash C} \ \forall\text{-L} \qquad \frac{\Delta \vdash B[y/x]}{\Delta \vdash \forall x.B} \ \forall\text{-R}$$

provided that y is not free in the lower sequent.

Fig. 2. A sequent calculus for a fragment of linear logic.

the account by Miller and Hodas [22], to which we refer for more details and motivations. It is possible, although slightly more technically involved, to give a more general and modern treatment of the proof-theory in terms of *focusing* [28].

A *substructural* logic differs from classical and intuitionistic logic by restricting or even dropping from its proof-theory one of the usual structural rules, namely weakening, contraction, and exchange. *Linear* logic [21] is probably the most well-known: by controlling the use of contraction and weakening we can view logical deduction no longer as an ever-expanding collection of persistent "truths", but as a way of manipulating *resources* that cannot be arbitrarily duplicated or thrown away.

A linear logic programming language such as Lolli extends conservatively the logic behind λProlog, that is (first-order) Hereditary Harrop formulæ (HHF), which can be seen as the language freely generated by $\top, \wedge, \Rightarrow$ and $\forall$. Therefore it is natural to refine HHF via the connectives $\top, \&, \otimes, \multimap, !, \forall$. We present the proof-theory of this language as a two-sided sequent calculus (Fig. 2) based on the judgment $\Delta \vdash B^2$, where B is a formula over the above connectives and Δ is a multi-set of formulas. We use "," to denote both multi-set union and adding a formula to a context; further, with $!\Delta$ we mean the multiset $\{!B \mid B \in \Delta\}$. Contraction and weakening are allowed only on unrestricted assumptions (rules !-W and !-C). Linear logic induces a related distinction between connectives, which now come in two flavors: additive and multiplicative. The former duplicate the context, e.g., additive conjunction (&-R), the latter split it, e.g., multiplicative conjunction ($\otimes$-R).

---

[2] We overload "$\vdash$" to denote provability for all the sequent systems in this paper, counting on the structure of antecedent and consequent to disambiguate.

$$\dfrac{\Delta \vdash G_1 \quad \Delta \vdash G_2}{\Delta \vdash G_1 \,\&\, G_2} \qquad \dfrac{}{\cdot \vdash 1} \qquad \dfrac{\Delta_1 \vdash G_1 \quad \Delta_2 \vdash G_2}{\Delta_1, \Delta_2 \vdash G_1 \otimes G_2} \qquad \dfrac{}{\Delta \vdash \top}$$

$$\dfrac{\Delta, \alpha \vdash G}{\Delta \vdash \alpha \multimap G} \qquad \dfrac{\cdot \vdash G}{\cdot \vdash \,!G} \qquad \dfrac{\Delta, !A, A \vdash G}{\Delta, !A \vdash G}$$

$$\dfrac{}{!\Delta, A \vdash A} \qquad \dfrac{\Delta \vdash G \quad G \multimap A \in grnd(\mathcal{P})}{\Delta \vdash A}$$

Fig. 3. Uniform proofs for second order LHHF

While this calculus is well-understood, it cannot be seen as an abstract logic programming language in the sense of [37], since it does not enjoy the uniform proof property: the latter allows one to see a cut-free sequent derivation $\Gamma \vdash G$ as the state of an interpreter trying to establish if G follows from Γ. More technically, a proof is *uniform* if every occurrence of a sequent with non-atomic succedent is the conclusion of a right introduction rule.

For the fragment in Fig. 2, the problem boils down to the non-permutability of the right rules for tensor and of-course over the left rules. Miller & Hodas' solution was to limit the occurrences of those troublesome operators. We go a little bit further, following large part of the literature [4,17,19], and adopt an additional minor restriction of linear Hereditary Harrop formulæ: we limit ourselves to implications with *atomic*, possibly banged, premises. We also drop universal goals, since our term language is first-order (as opposed to λProlog), making universal goals essentially useless. On the other hand, we introduce as goals (not as first class connectives) the tensor and the of-course modality. This allows us to view, as usual, intuitionistic implication as defined: $A \Rightarrow B$ is mapped to $!A \multimap B$. Having both forms (linear and unrestricted) of hypothetical judgments is an essential ingredient in the art of linear logic specifications. Programs are sets of the universal closure of clauses of the form $G \multimap A$, which are fixed and implicitly banged, since they can be used as many times as needed. The grammar of second-order LHHF follows:

Goals	G	$::= A \mid \top \mid 1 \mid \alpha \multimap G \mid \,!G \mid G_1 \otimes G_2 \mid G_1 \,\&\, G_2$
Clauses	D	$::= \forall(G \multimap A)$
Programs	$\mathcal{P}$	$::= \cdot \mid \mathcal{P}, D$
Assumption	α	$::= A \mid \,!A$
Context	Δ	$::= \cdot \mid \Delta, \alpha$
Atoms	A	$::= \ldots$

This reformulation of LHHF leads to the calculus in Fig. 3, which is closer to our intuition of a logic programming interpreter since the left rules have been replaced by *backchaining* (last rule) over all the ground instances (*grnd*) of a program. Note how the additive unit $\top$ allows one to discard any remaining assumption, while 1 holds only if all resources have been consumed. Similarly,

$$\frac{\Delta_I \setminus \Delta_O \vdash G_1 \quad \Delta_I \setminus \Delta_O \vdash G_2}{\Delta_I \setminus \Delta_O \vdash G_1 \& G_2} \qquad \frac{}{\Delta_I \setminus \Delta_I \vdash 1}$$

$$\frac{\Delta_I \setminus \Delta_M \vdash G_1 \quad \Delta_M \setminus \Delta_O \vdash G_2}{\Delta_I \setminus \Delta_O \vdash G_1 \otimes G_2} \qquad \frac{\Delta_O \subseteq \Delta_I}{\Delta_I \setminus \Delta_O \vdash \top}$$

$$\frac{\Delta_I, \alpha \setminus \Delta_O, \square \vdash G}{\Delta_I \setminus \Delta_O \vdash \alpha \multimap G} \qquad \frac{\Delta_I \setminus \Delta_I \vdash G}{\Delta_I \setminus \Delta_I \vdash !G}$$

$$\frac{}{\Delta_I, A \setminus \Delta_I, \square \vdash A} \qquad \frac{}{\Delta_I, !A \setminus \Delta_O, !A \vdash A}$$

$$\frac{\Delta_I \setminus \Delta_O \vdash G \quad G \multimap A \in grnd(\mathcal{P})}{\Delta_I \setminus \Delta_O \vdash A}$$

Fig. 4. The IO system for second order LHHF.

a bang can hold only if it does not depend on any resource. In the axiom rule, A is the only ephemeral assumption. Unrestricted assumptions can be copied at will.

By adapting the techniques in [22], we can show that second-order LHHF has the uniform proof property. However, the latter does not address the question of how to perform proof search in the presence of linear assumptions, a.k.a. the *resource management problem* [6]. The problem is firstly caused by multiplicative connectives that, under a goal-oriented strategy, require a potentially exponential partitioning of the given linear context, case in point the tensor right rule. Another source of non-determinism is the rule for $\top$, since it puts no constraint on the required context.

A solution to the first issue is based on *lazy* context splitting and it is known as the *IO system*: it was introduced in [22], and further refined in [6]: when we need to split a context (in our fragment only in the tensor case), we give to one of the sub-goal the whole input context (Δ_I): some of it will be consumed and the leftovers (Δ_O) returned to be used by the other sub-goal.

Figure 4 contains a version of the IO system for our language as described by the judgment $\Delta_I \setminus \Delta_O \vdash G$, where $\setminus$ is just a suggestive notation to separate input and output context. Following the literature and our implementation, we will signal that a resource has been consumed in the input context by replacing it with the placeholder "$\square$".

The IO system is known to be sound and complete w.r.t. uniform provability: $\Delta_I \setminus \Delta_O \vdash G$ iff $\Delta_I - \Delta_O \vdash G$, where "$-$" is context difference modulo $\square$ (see [22] for the definition). Given this relationship, the requirement for the linear context to be empty in the right rules for **1** and ! is realized by the notation $\Delta_I \setminus \Delta_I$. In particular, in the linear axiom rule, A is the only available resource, while in the intuitionistic case, $!A$ is not consumed. The tensor rule showcases lazy context splitting, while additive conjunction duplicates the linear context.

The handling of $\top$ is sub-optimal, since it succeeds with any subset of the input context. As well known, this could be addressed by using the notion of *slack* [6] to remove ⊤-non determinism. However, given the preferred style of our encodings (see Sect. 5), where additive unit is called only as a last step, this has so far not proved necessary.

4   The Proof-Theory of PBT

While PBT originated in a functional programming setting [14], at least two factors make a proof-theoretic reconstruction fruitful:

1. it fits nicely with a (co)inductive reading of rule-based presentations of a system-under-test;
2. it easily generalizes to richer logics.

If we view a property as a logical formula $\forall x[(\tau(x) \wedge P(x)) \supset Q(x)]$ where τ is a typing predicate, providing a counter-example consists of negating the property, and therefore searching for a proof of $\exists x[(\tau(x) \wedge P(x)) \wedge \neg Q(x)]$.

Stated in this way the problem points to a logic programming solution, and this means uniform proofs or more generally, proof-search in a *focused* sequent calculus [28], where the specification is a set of assumptions (typically sets of clauses) and the negated property is the query.

The connection of PBT with focused proof search is that in such a query the *positive phase* is represented by $\exists x$ and $(\tau(x) \wedge P(x))$. This corresponds to the generation of possible counter-examples under precondition P. That is followed by the *negative phase* (which corresponds to counter-example testing) and is represented by $\neg Q(x)$. This formalizes the intuition that generation may be arbitrarily hard, while testing is just a deterministic computation.

How do we supply external information to the positive phase? In particular, how do we steer data generation? This is where the theory of *foundational proof certificates* [12] (FPC) comes in. For the type-theoretically inclined, FPC can be understood as a generalization of proof-terms in the Curry-Howard tradition. They have been introduced to define and share a range of proof structures used in various theorem provers (e.g., resolution refutations, Herbrand disjuncts, tableaux, etc.). A FPC implementation consists of

1. a generic proof-checking kernel,
2. the specification of a certificate format, and
3. a set of predicates (called *clerks and experts*) that decorate the sequent rules used in the kernel and help to process the certificate.

In our setting, we can view those predicates as simple logic programs that guide the search for potential counter-examples using different generation strategies. The following special case may clarify the idea: consider two variations of the beloved Prolog vanilla meta-interpreter, where in the left-hand side we bound the derivation by its *height* and in the right-hand side we limit the number of clauses used (*size*): for the latter, N is input and M output, so the size will be $N - M$. For convenience we use numerals.

$$\frac{\Xi_1 : \Delta_I \setminus \Delta_O \vdash G_1 \quad \Xi_2 : \Delta_I \setminus \Delta_O \vdash G_2 \quad \&_e(\Xi, \Xi_1, \Xi_2)}{\Xi : \Delta_I \setminus \Delta_O \vdash G_1 \& G_2} \qquad \frac{\mathbf{1}_e(\Xi)}{\Xi : \Delta_I \setminus \Delta_I \vdash \mathbf{1}}$$

$$\frac{\Xi_1 : \Delta_I \setminus \Delta_M \vdash G_1 \quad \Xi_2 : \Delta_M \setminus \Delta_O \vdash G_2 \quad \otimes_e(\Xi, \Xi_1, \Xi_2)}{\Xi : \Delta_I \setminus \Delta_O \vdash G_1 \otimes G_2} \qquad \frac{\Delta_I \supseteq \Delta_O \quad \top_e(\Xi)}{\Xi : \Delta_I \setminus \Delta_O \vdash \top}$$

$$\frac{\Xi' : \Delta_I, \alpha \setminus \Delta_O, \Box \vdash G \quad \multimap_e(\Xi, \Xi')}{\Xi : \Delta_I \setminus \Delta_O \vdash \alpha \multimap G} \qquad \frac{\Xi' : \Delta_I \setminus \Delta_I \vdash G \quad !_e(\Xi, \Xi')}{\Xi : \Delta_I \setminus \Delta_I \vdash !G}$$

$$\frac{init_e(\Xi)}{\Xi : \Delta_I, A \setminus \Delta_I, \Box \vdash A} \qquad \frac{init!_e(\Xi)}{\Xi : \Delta_I, !A \setminus \Delta_O, !A \vdash A}$$

$$\frac{\Xi' : \Delta_I \setminus \Delta_O \vdash G \quad (G \multimap A) \in grnd(\mathcal{P}) \quad unfold_e(\Xi, \Xi', A, G)}{\Xi : \Delta_I \setminus \Delta_O \vdash A}$$

Fig. 5. FPC presentation of the IO system for second order Lolli

```
demo(_,true).                 demo(N,N,true).
demo(H,(G1,G2)) :-            demo(N,M,(G1,G2)) :-
 demo(H,G1),demo(H,G2).        demo(N,T,G1),demo(T,M,G2).
demo(s(H),A)      :-          demo(s(N),M,A)      :-
 clause(A,G),demo(H,G).        clause(A,G),demo(N,M,G).
```

Not only is this code repetitious, but it reflects just two specific derivations strategies. We can abstract the pattern by replacing the concrete bounds with a variable to be instantiated with a specific certificate format and add for each case/rule a predicate that will direct the search according to the given certificate.

```
demo(Cert,true)    :-
  trueE(Cert).
demo(Cert,(G1,G2)) :-
 andE(Cert,Cert1,Cert2),
 demo(Cert1,G1),demo(Cert2,G2).
demo(Cert,A)       :-
 unfoldE(Cert,Cert1),
 clause(A,G),demo(Cert1,G).
```

Then, it is just a matter to provide the predicates, implicitly fixing the certificate format:

```
trueE(height(_)).
trueE(size(N,N)).
andE(height(H),height(H),height(H)).
andE(size(N,M),size(N,T),size(T,M)).
unfoldE(height(s(H)),height(H)).
unfoldE(size(s(N)),M),size(N,M)).
```

With this intuition in place, we can take the final step by augmenting each inference rule of the system in Fig. 4 with an additional premise involving an expert predicate, a certificate $\varXi$, and possibly resulting certificates $(\varXi', \varXi_1, \varXi_2)$, reading the rules from conclusion to premises. Operationally, the certificate $\varXi$ is an input in the conclusion of a rule and the continuations are computed by the expert to be handed over to the premises, if any. We sum up the rules in Fig. 5.

As we have said, the FPC methodology requires to describe a format for the certificate. Since in this paper we use FPC only to guide proof-search, we fix the following three formats and we allow their composition, known as *pairing*:

$$\text{Certificates } \varXi ::= n \mid \langle n, m \rangle \mid d \mid (\varXi, \varXi)$$

Following on the examples above, the first certificate is just a natural number (*height*), while the second consists of a pair of naturals (*size*). In the third case, d stands for a *distribution* of weights to clauses in a predicate definition, to be used for random generation; if none is given, we assume a uniform distribution. Crucially, we can compose certificates, so that for example we can offer random generation bounded by the height of the derivation; pairing is a simple, but surprisingly effective combinator [3].

Each certificate format is accompanied by the implementation of the predicates that process the certificate in question. We exemplify the FPC discipline with a selection of rules instantiated with the *size* certificates. If we run the judgment $\langle n, m \rangle : \varDelta_I \setminus \varDelta_O \vdash G$, the inputs are n, $\varDelta_I$ and G, while $\varDelta_O$ and m will be output.

$$\frac{\langle n-1, m \rangle : \varDelta_I \setminus \varDelta_O \vdash G \quad (A \leftarrow G) \in \mathrm{grnd}(\mathcal{P}) \quad n > 0}{\langle n, m \rangle : \varDelta_I \setminus \varDelta_O \vdash A} \qquad \langle n, n \rangle : \varDelta_I \setminus \varDelta_I \vdash 1$$

$$\frac{\langle i, m \rangle : \varDelta_I \setminus \varDelta_M \vdash G_1 \quad \langle m, o \rangle : \varDelta_M \setminus \varDelta_O \vdash G_2}{\langle i, o \rangle : \varDelta_I \setminus \varDelta_O \vdash G_1 \otimes G_2}$$

$$\frac{\langle n, m \rangle : \varDelta_I \setminus \varDelta_O \vdash G_1 \quad \langle n, m \rangle : \varDelta_I \setminus \varDelta_O \vdash G_2}{\langle n, m \rangle : \varDelta_I \setminus \varDelta_O \vdash G_1 \,\&\, G_2}$$

Here (as in all the formats considered in this paper), most experts are rather simple; they basically hand over the certificate according to the connective. This is the case of $\&$ and 1, where the expert copies the bound and its action is implicit in the instantiation of the certificates in the premises. In the tensor rule, the certificate mimics context splitting. The *unfold* expert, instead, is more interesting: not only it decreases the bound, provided we have not maxed out on the latter, but it is also in charge of selecting the next goal: for bounded search via chronological backtracking, for random data generation via random backtracking: every time the derivation reaches an atom, we permute its definition and pick a matching clause according to the distribution described by the certificate. Other strategies are possible, as suggested in [18]: for example, permuting the definition just once at the beginning of generation, or even randomizing the conjunctions in the body of a clause.

Note that we have elected *not* to delegate to the experts resource management: while possible, it would force us to pair such certificate with any other one. As detailed in [4], more sophisticated FPC capture other features of PBT, such as shrinking and bug-provenance, and will not be repeated here.

We are now ready to account for the soundness property from the example in Sect. 2. By analogy, this applies to certificate-driven PBT with a liner IO kernel in general. Let Ξ be here the height certificate with bound 4 and `form(_)` a unary predicate describing the syntax of implicational formulæ, which we use as a generator. Testing the property amounts to the following query in a host language that implements the kernel:

$$\exists F. \ (\Xi : \cdot \setminus \cdot \vdash \texttt{form(F)}) \wedge (\Xi : \cdot \setminus \cdot \vdash \texttt{pv(F)}) \wedge \neg (\Xi : \cdot \setminus \cdot \vdash \texttt{pvb(F)})$$

In our case, the meta-language is simply Prolog, where we encode the kernel with a predicate `prove/4` and to check for un-provability negation-as-failure suffices, as argued in [4].

```
C = height(4),prove(C,[],[],form(F)),
    prove(C,[],[],pv(F)),\+ prove(C,[],[],pvb(F)).
```

5   Case Study

IMP is a model of a minimalist Turing-complete imperative programming language, featuring instructions for assignment, sequencing, conditional and loop. It has been extensively used in teaching and in mechanizations (viz. formalized textbooks such as *Software Foundations* and *Concrete Semantics*[3]). Here we follow Leroy's account [27], but add a basic type system to distinguish arithmetical from Boolean expressions.

IMP is a good candidate for a linear logic encoding, since its operational semantics is, of course, state-based, while its syntax (see below) is simple enough not to require a sophisticated treatment of binders.

expr ::=	var	*variable*
|	i	*integer constant*
|	b	*Boolean constant*
|	expr + expr	*addition*
|	expr − expr	*subtraction*
|	expr ∗ expr	*multiplication*
|	expr ∧ expr	*conjunction*
|	expr ∨ expr	*disjunction*
|	¬ expr	*negation*
|	expr == expr	*equality*

val ::=			ty ::=		
|	vi	*integer value*	|	tint	*integers type*
|	vb	*Boolean value*	|	tbool	*Bool type*

---

[3] softwarefoundations.cis.upenn.edu and concrete-semantics.org.

```
cmd ::= skip                          no op
      | cmd ; cmd                     sequence
      | if expr then cmd else cmd     conditional
      | while expr do cmd             loop
      | var = expr                    assignment
```

The relevant judgments describing the dynamic and static semantics of IMP are:

$\sigma \vdash e \Downarrow v$ big step evaluation of expressions;
$(c, \sigma) \Downarrow \sigma'$ big step execution of commands;
$(c, \sigma) \rightsquigarrow (c', \sigma')$ small step execution of commands and its Kleene closure;
$\Gamma \vdash e : \tau$ well-typed expressions and $v : \tau$ well-typed values;
$\Gamma \vdash c$ well-typed commands and $\Gamma : \sigma$ well-typed states;

5.1 On Linear Encodings

In traditional accounts, a state σ is a (finite) map between variables and values. Linear logic takes a "distributed" view and represents a state as a multi-set of linear assumptions. Since this is central to our approach, we make explicit the (overloaded) encoding function $\ulcorner \cdot \urcorner$ on states. Its action on values is as expected and therefore omitted:

$$\sigma ::= \cdot \mid \sigma, x \mapsto v$$
$$\ulcorner \cdot \urcorner = \emptyset$$
$$\ulcorner \sigma, x \mapsto v \urcorner = \ulcorner \sigma \urcorner, var(x, \ulcorner v \urcorner)$$

When encoding state-based computations such as evaluation and execution in a Lolli-like language, it is almost forced on us to use a *continuation-passing style* (CPS [47]): by sequencing the computation, we get a handle on how to express "what to compute next", and this turns out to be the right tool to encode the operational semantics of state update, the more when the modeled semantics has side-effects, lest adequacy is lost.

Yet, even under the CPS-umbrella, there are choices: e.g., whether to adopt an encoding that privileges *additive* connectives, in particular when using the state in a non-destructive way. In the additive style, the state is duplicated with & and then eventually disposed of via $\top$ at the leaves of the derivation.

This is well-understood, but it would lead to the reification of the continuation as a data structure and the introduction of an additional layer of instructions to manage the continuation: for an example, see the static and dynamic semantics of MiniMLR in [7][4].

Mixing additive and multiplicative connectives asks for a more sophisticated resource management system; this is a concern, given the efficiency requirements that testing brings to the table: the idea behind "QuickCheck", and hence its name, is that an outcome should be produced quickly.

---

[4] This can be circumvented by switching to a more expressive logic, either by internalizing the continuation as an ordered context [46] or by changing representation via forward chaining (*destination-passing style*) [29].

A solution comes from the notion of *logical* continuation advocated by Chirimar [13], which affords us the luxury to never duplicate the state. Logical continuations need higher-order logic (or can be simulated in an un-typed setting such as Prolog). Informally, the idea is to transform every atom A of type $(\tau_1 * \cdots * \tau_n) \to o$ into a new one $\hat{A}$ of type $(\tau_1 * \cdots * \tau_n * o) \to o$ where we accumulate in the additional argument the body of the definition of A as a nested goal. Facts are transformed so that the continuation becomes the precondition.

For example, consider a fragment of the rules for the evaluation judgment $\sigma \vdash m \Downarrow v$ and its CPS-encoding:

$$\frac{x \mapsto v \in \sigma}{\sigma \vdash x \Downarrow v} \; e/v \qquad \frac{}{\sigma \vdash n \Downarrow n} \; e/n$$

$$\frac{\sigma \vdash e_1 \Downarrow v_1 \quad \sigma \vdash e_2 \Downarrow v_2 \quad \text{plus } v_1 \; v_2 \; v}{\sigma \vdash e_1 + e_2 \Downarrow v} \; e/p$$

```
eval(v(X),N,K)           o- var(X,N) x (var(X,N) -o K).
eval(i(N),vi(N),K)       o- K.
eval(plus(E1,E2),vi(V),K) o-
    eval(E1,vi(V1),eval(E2,vi(V2),bang(sum(V1,V2,V,K)))).
```

In the variable case, the value for X is read (and consumed) in the linear context and consequently reasserted; then we call the continuation in the restored state. Evaluating a constant i(N) will have the side-effect of instantiating N in K. The clause for addition showcases the sequencing of goals inside the logical continuation, where the sum predicate is "banged" as a computation that does not need the state.

The *adequacy* statement for CPS-evaluation reads: $\sigma \vdash m \Downarrow v$ iff the sequent $\ulcorner \sigma \urcorner \vdash \texttt{eval}(\ulcorner m \urcorner, \ulcorner v \urcorner, \top)$ has a uniform proof, where the initial continuation $\top$ cleans up $\ulcorner \sigma \urcorner$ upon success. As well-know, we need to generalize the statement to arbitrary continuations for the proof to go through.

It is instructive to look at a direct additive encoding as well:

```
ev(v(X),V)           o- var(X,V) x erase.
ev(i(N),vi(N))       o- erase.
ev(plus(E1,E2),vi(V)) o- ev(E1,vi(V1)) &
                         ev(E2,vi(V2)) &
                         bang(sum(V1,V2,V)).
```

While this seems appealingly simpler, it breaks down when the state is updated and not just read; consider the operational semantics of assignment and its CPS-encoding:

$$\frac{\sigma \vdash m \Downarrow v}{(\sigma, x := m) \Downarrow \sigma \oplus \{x \mapsto v\}}$$

```
ceval(asn(X,E),K) o-
            eval(E,V, (var(X,_) x (var(X,V) -o K))).
```

The continuation is in charge of both having something to compute after the assignment returns, but also of sequencing in the right order reading the state via evaluation, and updating via the embedded implication. An additive encoding using & would not be adequate, since the connective's commutativity is at odd with side-effects.

At the top level, we initialize the execution of programs (seen as a sequence of commands) by using as initial continuation a predicate `collect` that consumes the final state and returns it in a reified format.

```
main(P,Vars,S) o- ceval(P,collect(Vars,S)).
```

We are now in the position of addressing the meta-theory of our system-under-study via testing. We list the more important properties among those that we have considered. All statements are universally quantified:

srv subject reduction for evaluation: $\Gamma \vdash m : \tau \longrightarrow \sigma \vdash m \Downarrow v \longrightarrow \Gamma : \sigma \longrightarrow v : \tau$;

dtx determinism of execution: $(\sigma, c) \Downarrow \sigma_1 \longrightarrow (\sigma, c) \Downarrow \sigma_2 \longrightarrow \sigma_1 \approx \sigma_2$;

srx subject reduction for execution: $\Gamma \vdash c \longrightarrow \Gamma : \sigma \longrightarrow (\sigma, c) \Downarrow \sigma' \longrightarrow \Gamma : \sigma'$;

pr progress for small step execution: $\Gamma \vdash c \longrightarrow \Gamma : \sigma \longrightarrow c = \mathrm{skip} \vee \exists c' \, \sigma', (c, \sigma) \rightsquigarrow (c', \sigma')$;

eq equivalence of small and big step execution (assuming determinism of both): $(\sigma, c) \Downarrow \sigma_1 \longrightarrow (c, \sigma_1) \rightsquigarrow^* (\mathrm{skip}, \sigma_2) \longrightarrow \sigma_1 \approx \sigma_2$.

We have also encoded the compilation of IMP to a stack machine and (mutation) tested forward and backward simulation of compilation w.r.t. source and target execution [27]. We have added a simple type discipline for the assembly language in the spirit of Typed Assembly Languages [39] and tested preservation and progress, to exclude underflows in the execution of a well-typed stack machine. Details can be found in the accompanying repository[5].

5.2   Experimental Evaluation

A word of caution before discussing our experiments: first, we have spent almost no effort in crafting nor tuning custom generators; in fact, they are simply FPC-driven regular unary logic programs [52] with a very minor massage. Compare this with the amount of ingenuity poured in writing generators in [23] or with the model-checking techniques of [48]. Secondly, our interpreter is a Prolog meta-interpreter and while we have tried to exploit Prolog's indexing, there are obvious ways to improve its efficiency, from partial evaluation to better data structures for contexts.

Of the many experiments that we have run and are available in the dedicated repository, we list here only a few, with no pretense of completeness. In those, we have adopted a certain exhaustive generation strategy (*size*), then paired it

---

[5] https://github.com/Tovy97/Towards-Substructural-Property-Based-Testing/tree/master/Lolli/Assembly.

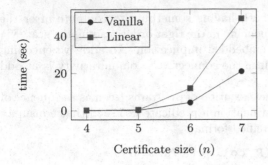

Fig. 6. Testing property **eq** with certificate $\langle n, \_ \rangle$

	dtx	srx	srv	pr	eq	cex
M1	pass	pass	pass	pass	pass	
M2	found	pass	pass	pass	found	w := 0 - 1
M3	pass	pass	pass	pass	pass	
M4	pass	found	found	pass	pass	x := tt /\ tt
M5	pass	pass	pass	pass	pass	
M6	found	pass	pass	pass	found	if x = x then {w := 0} else {w := 1}
M7	pass	pass	pass	pass	pass	
M8	pass	pass	pass	pass	pass	
M9	pass	pass	pass	pass	pass	

Fig. 7. Mutation testing

with *height*. We have used consistently certain bounds that experimentally have shown to be effective in generating enough interesting data.

To establish a fair baseline, we have also implemented a *state-passing* version of our benchmarks driven by a FPC-lead vanilla meta-interpreter.

We have run the experiments on a laptop with an Intel i7-7500U CPU and 16 GB of RAM running WSL (Ubuntu 20.04) over Windows 10, using SWI-Prolog 8.2.4. All times are in seconds, as reported by SWI's `time/1`. They are the average of five measurements.

First we compare the time to test a sample property ("**eq**", the equivalence of big and small step execution) over a bug-free model both with linear and vanilla PBT. On the left of Fig. 6 we plot the time proportionally to the certificate size. On the right we list the number of generated programs and the percentage of those that converge within a bound given by a polynomial function over the certificate size (column "coverage"). The linear interpreter performs worse than the state-passing one, but not dramatically so. This is to be expected, since the vanilla meta-interpreter does not do any context management: in fact, it does not use logical contexts at all.

Next, to gauge the effectiveness in catching bugs, we use, as customary, *mutation analysis* [25], whereby single intentional mistakes are inserted into the system under study. A testing suite is deemed as good as its capability of detecting those bugs (*killing a mutant*). Most of the literature about mutation analysis revolves around automatic mutant analysis for imperative code, certainly not linear logical specifications of object logics. Therefore, we resort to the *manual* design of a small number of mutants, with all the limitations entailed. Note, however, that this is the approach taken by the testing suite[6] of a leading tool such as *PLT-Redex* [16].

We list in Table 1 a selection of the mutations that we have implemented, together with a categorization, borrowed from the classification of mutations for Prolog-like languages in [38]. We also report the judgment where the mutation occurs.

Clause mutations: deletion of a predicate in the body of a clause, deleting the whole clause if a fact.

Operator mutations: arithmetic and relational operator mutation.

Variable mutations: replacing a variable with an (anonymous) variable and vice versa.

Constant mutations: replacing a constant by a constant (of the same type), or by an (anonymous) variable and vice versa.

Table 1. List of mutations

M1 (eval, C) mutation in the definition of addition
M2 (eval, Cl) added another clause to the definition of subtraction
M3 (eval, O) substitution of − for * in arithmetic definitions
M4 (eval, O) similar to M1 but for conjunction
M5 (exec, V) bug on assignment
M6 (exec, Cl) switch branches in if-then-else
M7 (exec, Cl) deletion of one of the `while` rule
M8 (type, C) wrong output type in rule for addition
M9 (type, C) wrong input type in rule for disjunction

Figure 7 summarizes the outcome of mutation testing, where "found" indicates that a counter-example (cex) has been found and "pass" that the bound has been exhausted. In the first case, we report counter-examples in the last column, after pretty-printing. Since this is accomplished in milliseconds, we omit the precise timing information. Note that counter-examples found by exhaustive search are minimal by construction.

The results seem at first disappointing (3 mutants out of 9 being detected), until we realize that it is not so much a question of our tool failing to kill mutants, but of the above properties being too coarse. Consider for example mutation M3: being a type-preserving operation swap in the evaluation of expressions, this will

---

[6] https://docs.racket-lang.org/redex/benchmark.html.

certainly not lead to a failure of subject reduction, nor invalidate determinism of evaluation. On the other hand all mutants are easily killed with model-based testing, that is taking as properties soundness ($L \to C$) and completeness ($C \to L$) of the top-level judgments (exec/type) where mutations occur w.r.t. their bug-free versions executed under the vanilla interpreter. This is reported in Fig. 8.

	exec: $C \to L$	exec: $L \to C$	cex
No Mut	pass in 2.40	pass in 6.56	
M1	found in 0.06	pass in 6.45	w := 0 + 0
M2	pass in 2.40	found in 0.04	w := 0 - 1
M3	found in 0.06	found in 0.06	w := 0 * 1
M4	found in 0.06	found in 0.04	y := tt /\ tt
M5	found in 0.00	pass in 5.15	w := 0; w := 1
M6	pass in 2.34	found in 0.17	if y = y then {w := 0} else {w := 1}
M7	found in 0.65	pass in 0.82	while y = y /\ y = w do {y := tt}

	type: $C \to L$	type: $L \to C$	cex
No Mut	pass in 0.89	pass in 0.87	
M8	found in 0.03	pass in 0.84	w := 0 + 0
M9	found in 0.04	pass in 0.71	y := tt \/ tt

Fig. 8. Model-based testing of IMP mutations

6 Related Work and Conclusions

The success of QuickCheck has lead many proof assistants to adopt some form of PBT or more in general of counterexamples search. The system where proofs and disproofs are best integrated is arguably Isabelle/HOL, which offers a combination of random, exhaustive and symbolic testing [5] together with a model finder [2]. A decade later *QuickChick* [42] has been added to Coq as a porting of PBT compatible with the severe constraints of constructive type theory. However, these PBT tools tend to be limited to executable total specifications, while many judgments are partial and/or non-terminating. An exception is the approach in [31], which brings relational PBT to Coq.

As far as the meta-theory of programming languages is concerned, PLT-Redex [16] is an executable DSL for mechanizing semantic models built on top of the programming environment *DrRacket*. Its usefulness has been demonstrated in several impressive case studies [26]. αCheck [10,11] is a close ancestor of the present work, since it is based on a proof-theoretic view of PBT, although it wires in a fixed generation strategy. Moreover, the system goes beyond the confine of classical or intuitionistic logic and embraces *nominal* logic as a way to give a logical account of encoding models where *binding* signatures matter [9].

While substructural logics are a recurring thread in current PL theory (see for example session types and separation logic) and while linear logic programming languages have been extensively used to represent such models [20,44,49], formal *verification* via linear logic frameworks, as we have mentioned, is still in its infancy. Schürmann et al. [33] have designed $\mathcal{L}_\omega^+$, a linear meta-logics conservatively extending the meta-theory of Twelf and Pientka et al. [20] have introduced *LINCX*, a linear version of contextual modal type theory to be used within Beluga.

However most case studies, as elegant as they are, are still on paper, viz. type soundness of MiniML with references and cut-elimination for (object) linear logic (LLF [7,33]). Martin's dissertation [32] offers a thorough investigation of the verification of the meta-theory of MiniML with references in Isabelle/HOL's Hybrid library, in several styles, including linear and ordered specifications. A more extensive use of Hybrid, this time on top of Coq, is the recent verification of type soundness of the *proto-Quipper* quantum functional programming language in a Lolli-like specification logic [30].

In this paper we have argued for the extension of property-based testing to substructural logics to overcome the current lack of reasoning tools in the field. We have taken the first step by implementing a PBT system for specifications written in linear Hereditary Harrop formulæ, the language underlying Lolli. We have adapted the FPC architecture to model various generation strategies. We have validated our approach by encoding the meta-theory of IMP and its compilation with a dimple mutation analysis. With all the caution that our setup entails, the experiments show that linear PBT is effective w.r.t. mutations and while it under-performs vanilla PBT over bug-free models, there are immediate avenues for improvement.

There is so much future work that it is almost overwhelming: first item, from the system point of view, is abandoning the meta-interpretation approach, and then a possible integration with Abella. Theoretically, our plan is to extend our framework to richer linear logic languages, featuring ordered logic up to concurrency, as well as supporting different operational semantics, to begin with bottom-up evaluation.

Source code can be found at https://github.com/Tovy97/Towards-Substruct ural-Property-Based-Testing.

Acknowledgments. We are grateful to Dale Miller for many discussions and in particular for suggesting the use of logical continuations. Thanks also to Jeff Polakow for his comments on a draft version of this paper.

References

1. Baelde, D., et al.: Abella: a system for reasoning about relational specifications. J. Formaliz. Reason. **7**(2), 1–89 (2014)
2. Blanchette, J.C., Bulwahn, L., Nipkow, T.: Automatic proof and disproof in Isabelle/HOL. In: Tinelli, C., Sofronie-Stokkermans, V. (eds.) FroCoS 2011. LNCS (LNAI), vol. 6989, pp. 12–27. Springer, Heidelberg (2011). https://doi.org/10.1007/978-3-642-24364-6_2
3. Blanco, R., Chihani, Z., Miller, D.: Translating between implicit and explicit versions of proof. In: de Moura, L. (ed.) CADE 2017. LNCS (LNAI), vol. 10395, pp. 255–273. Springer, Cham (2017). https://doi.org/10.1007/978-3-319-63046-5_16

4. Blanco, R., Miller, D., Momigliano, A.: Property-based testing via proof reconstruction. In: PPDP, pp. 5:1–5:13. ACM (2019)
5. Bulwahn, L.: The new Quickcheck for Isabelle. In: Hawblitzel, C., Miller, D. (eds.) CPP 2012. LNCS, vol. 7679, pp. 92–108. Springer, Heidelberg (2012). https://doi.org/10.1007/978-3-642-35308-6_10
6. Cervesato, I., Hodas, J.S., Pfenning, F.: Efficient resource management for linear logic proof search. Theor. Comput. Sci. **232**(1–2), 133–163 (2000)
7. Cervesato, I., Pfenning, F.: A linear logical framework. In: LICS, pp. 264–275. IEEE Computer Society (1996)
8. Cervesato, I., Pfenning, F., Walker, D., Watkins, K.: A concurrent logical framework ii: examples and applications. Technical report, CMU (2002)
9. Cheney, J.: Toward a general theory of names: binding and scope. In: MERLIN, pp. 33–40. ACM (2005)
10. Cheney, J., Momigliano, A.: αCheck: a mechanized metatheory model checker. Theory Pract. Logic Program. **17**(3), 311–352 (2017)
11. Cheney, J., Momigliano, A., Pessina, M.: Advances in property-based testing for αProlog. In: Aichernig, B.K.K., Furia, C.A.A. (eds.) TAP 2016. LNCS, vol. 9762, pp. 37–56. Springer, Cham (2016). https://doi.org/10.1007/978-3-319-41135-4_3
12. Chihani, Z., Miller, D., Renaud, F.: A semantic framework for proof evidence. J. Autom. Reason. **59**(3), 287–330 (2017)
13. Chirimar, J.: Proof theoretic approach to specification languages. Ph.D. thesis. University of Pennsylvania (1995)
14. Claessen, K., Hughes, J.: QuickCheck: a lightweight tool for random testing of Haskell programs. In: Proceedings of the 2000 ACM SIGPLAN International Conference on Functional Programming (ICFP 2000), pp. 268–279. ACM (2000)
15. Dubois, C.: Proving ML type soundness within Coq. In: Aagaard, M., Harrison, J. (eds.) TPHOLs 2000. LNCS, vol. 1869, pp. 126–144. Springer, Heidelberg (2000). https://doi.org/10.1007/3-540-44659-1_9
16. Felleisen, M., Findler, R.B., Flatt, M.: Semantics Engineering with PLT Redex. The MIT Press, Cambridge (2009)
17. Felty, A.P., Momigliano, A.: Hybrid - a definitional two-level approach to reasoning with higher-order abstract syntax. J. Autom. Reason. **48**(1), 43–105 (2012)
18. Fetscher, B., Claessen, K., Pałka, M., Hughes, J., Findler, R.B.: Making random judgments: automatically generating well-typed terms from the definition of a type-system. In: Vitek, J. (ed.) ESOP 2015. LNCS, vol. 9032, pp. 383–405. Springer, Heidelberg (2015). https://doi.org/10.1007/978-3-662-46669-8_16
19. Gacek, A., Miller, D., Nadathur, G.: A two-level logic approach to reasoning about computations. J. Autom. Reason. **49**(2), 241–273 (2012)
20. Georges, A.L., Murawska, A., Otis, S., Pientka, B.: LINCX: a linear logical framework with first-class contexts. In: Yang, H. (ed.) ESOP 2017. LNCS, vol. 10201, pp. 530–555. Springer, Heidelberg (2017). https://doi.org/10.1007/978-3-662-54434-1_20
21. Girard, J.-Y.: Linear logic. Theor. Comput. Sci. **50**(1), 1–102 (1987)
22. Hodas, J., Miller, D.: Logic programming in a fragment of intuitionistic linear logic. Inf. Comput. **110**(2), 327–365 (1994)
23. Hritcu, C., et al.: Testing noninterference, quickly. In: Proceedings of the 18th ACM SIGPLAN International Conference on Functional Programming, ICFP 2013, pp. 455–468. ACM, New York, NY, USA (2013)
24. Hughes, J.: QuickCheck testing for fun and profit. In: Hanus, M. (ed.) PADL 2007. LNCS, vol. 4354, pp. 1–32. Springer, Heidelberg (2006). https://doi.org/10.1007/978-3-540-69611-7_1

25. Jia, Y., Harman, M.: An analysis and survey of the development of mutation testing. IEEE Trans. Softw. Eng. **37**(5), 649–678 (2011)
26. Klein, C., et al.: Run your research: on the effectiveness of lightweight mechanization. In: Proceedings of the 39th Annual ACM SIGPLAN-SIGACT Symposium on Principles of Programming Languages, POPL '12, pp. 285–296. ACM, New York, NY, USA (2012)
27. Leroy, X.: Mechanized semantics - with applications to program proof and compiler verification. In: Logics and Languages for Reliability and Security, volume 25 of NATO Science for Peace and Security Series - D: Information and Communication Security, pp. 195–224. IOS Press (2010)
28. Liang, C., Miller, D.: Focusing and polarization in linear, intuitionistic, and classical logics. Theor. Comput. Sci. **410**(46), 4747–4768 (2009)
29. López, P., Pfenning, F., Polakow, J., Watkins, K.: Monadic concurrent linear logic programming. In: PPDP, pp. 35–46. ACM (2005)
30. Mahmoud, M.Y., Felty, A.P.: Formalization of metatheory of the quipper quantum programming language in a linear logic. J. Autom. Reason. **63**(4), 967–1002 (2019)
31. Manighetti, M., Miller, D., Momigliano, A.: Two applications of logic programming to Coq. In: TYPES, volume 188 of LIPIcs, pp. 10:1–10:19. Schloss Dagstuhl - Leibniz-Zentrum für Informatik (2020)
32. Martin, A.: Reasoning using higher-order abstract syntax in a higher-order logic proof environment: improvements to hybrid and a case study. Ph.D. thesis. University of Ottawa (2010). https://ruor.uottawa.ca/handle/10393/19711
33. McCreight, A., Schürmann, C.: A meta linear logical framework. Electron. Notes Theor. Comput. Sci. **199**, 129–147 (2008)
34. McDowell, R., Miller, D.: Reasoning with higher-order abstract syntax in a logical framework. ACM Trans. Comput. Log. **3**(1), 80–136 (2002)
35. Michaylov, S., Pfenning, F.: Natural semantics and some of its meta-theory in Elf. In: Eriksson, L.-H., Hallnäs, L., Schroeder-Heister, P. (eds.) ELP 1991. LNCS, vol. 596, pp. 299–344. Springer, Heidelberg (1992). https://doi.org/10.1007/BFb0013612
36. Miller, D.: Forum: a multiple-conclusion specification logic. Theor. Comput. Sci. **165**(1), 201–232 (1996)
37. Miller, D., Nadathur, G., Pfenning, F., Scedrov, A.: Uniform proofs as a foundation for logic programming. Ann. Pure Appl. Log. **51**, 125–157 (1991)
38. Momigliano, A., Ornaghi, M.: The blame game for property-based testing. In: CILC, volume 2396 of CEUR Workshop Proceedings, pp. 4–13. CEUR-WS.org (2019)
39. Morrisett, J.G., Walker, D., Crary, K., Glew, N.: From system F to typed assembly language. ACM Trans. Program. Lang. Syst. **21**(3), 527–568 (1999)
40. Nigam, V., Miller, D.: Algorithmic specifications in linear logic with subexponentials. In: PPDP, pp. 129–140. ACM (2009)
41. Paoli, F.: Substructural Logics: A Primer. Kluwer, Alphen aan den Rijn (2002)
42. Paraskevopoulou, Z., Hriţcu, C., Dénès, M., Lampropoulos, L., Pierce, B.C.: Foundational property-based testing. In: Urban, C., Zhang, X. (eds.) ITP 2015. LNCS, vol. 9236, pp. 325–343. Springer, Cham (2015). https://doi.org/10.1007/978-3-319-22102-1_22
43. Pfenning, F.: Logical frameworks. In: Robinson, A., Voronkov, A. (eds.), Handbook of Automated Reasoning. Elsevier Science Publishers (1999)
44. Pfenning, F., Simmons, R.J.: Substructural operational semantics as ordered logic programming. In: LICS, pp. 101–110. IEEE Computer Society (2009)

45. Pientka, B., Dunfield, J.: Beluga: a framework for programming and reasoning with deductive systems (system description). In: Giesl, J., Hähnle, R. (eds.) IJCAR 2010. LNCS (LNAI), vol. 6173, pp. 15–21. Springer, Heidelberg (2010). https://doi.org/10.1007/978-3-642-14203-1_2
46. Polakow, J.: Linear logic programming with an ordered context. In: PPDP, pp. 68–79. ACM (2000)
47. Reynolds, J.C.: The discoveries of continuations. LISP Symb. Comput. **6**(3–4), 233–248 (1993)
48. Roberson, M., Harries, M., Darga, P.T., Boyapati, C.: Efficient software model checking of soundness of type systems. In: Harris, G.E. (ed.), OOPSLA, pp. 493–504. ACM (2008)
49. Schack-Nielsen, A., Schürmann, C.: Celf – a logical framework for deductive and concurrent systems (system description). In: Armando, A., Baumgartner, P., Dowek, G. (eds.) IJCAR 2008. LNCS (LNAI), vol. 5195, pp. 320–326. Springer, Heidelberg (2008). https://doi.org/10.1007/978-3-540-71070-7_28
50. Tarau, P.: A combinatorial testing framework for intuitionistic propositional theorem provers. In: Alferes, J.J., Johansson, M. (eds.) PADL 2019. LNCS, vol. 11372, pp. 115–132. Springer, Cham (2019). https://doi.org/10.1007/978-3-030-05998-9_8
51. Wadler, P.: Linear types can change the world! In: Programming Concepts and Methods, p. 561. North-Holland (1990)
52. Yardeni, E., Shapiro, E.: A type system for logic programs. J. Log. Program. **10**(2), 125–153 (1991)

The Next 700 Program Transformers

Geoff Hamilton[⊠][iD]

School of Computing, Dublin City University, Dublin, Ireland
geoffrey.hamilton@dcu.ie

Abstract. In this paper, we describe a hierarchy of program transformers, capable of performing fusion to eliminate intermediate data structures, in which the transformer at each level of the hierarchy builds on top of those at lower levels. The program transformer at level 1 of the hierarchy corresponds to positive supercompilation, and that at level 2 corresponds to distillation. We give a number of examples of the application of our transformers at different levels in the hierarchy and look at the speedups that are obtained. We determine the maximum speedups that can be obtained at each level, and prove that the transformers at each level terminate.

Keywords: transformation hierarchy · supercompilation · distillation · speedups

1 Introduction

It is well known that programs written using functional programming languages often make use of intermediate data structures and thus can be inefficient. Several program transformation techniques have been proposed to eliminate some of these intermediate data structures; for example *partial evaluation* [14], *deforestation* [30] and *supercompilation* [27]. *Positive supercompilation* [26] is a variant of Turchin's supercompilation [27] that was introduced in an attempt to study and explain the essentials of Turchin's supercompiler. Although strictly more powerful than both partial evaluation and deforestation, Sørensen has shown that positive supercompilation (without the identification of common sub-expressions in generalisation), and hence also partial evaluation and deforestation, can only produce a linear speedup in programs [24]. Even with the identification of common sub-expressions in generalisation, superlinear speedups are obtained for very few interesting programs, and many obvious improvements cannot be made without the use of so-called 'eureka' steps [4].

Example 1. Consider the function call *nrev xs* shown in Fig. 1. This reverses the list *xs*, but the recursive function call (*nrev xs'*) is an intermediate data structure, so in terms of time and space usage, it is quadratic with respect to the length of the list *xs*. A more efficient function that is linear with respect to the length of the list *xs* is the function *qrev* shown in Fig. 1.

A number of algebraic transformations have been proposed that can perform this transformation (e.g. [29]), making essential use of eureka steps requiring

© Springer Nature Switzerland AG 2022
E. De Angelis and W. Vanhoof (Eds.): LOPSTR 2021, LNCS 13290, pp. 113–134, 2022.
https://doi.org/10.1007/978-3-030-98869-2_7

$$nrev \; xs$$
where
$$
\begin{aligned}
nrev \; xs \quad &= \textbf{case} \; xs \; \textbf{of} \\
&\quad Nil \qquad\qquad \Rightarrow Nil \\
&\quad Cons \; x' \; xs' \Rightarrow append \; (nrev \; xs') \; (Cons \; x' \; Nil) \\
append \; xs \; ys &= \textbf{case} \; xs \; \textbf{of} \\
&\quad Nil \qquad\qquad \Rightarrow ys \\
&\quad Cons \; x' \; xs' \Rightarrow Cons \; x' \; (append \; xs' \; ys)
\end{aligned}
$$

$$qrev \; xs$$
where
$$
\begin{aligned}
qrev \; xs \quad\;\; &= qrev' \; xs \; Nil \\
qrev' \; xs \; ys &= \textbf{case} \; xs \; \textbf{of} \\
&\quad Nil \qquad\qquad \Rightarrow ys \\
&\quad Cons \; x' \; xs' \Rightarrow qrev' \; xs' \; (Cons \; x' \; ys)
\end{aligned}
$$

Fig. 1. Alternative Definitions of List Reversal

human insight and not easy to automate; for the given example this can be achieved by appealing to a specific law stating the associativity of the *append* function. However, none of the generic program transformation techniques mentioned above are capable of performing this transformation.

The *distillation* algorithm [9,11] was originally motivated by the need for automatic techniques that avoid the reliance on eureka steps to perform transformations such as the above. In positive supercompilation, generalisation and folding are performed only on expressions, while in distillation, generalisation and folding are also performed on recursive function representations (*process trees*). This allows a number of improvements to be obtained using distillation that cannot be obtained using positive supercompilation.

The process trees that are generalised and folded in distillation are in fact those produced by positive supercompilation, so we can see that the definition of distillation is built on top of positive supercompilation. This suggests the existence of a hierarchy of program transformers, where the transformer at each level is built on top of those at lower levels, and more powerful transformations are obtained as we move up through this hierarchy. In this paper, we define such a hierarchy inductively, with positive supercompilation at level 1, distillation at level 2 and each new level defined in terms of the previous ones. Each of the transformers is capable of performing *fusion* to eliminate intermediate data structures by fusing nested function calls. As we move up through the hierarchy, deeper nestings of function calls can be fused, thus removing more intermediate data structures.

The remainder of this paper is structured as follows. In Sect. 2, we define the higher-order functional language on which the described transformations are performed. In Sect. 3, we give an overview of process trees and define a number of operations on them. In Sect. 4, we define the program transformer hierarchy, where the transformer at level 0 corresponds to the identity transformation, and each successive transformer is defined in terms of the previous ones. In Sect. 5, we give examples of transformations that can be performed at different levels in our hierarchy. In Sect. 6, we consider the efficiency improvements that can be obtained as we move up through this hierarchy. In Sect. 7, we prove that each of the transformers in our hierarchy terminates. In Sect. 8, we consider related work and Sect. 9 concludes and considers possibilities for further work.

2 Language

In this section, we describe the call-by-name higher-order functional language that will be used throughout this paper.

Definition 1 (Language Syntax). The syntax of this language is as shown in Fig. 2.

$$prog ::= e_0 \textbf{ where } h_1 = e_1 \ldots h_n = e_n \quad \text{Program}$$

$$
\begin{array}{lll}
e & ::= x & \text{Variable} \\
& \mid c\ e_1 \ldots e_n & \text{Constructor Application} \\
& \mid \lambda x.e & \text{λ-Abstraction} \\
& \mid f & \text{Function Call} \\
& \mid e_0\ e_1 & \text{Application} \\
& \mid \textbf{case } e_0 \textbf{ of } p_1 \Rightarrow e_1 \ldots p_n \rightarrow e_n & \text{Case Expression}
\end{array}
$$

$$h \quad ::= f\ x_1 \ldots x_n \qquad\qquad\qquad \text{Function Header}$$

$$p \quad ::= c\ x_1 \ldots x_n \qquad\qquad\qquad \text{Pattern}$$

Fig. 2. Language Syntax

Programs in the language consist of an expression to evaluate and a set of function definitions. An expression can be a variable, constructor application, λ-abstraction, function call, application or **case**. Variables introduced by function definitions, λ-abstractions and **case** patterns are *bound*; all other variables are *free*. We assume that bound variables are represented using De Bruijn indices. An expression that contains no free variables is said to be *closed*. We write $e \equiv e'$ if e and e' differ only in the names of bound variables.

Each constructor has a fixed arity; for example *Nil* has arity 0 and *Cons* has arity 2. In an expression $c\ e_1 \ldots e_n$, n must equal the arity of c. The patterns in **case** expressions may not be nested. No variable may appear more than once within a pattern. We assume that the patterns in a **case** expression are non-overlapping and exhaustive. It is also assumed that erroneous terms such as $(c\ e_1 \ldots e_n)\ e$ where c is of arity n and **case** $(\lambda x.e)$ **of** $p_1 \Rightarrow e_1 \ldots p_k \Rightarrow e_k$ cannot occur.

Definition 2 (Substitution). We use the notation $\theta = \{x_1 \mapsto e_1, \ldots, x_n \mapsto e_n\}$ to denote a *substitution*. If e is an expression, then $e\theta = e\{x_1 \mapsto e_1, \ldots, x_n \mapsto e_n\}$ is the result of simultaneously substituting the expressions $e_1, \ldots, e_n$ for the corresponding variables $x_1, \ldots, x_n$, respectively, in the expression e while ensuring that bound variables are renamed appropriately to avoid name capture. A *renaming* denoted by σ is a substitution of the form $\{x_1 \mapsto x_1', \ldots, x_n \mapsto x_n'\}$.

Definition 3 (Shallow Reduction Context). A shallow reduction context $\mathcal{C}$ is an expression containing a single hole $\bullet$ in the place of the redex, which can have one of the two following possible forms:

$$\mathcal{C} ::= \bullet \; e \mid \textbf{case} \; \bullet \; \textbf{of} \; p_1 \Rightarrow e_1 \ldots p_n \Rightarrow e_n$$

Definition 4 (Evaluation Context). An evaluation context $\mathcal{E}$ is represented as a sequence of shallow reduction contexts (known as a *zipper* [13]), representing the nesting of these contexts from innermost to outermost within which the redex is contained. An evaluation context can therefore have one of the two following possible forms:

$$\mathcal{E} ::= \langle\rangle \mid \langle \mathcal{C} : \mathcal{E} \rangle$$

Definition 5 (Insertion into Evaluation Context). The insertion of an expression e into an evaluation context κ, denoted by $\kappa \bullet e$, is defined as follows:

$$
\begin{aligned}
\langle\rangle \bullet e &= e \\
\langle (\bullet \; e') : \kappa \rangle \bullet e &= \kappa \bullet (e \; e') \\
\langle (\textbf{case} \; \bullet \; \textbf{of} \; p_1 \Rightarrow e_1 \ldots p_n \Rightarrow e_n) : \kappa \rangle \bullet e & \\
&= \kappa \bullet (\textbf{case} \; e \; \textbf{of} \; p_1 \Rightarrow e_1 \ldots p_n \Rightarrow e_n)
\end{aligned}
$$

Definition 6 (Language Semantics). The normal order reduction semantics for programs in our language is defined by $\mathcal{N}_p[\![p]\!]$ as shown in Fig. 3, where it is assumed the program p contains no free variables. Within the rules $\mathcal{N}_e$, κ denotes the context of the expression under scrutiny and Δ is the set of function definitions. We always evaluate the redex of an expression within the context κ.

$$\mathcal{N}_p[\![e_0 \; \textbf{where} \; h_1 = e_1 \ldots h_n = e_n]\!] = \mathcal{N}_e[\![e_0]\!] \; \langle\rangle \; \{h_1 = e_1, \ldots, h_n = e_n\}$$

$$
\begin{aligned}
&\mathcal{N}_e[\![c \; e_1 \ldots e_n]\!] \; \langle\rangle \; \Delta = c \; (\mathcal{N}_e[\![e_1]\!] \; \langle\rangle \; \Delta) \ldots (\mathcal{N}_e[\![e_n]\!] \; \langle\rangle \; \Delta) \\
&\mathcal{N}_e[\![c \; e_1 \ldots e_n]\!] \; \langle (\textbf{case} \; \bullet \; \textbf{of} \; p_1 \Rightarrow e_1' \ldots p_k \Rightarrow e_k') : \kappa \rangle \; \Delta = \\
&\quad \mathcal{N}_e[\![e_i'\{x_1 \mapsto e_1, \ldots, x_n \mapsto e_n\}]\!] \; \kappa \; \Delta \\
&\quad \text{where} \; \exists i \in \{1 \ldots k\}.p_i = c \; x_1 \ldots x_n \\
&\mathcal{N}_e[\![\lambda x.e]\!] \; \langle\rangle \; \Delta = \lambda x.(\mathcal{N}_e[\![e]\!] \; \langle\rangle \; \Delta) \\
&\mathcal{N}_e[\![\lambda x.e]\!] \; \langle (\bullet \; e') : \kappa \rangle \; \Delta = \mathcal{N}_e[\![e\{x \mapsto e'\}]\!] \; \kappa \; \Delta \\
&\mathcal{N}_e[\![f]\!] \; \kappa \; \Delta = \mathcal{N}_e[\![\lambda x_1 \ldots x_n.e]\!] \; \kappa \; \Delta \\
&\quad \text{where} \; (f \; x_1 \ldots x_n = e) \in \Delta \\
&\mathcal{N}_e[\![e_0 \; e_1]\!] \; \kappa \; \Delta = \mathcal{N}_e[\![e_0]\!] \; \langle (\bullet \; e_1) : \kappa \rangle \; \Delta \\
&\mathcal{N}_e[\![\textbf{case} \; e_0 \; \textbf{of} \; p_1 \Rightarrow e_1 \ldots p_n \Rightarrow e_n]\!] \; \kappa \; \Delta = \\
&\quad \mathcal{N}_e[\![e_0]\!] \; \langle (\textbf{case} \; \bullet \; \textbf{of} \; p_1 \Rightarrow e_1 \ldots p_n \Rightarrow e_n) : \kappa \rangle \; \Delta
\end{aligned}
$$

Fig. 3. Language Semantics

3   Process Trees

The output of each of the transformers in our hierarchy are represented by *process trees*, as defined in [25]. Within these process trees, the nodes are labelled with expressions. We write $e \to t_1, \ldots, t_n$ for a process tree where the root node is labelled with the expression e, and $t_1, \ldots, t_n$ are the sub-trees of this root node. We also write $e \to \epsilon$ for a terminal node that has no sub-trees. We use $root(t)$ to denote the expression labelling the root node of process tree t. Process trees may also contain three special kinds of node:

- *Unfold nodes*: these are of the form $h \to t$, where h is a function header and t is the process tree resulting from transforming an expression after unfolding.
- *Fold nodes*: these are of the form $h \to \epsilon$, where folding has been performed with respect to a previous unfold node and the corresponding function headers are renamings of each other.
- *Generalisation nodes*: these are of the form $(x_0 \ x_1 \ldots x_n) \to t_0, t_1, \ldots, t_n$. This represents the result of a process tree generalisation, where the sub-trees $t_1 \ldots t_n$ have been extracted and replaced by the corresponding variables $x_1 \ldots x_n$ in the process tree t_0 that is represented by x_0.

Variables introduced by λ-abstractions, case patterns and generalisation nodes in process trees are bound; all other variables are free. We assume that bound variables are represented using De Bruijn indices. We use $fv(t)$ to denote the free variables of process tree t.

Definition 7 (Renaming of Process Trees). If t is a process tree, then the renaming $t\sigma$ is obtained by applying the renaming σ to the expressions labelling all nodes in t, while ensuring that bound variables are renamed appropriately to avoid name capture.

When transforming an expression with a function in the redex at level $k+1$, the expression is first transformed using a level k transformer. The resulting process tree is then compared to previously encountered process trees generated at level k. If it is a *renaming* of a previous one, then *folding* is performed, and if it is an *embedding* of a previous one, then *generalisation* is performed. The use of process trees in this comparison allows us to abstract away from the number and order of the parameters in functions, and instead focus on their recursive structure. We therefore define renaming, embedding and generalisation on process trees.

Definition 8 (Process Tree Renaming). Process tree t is a *renaming* of process tree t' if there is a renaming σ (which also renames functions) such that $t\sigma \cong t'$, where the relation $\cong$ is defined as follows:

$$(\phi(e_1 \ldots e_n) \to t_1, \ldots, t_n) \cong (\phi(e'_1 \ldots e'_n) \to t'_1, \ldots, t'_n), \text{ if } \forall i \in \{1 \ldots n\}. t_i \cong t'_i$$

Two process trees are therefore related by this equivalence relation if the pair of expressions in the corresponding root nodes have the same top-level syntactic constructor ϕ (a variable, constructor, lambda-abstraction, function name, application or **case**), and the corresponding sub-trees are also related. This includes the pathological case where the nodes have no sub-trees (such as free variables which must have the same name, and bound variables which must have the same de Bruijn index).

In order to ensure the termination of our transformation, we have to perform *generalisation*. This generalisation is performed when a process tree is encountered that is an *embedding* of a previous one. The form of embedding which we use to determine whether to perform generalisation is known as *homeomorphic embedding*. The homeomorphic embedding relation was derived from results by Higman [12] and Kruskal [19] and was defined within term rewriting systems [5] for detecting the possible divergence of the term rewriting process. Variants of this relation have been used to ensure termination within positive supercompilation [25], partial evaluation [21] and partial deduction [3,20]. The homeomorphic embedding relation is a *well-quasi-order*.

Definition 9 (Well-Quasi Order). A well-quasi order on a set S is a reflexive, transitive relation $\leq_S$ such that for any infinite sequence $s_1, s_2, \ldots$ of elements from S there are numbers i, j with $i < j$ and $s_i \leq_S s_j$.

The homeomorphic embedding relation on process trees is defined as follows.

Definition 10 (Process Tree Embedding). Process tree t is *embedded* in process tree t' if there is a renaming σ (which also renames functions) such that $t\sigma \trianglelefteq t'$, where the relation $\trianglelefteq$ is defined as follows:

$$(\phi(e_1 \ldots e_n) \to t_1, \ldots, t_n) \trianglelefteq (\phi(e'_1 \ldots e'_n) \to t'_1, \ldots, t'_n), \text{ if } \forall i \in \{1 \ldots n\}.t_i \trianglelefteq t'_i$$

$$t \trianglelefteq (e \to t_1, \ldots, t_n), \text{ if } \exists i \in \{1 \ldots n\}.t \trianglelefteq t_i$$

The first rule is a *coupling* rule, where the pair of expressions in the root nodes must have the same top-level syntactic constructor ϕ, and the corresponding sub-trees of the root nodes must also be related to each other. This includes the pathological case where the root nodes have no sub-trees (such as free variables which must have the same name, and bound variables which must have the same de Bruijn index). The second rule is a *diving* rule; this relates a process-tree with a sub-tree of a larger process tree. We write $t \preceq t'$ if $t \trianglelefteq t'$ and the coupling rule can be applied at the top level.

The use of this embedding relation ensures that in any infinite sequence of process trees $t_0, t_1, \ldots$ encountered during transformation there definitely exists some $i < j$ where t_i is embedded in t_j, so an embedding must eventually be encountered and transformation will not continue indefinitely without the need for generalisation or folding.

Definition 11 (Non-Decreasing Variable). Variable x is *non-decreasing* between process trees t and t' if there is a renaming σ such that $t\sigma \preceq t'$ and $(x \mapsto x) \in \sigma$.

Example 2. Consider the two process trees in Fig. 4 that are produced by our level 1 transformer for the expressions *append xs (Cons x Nil)* and *append (append xs' (Cons x' Nil)) (Cons x Nil)* respectively. The renaming $\{f \mapsto f', x \mapsto x, xs \mapsto xs'\}$ can be applied to process tree (1) so that it is embedded in process tree (2) by the relation $\preceq$. The variable x is therefore non-decreasing between these two process trees.

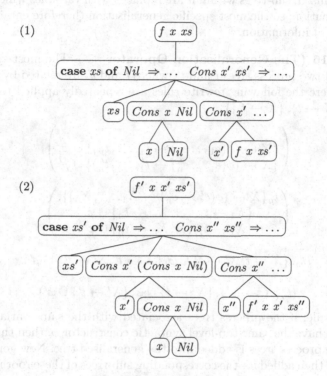

Fig. 4. Embedded Process Trees

The generalisation of a process tree involves replacing sub-trees with generalisation variables and creating *process tree substitutions*.

Definition 12 (Process Tree Substitution). We use the notation $\varphi = \{X_1 \mapsto t_1, \ldots, X_n \mapsto t_n\}$ to denote a *process tree substitution*. If t is an process tree, then $t\varphi = t\{X_1 \mapsto t_1, \ldots, X_n \mapsto t_n\}$ is the result of simultaneously substituting the sub-trees $t_1, \ldots, t_n$ for the corresponding tree variables $X_1, \ldots, X_n$, respectively, in the process tree t while ensuring that bound variables are renamed appropriately to avoid name capture.

Definition 13 (Process Tree Instance). Process tree t' is an *instance* of process tree t if there is a process tree substitution φ such that $t\varphi \cong t'$.

Definition 14 (Generalisation). A *generalisation* of process trees t and t' is a triple (t_g, φ, φ') where φ and φ' are process tree substitutions such that $t_g\varphi \cong t$ and $t_g\varphi' \cong t'$.

Definition 15 (Most Specific Generalisation). A *most specific generalisation* of process trees t and t' is a generalisation $(t_g, \varphi_1, \varphi_2)$ such that for every other generalisation $(t'_g, \varphi'_1, \varphi'_2)$ of t and t', t_g is an instance of t'_g. When a process tree is generalised, sub-trees within it are replaced with variables which implies a loss of information, so the most specific generalisation therefore entails the least possible loss of information.

Definition 16 (The Generalisation Operator $\sqcap$). The most specific generalisation of two process trees t and t', where t and t' are related by $\preceq$, is given by $t \sqcap t'$, where the following rewrite rules are repeatedly applied to the initial triple $(X, \{X \mapsto t\}, \{X \mapsto t'\})$:

$$\begin{pmatrix} t_g, \\ \{X \mapsto (\phi(e_1 \ldots e_n) \to t_1, \ldots, t_n)\} \cup \varphi, \\ \{X \mapsto (\phi(e'_1 \ldots e'_n) \to t'_1, \ldots, t'_n)\} \cup \varphi' \end{pmatrix}$$
$$\Downarrow$$
$$\begin{pmatrix} t_g\{X \mapsto (\phi(e'_1 \ldots e'_n) \to X_1, \ldots, X_n)\}, \\ \{X_1 \mapsto t_1, \ldots, X_n \mapsto t_n\} \cup \varphi, \\ \{X_1 \mapsto t'_1, \ldots, X_n \mapsto t'_n\} \cup \varphi' \end{pmatrix}$$

$$(t_g, \{X \mapsto t, X' \mapsto t\} \cup \varphi, \{X \mapsto t', X' \mapsto t'\} \cup \varphi')$$
$$\Downarrow$$
$$(t_g\{X \mapsto X'\}, \{X' \mapsto t\} \cup \varphi, \{X' \mapsto t'\} \cup \varphi')$$

In the first rule, if the process trees associated with the same variable in each environment have the same top-level syntactic constructor ϕ, then the root node of one of the process trees is added into the generalised tree. New generalisation variables are then added for the corresponding sub-trees of these root nodes. Note that it does not matter which of the original two process trees the expressions in the resulting generalised process tree come from, so long as they all come from one of them (so the corresponding unfold and fold nodes still match); the resulting residualised program will be the same. The second rule identifies common substitutions that were previously given different names.

Theorem 1 (Most Specific Generalisation). If process trees t and t' are related by $\preceq$, then the generalisation procedure $t \sqcap t'$ terminates and calculates the most specific generalisation.

Proof. To prove that the generalisation procedure terminates, we show that within each rewrite rule, either the size of the environments φ and φ' is reduced, or the size of the terms contained in these environments is reduced. Since the values are well-founded, the rewrite rules can only be applied finitely many times.

The proof that the result of the procedure is indeed a generalisation is by induction. The initial triple is trivially a generalisation, and for each of the rewrite rules, if the input triple is a generalisation, then the output triple must also be a generalisation.

The proof that the result of the procedure is a most specific generalisation is by contradiction. If the resulting triple $(t, \varphi_1, \varphi_2)$ is not a most specific generalisation, then there must exist a most specific generalisation $(t', \varphi_1', \varphi_2')$ and a tree substitution φ such that $t\varphi \cong t'$, but no tree substitution φ' such that $t'\varphi' \cong t$. This will be the case if either φ is not a renaming, so contains a substitution of the form $X \mapsto (\phi(e_1 \ldots e_n) \rightarrow t_1, \ldots, t_n$, or it identifies two variables within t. In the first case, the first rewrite rule would have been applied to further generalise, and in the second case, the second rewrite rule would have been applied to identify the variables. Thus there is a contradiction, so the generalisation computed by the procedure must be the most specific.

Example 3. The result of generalising the two process trees in Fig. 4 is shown in Fig. 5, with the mismatched nodes replaced by the generalisation variable X.

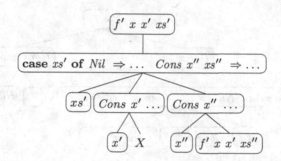

Fig. 5. Generalised Process Tree

Definition 17 (Generalisation Node Construction). The construction of a generalisation node for process tree t', where there is a process tree t such that $t \preceq t'$, is given by $t \uparrow t'$, which is defined as follows.

$t \uparrow t' = (x_0\ x_1 \ldots x_n) \rightarrow t_0, t_1, \ldots, t_n$
where $t \sqcap t' = (t_0', \{X_1 \mapsto t_1', \ldots, X_n \mapsto t_n'\}, \{X_1 \mapsto t_1'', \ldots, X_n \mapsto t_n''\})$
$\quad \{x_0 \mapsto t_0, x_1 \mapsto t_1, \ldots, x_n \mapsto t_n\} = \mathcal{G}^n(t \sqcap t')$

$\mathcal{G}^0(t_0, \{\}, \{\}) = \{x_0 \mapsto t_0\}$ (x_0 is fresh)
$\mathcal{G}^k(t_0, \{X_k \mapsto x\ x_1 \ldots x_n\} \cup \varphi, \{X_k \mapsto t\} \cup \varphi') =$
$\quad \{x \mapsto \lambda x_1 \ldots x_n.t\} \cup \mathcal{G}^{k-1}(t_0\{X_k \mapsto (x\ x_1 \ldots x_n) \rightarrow \epsilon\}, \varphi, \varphi'),$
$\quad\quad\quad\quad\quad\quad\quad\quad\quad\quad\quad\quad\quad\quad\quad\quad\quad$ if x is non-decreasing
$\mathcal{G}^k(t_0, \{X_k \mapsto t\} \cup \varphi, \{X_k \mapsto t'\} \cup \varphi') =$
$\quad \{x_k \mapsto \lambda x_1 \ldots x_n.t'\} \cup \mathcal{G}^{k-1}(t_0\{X \mapsto (x_k\ x_1 \ldots x_n) \rightarrow \epsilon\}, \varphi, \varphi')$ (x_k is fresh)
$\quad$ where $\{x_1 \ldots x_n\} = fv(t)$

The rules $\mathcal{G}^n$ return an environment $\{x_0 \mapsto t_0, x_1 \mapsto t_1, \ldots, x_n \mapsto t_n\}$ from which the corresponding generalisation node $(x_0\ x_1 \ldots x_n) \rightarrow t_0, t_1, \ldots, t_n$ is constructed. The rules are applied to the triple (t_0, φ, φ') resulting from the generalisation of the process trees t and t'. They work through each of the corresponding generalisation variables in the environments φ and φ' in turn. In the first rule, when both generalisation environments are exhausted, we are left with the generalised process tree t_0 in which appropriate values have been substituted for the generalisation variables; this is associated with the fresh variable x_0. In the final rule, the extracted sub-tree is abstracted over its variables (so that these are not extracted outside of their binders), and associated with the fresh variable x_k; the generalisation variable in the generalised process tree is replaced with a corresponding application of x_k. In the second rule, if we have an instance of the application of the variable x, and x is non-decreasing, then the same variable is reused in the generalisation.

Example 4. The result of applying the generalisation node constructor to the result of generalising the two process trees in Fig. 4 is shown in Fig. 6.

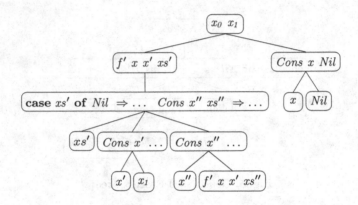

Fig. 6. Generalised Process Tree With Generalisation Node

We now show how a program can be residualised from a process tree.

Definition 18 (Residualisation). A program can be residualised from a process tree t as $\mathcal{R}_p[\![t]\!]$ using the rules as shown in Fig. 7.

Within the rules $\mathcal{R}_e$, the parameter ρ contains the unfold node function headers and the corresponding new function headers that are created for them. The rules return a residual expression along with a set of newly created function definitions. In rule (2), on encountering an unfold node, a new function header is created, associated with the unfold node function header, and added to ρ. Note that this new function header may not have the same variables as the one in the unfold node, as new variables may have been added to the sub-tree as a result of generalisation. In rule (3), on encountering a fold node, a recursive call of the function associated with the unfold node function header in ρ is created. In rule (9), on encountering a generalisation node, the sub-trees of the node are residualised separately, and then the expressions residualised from the extracted

(1) $\mathcal{R}_p[\![t]\!] = e_0$ **where** $h_1 = e_1, \ldots, h_n = e_n$
   where $\mathcal{R}_e[\![t]\!] \; \{\} = (e_0, \{h_1 = e_1, \ldots, h_n = e_n\})$

(2) $\mathcal{R}_e[\![h \to t]\!] \; \rho = (h', \{h' = e\} \cup \Delta)$
   where $\mathcal{R}_e[\![t]\!] \; (\rho \cup \{h = h'\}) = (e, \Delta)$
   $h' = f \; x_1 \ldots x_n$ (f is fresh, $\{x_1 \ldots x_n\} = fv(t)$)

(3) $\mathcal{R}_e[\![h \to \epsilon]\!] \; \rho = (h''\sigma, \{\})$
   where $(h' = h'') \in \rho \wedge h \equiv h'\sigma$

(4) $\mathcal{R}_e[\![x \to \epsilon]\!] \; \rho = (x, \{\})$

(5) $\mathcal{R}_e[\![(c \; e_1 \ldots e_n) \to t_1, \ldots, t_n]\!] \; \rho = (c \; e_1' \ldots e_n', \overset{n}{\underset{i=1}{\biguplus}} \Delta_i)$
   where $\forall i \in \{1 \ldots n\}. \mathcal{R}_e[\![t_i]\!] \; \rho = (e_i', \Delta_i)$

(6) $\mathcal{R}_e[\![(\lambda x.e) \to t]\!] \; \rho = (\lambda x.e', \Delta)$
   where $\mathcal{R}_e[\![t]\!] \; \rho = (e', \Delta)$

(7) $\mathcal{R}_e[\![(e_0 \; e_1) \to t_0, t_1]\!] \; \rho = (e_0' \; e_1', \overset{2}{\underset{i=1}{\biguplus}} \Delta_i)$
   where $\forall i \in \{0 \ldots 1\}. \mathcal{R}_e[\![t_i]\!] \; \rho = (e_i', \Delta_i)$

(8) $\mathcal{R}_e[\![(\mathbf{case} \; e_0 \; \mathbf{of} \; p_1 \Rightarrow e_1 \ldots p_n \Rightarrow e_n) \to t_0, \ldots, t_n]\!] \; \rho =$
   $(\mathbf{case} \; e_0' \; \mathbf{of} \; p_1 \Rightarrow e_1' \ldots p_n \Rightarrow e_n', \overset{n}{\underset{i=0}{\biguplus}} \Delta_i)$
   where $\forall i \in \{0 \ldots n\}. \mathcal{R}_e[\![t_i]\!] \; \rho = (e_i', \Delta_i)$

(9) $\mathcal{R}_e[\![(x_0 \; x_1 \ldots x_n) \to t_0, t_1, \ldots, t_n]\!] \; \rho = e_0\{x_1 \mapsto e_1, \ldots, x_n \mapsto e_n\}, \overset{n}{\underset{i=0}{\biguplus}} \Delta_i)$
   where $\forall i \in \{0 \ldots n\}. \mathcal{R}_e[\![t_i]\!] \; \rho = (e_i, \Delta_i)$

Fig. 7. Rules For Residualisation

sub-trees $t_1 \ldots t_n$ are substituted back into the result of residualising the main body t_0.

Example 5. The program shown in Fig. 8 is obtained by applying the residualisation rules to the process tree shown in Fig. 6.

$f \; x' \; xs' \; (Cons \; x \; Nil)$
where
$f \; x \; xs \; ys = \mathbf{case} \; xs \; \mathbf{of}$
$\qquad\qquad Nil \qquad\qquad \Rightarrow Cons \; x \; ys$
$\qquad\qquad Cons \; x' \; xs' \Rightarrow Cons \; x' \; (f \; x \; xs' \; ys)$

Fig. 8. Result of Residualisation

4   A Hierarchy of Program Transformers

In this section, we define our hierarchy of transformers. The level k transformer is defined as $\mathcal{T}_p^k[\![p]\!]$, where p is the program to be transformed. It is assumed that the input program contains no λ-abstractions; these can be replaced by named functions. The output of the transformer is a process tree from which the transformed program can be residualised.

4.1   Level 0 Transformer

Level 0 in our hierarchy just maps a program to a corresponding process tree without performing any reductions as shown in Fig. 9.

(1) $\mathcal{T}_p^0[\![e_0 \text{ where } h_1 = e_1, \ldots, h_n = e_n]\!] = \mathcal{T}_e^0[\![e_0]\!] \; \{\} \; \{h_1 = e_1, \ldots, h_n = e_n\}$

(2) $\mathcal{T}_e^0[\![x]\!] \; \rho \; \Delta = x \rightarrow \epsilon$
(3) $\mathcal{T}_e^0[\![c \; e_1 \ldots e_n]\!] \; \rho \; \Delta = (c \; e_1 \ldots e_n) \rightarrow (\mathcal{T}_e^0[\![e_1]\!] \; \rho \; \Delta), \ldots, (\mathcal{T}_e^0[\![e_n]\!] \; \rho \; \Delta)$
(4) $\mathcal{T}_e^0[\![\lambda x.e]\!] \; \rho \; \Delta = (\lambda x.e) \rightarrow (\mathcal{T}_e^0[\![e]\!] \; \rho \; \Delta)$
(5) $\mathcal{T}_e^0[\![f]\!] \; \rho \; \Delta = \begin{cases} f \rightarrow \epsilon, & \text{if } f \in \rho \\ f \rightarrow (\mathcal{T}_e^0[\![\lambda x_1 \ldots x_n.e]\!] \; (\rho \cup \{f\}) \; \Delta), \text{otherwise} \\ \text{where } (f \; x_1 \ldots x_n = e) \in \Delta \end{cases}$
(6) $\mathcal{T}_e^0[\![e_0 \; e_1]\!] \; \rho \; \Delta = (e_0 \; e_1) \rightarrow (\mathcal{T}_e^0[\![e_0]\!] \; \rho \; \Delta), (\mathcal{T}_e^0[\![e_1]\!] \; \rho \; \Delta)$
(7) $\mathcal{T}_e^0[\![\text{case } e_0 \text{ of } p_1 \Rightarrow e_1 \ldots p_k \Rightarrow e_k]\!] \; \rho \; \Delta =$
    $(\text{case } e_0 \text{ of } p_1 \Rightarrow e_1 \ldots p_k \Rightarrow e_k) \rightarrow (\mathcal{T}_e^0[\![e_0]\!] \; \rho \; \Delta), \ldots, (\mathcal{T}_e^0[\![e_k]\!] \; \rho \; \Delta)$

Fig. 9. Level 0 Transformation Rules

Within the rules $\mathcal{T}_e^0$, ρ is the set of previously encountered function calls and Δ is the set of function definitions. If a function call is re-encountered, no further nodes are added to the process tree. Thus, the constructed process tree will always be a finite representation of the program.

4.2   Level $k + 1$ Transformers

Each subsequent level $(k + 1)$ in our hierarchy is built on top of the previous levels. The rules for level $k + 1$ transformation of program p are defined by $\mathcal{T}_p^{k+1}[\![p]\!]$ as shown in Fig. 10.

Within these rules, κ denotes the context of the expression under scrutiny and ρ contains memoised process trees and their associated new function headers. For most of the level $k+1$ transformation rules, normal order reduction is applied to the current term, as for the semantics given in Fig. 3.

In rule (3), if the context surrounding a variable redex is a **case**, then information is propagated to each branch of the **case** to indicate that this variable has the value of the corresponding branch pattern.

(1) $\mathcal{T}_p^{k+1}[\![e_0 \textbf{ where } h_1 = e_1, \ldots, h_n = e_n]\!] = \mathcal{T}_e^{k+1}[\![e_0]\!] \; \langle\rangle \; \{\} \; \{h_1 = e_1, \ldots, h_n = e_n\}$

(2) $\mathcal{T}_e^{k+1}[\![x]\!] \; \langle\rangle \; \rho \; \Delta = x \to \epsilon$

(3) $\mathcal{T}_e^{k+1}[\![x]\!] \; \langle(\textbf{case } \bullet \textbf{ of } p_1 \Rightarrow e_1 \ldots p_n \Rightarrow e_n) : \kappa\rangle \; \rho \; \Delta =$
$\quad \mathcal{T}_\kappa^{k+1}[\![x \to \epsilon]\!] \; \langle(\textbf{case } \bullet \textbf{ of } p_1 \Rightarrow (\kappa \bullet e_1)\{x \mapsto p_1\} \ldots p_n \Rightarrow (\kappa \bullet e_n)\{x \mapsto p_n\}) : \langle\rangle\rangle \; \rho \; \Delta$

(4) $\mathcal{T}_e^{k+1}[\![x]\!] \; \langle(\bullet \; e) : \kappa\rangle \; \rho \; \Delta = \mathcal{T}_\kappa^{k+1}[\![x \to \epsilon]\!] \; \langle(\bullet \; e) : \kappa\rangle \; \rho \; \Delta$

(5) $\mathcal{T}_e^{k+1}[\![c \; e_1 \ldots e_n]\!] \; \langle\rangle \; \rho \; \Delta =$
$\quad (c \; e_1 \ldots e_n) \to (\mathcal{T}_e^{k+1}[\![e_1]\!] \; \langle\rangle \; \rho \; \Delta), \ldots, (\mathcal{T}_e^{k+1}[\![e_n]\!] \; \langle\rangle \; \rho \; \Delta)$

(6) $\mathcal{T}_e^{k+1}[\![c \; e_1 \ldots e_n]\!] \; \langle(\textbf{case } \bullet \textbf{ of } p_1 \Rightarrow e_1' \ldots p_k \Rightarrow e_k') : \kappa\rangle \; \rho \; \Delta =$
$\quad \mathcal{T}_e^{k+1}[\![e_i'\{x_1 \mapsto e_1, \ldots, x_n \mapsto e_n\}]\!] \; \kappa \; \rho \; \Delta$
$\quad \text{where } \exists i \in \{1 \ldots k\}.p_i = c \; x_1 \ldots x_n$

(7) $\mathcal{T}_e^{k+1}[\![\lambda x.e_0]\!] \; \langle\rangle \; \rho \; \Delta = (\lambda x.e_0) \to (\mathcal{T}_e^{k+1}[\![e_0]\!] \; \langle\rangle \; \rho \; \Delta)$

(8) $\mathcal{T}_e^{k+1}[\![\lambda x.e_0]\!] \; \langle(\bullet \; e_1) : \kappa\rangle \; \rho \; \Delta = \mathcal{T}_e^{k+1}[\![e_0\{x \mapsto e_1\}]\!] \; \kappa \; \rho \; \Delta$

(9) $\mathcal{T}_e^{k+1}[\![f]\!] \; \kappa \; \rho \; \Delta = \begin{cases} h\sigma \to \epsilon, & \text{if } \exists(h = t') \in \rho, \sigma.t'\sigma \cong t \\ \mathcal{T}_\varphi^{k+1}[\![t'\sigma \uparrow t]\!], & \text{if } \exists(h = t') \in \rho, \sigma.t'\sigma \preceq t \\ h \to \mathcal{T}_e^{k+1}[\![\lambda x_1 \ldots x_n.e]\!] \; \kappa \; (\rho \cup \{h = t\}) \; \Delta, & \text{otherwise} \\ \quad \text{where } (f \; x_1 \ldots x_n = e) \in \Delta \\ \quad h = f' \; x_1' \ldots x_k' \; (f' \text{ is fresh}, \{x_1' \ldots x_k'\} = fv(t)) \end{cases}$
$\quad \text{where } t = \mathcal{T}_e^k[\![f]\!] \; \kappa \; \{\} \; \Delta$

(10) $\mathcal{T}_e^{k+1}[\![e_0 \; e_1]\!] \; \kappa \; \rho \; \Delta = \mathcal{T}_e^{k+1}[\![e_0]\!] \; \langle(\bullet \; e_1) : \kappa\rangle \; \rho \; \Delta$

(11) $\mathcal{T}_e^{k+1}[\![\textbf{case } e_0 \textbf{ of } p_1 \Rightarrow e_1 \ldots p_n \Rightarrow e_n]\!] \; \kappa \; \rho \; \Delta =$
$\quad \mathcal{T}_e^{k+1}[\![e_0]\!] \; \langle(\textbf{case } \bullet \textbf{ of } p_1 \Rightarrow e_1 \ldots p_n \Rightarrow e_n) : \kappa\rangle \; \rho \; \Delta$

(12) $\mathcal{T}_\kappa^{k+1}[\![t]\!] \; \langle\rangle \; \rho \; \Delta = t$

(13) $\mathcal{T}_\kappa^{k+1}[\![t]\!] \; (\kappa = \langle(\bullet \; e) : \kappa'\rangle) \; \rho \; \Delta =$
$\quad \mathcal{T}_\kappa^{k+1}[\![(\kappa \bullet root(t)) \to t, (\mathcal{T}_e^{k+1}[\![e]\!] \; \langle\rangle \; \rho \; \Delta)]\!] \; \kappa' \; \rho \; \Delta$

(14) $\mathcal{T}_\kappa^{k+1}[\![t]\!] \; (\kappa = \langle(\textbf{case } \bullet \textbf{ of } p_1 \Rightarrow e_1 \ldots p_n \Rightarrow e_n) : \kappa'\rangle) \; \rho \; \Delta =$
$\quad (\kappa \bullet root(t)) \to t, (\mathcal{T}_e^{k+1}[\![e_1]\!] \; \kappa' \; \rho \; \Delta), \ldots, (\mathcal{T}_e^{k+1}[\![e_n]\!] \; \kappa' \; \rho \; \Delta)$

(15) $\mathcal{T}_\varphi^{k+1}[\![(x_0 \; x_1 \ldots x_n) \to t_0, t_1, \ldots, t_n]\!] = (x_0 \; x_1 \ldots x_n) \to t_0', t_1', \ldots, t_n'$
$\quad \text{where } \forall i \in \{0 \ldots n\}.t_i' = \mathcal{T}_p^{k+1}[\![\mathcal{R}_p[\![t_i]\!]]\!]$

Fig. 10. Level $k + 1$ Transformation Rules

In rule (6), if the context surrounding a constructor application redex is a **case**, then pattern matching is performed and the appropriate branch of the **case** is selected, thus removing the constructor application. This is where our transformers actually remove intermediate data structures.

In rule (9), if the redex of the current term is a function, then it is transformed by the transformer one level lower in the hierarchy (level k) producing a process tree; this is therefore where the transformer builds on all the transformers at lower levels. This level k process tree is compared to the previous process trees produced at level k (contained in ρ). If the process tree is a *renaming* of a previous one, then *folding* is performed, and a fold node is created using a recursive call of the function associated with the renamed process tree in ρ. If the process tree is an *embedding* of a previous one, then *generalisation* is performed; the result of this generalisation is then further transformed. Otherwise, the current process tree is memoised by being associated with a new function call in ρ; an unfold node is created with this new function call in the root node, with the result of transforming the unfolding of the current term as its sub-tree.

The rules $\mathcal{T}_\kappa^{k+1}$ are defined on a process tree and a surrounding context. These rules are applied when the normal-order reduction of the input program becomes 'stuck' as a result of encountering a variable in the redex position. In this case, the surrounding context is further transformed.

The rule $\mathcal{T}_\varphi^{k+1}$ is applied to a newly constructed generalisation node; all the sub-trees of the node are residualised and further transformed.

5   Examples

In this section, we look at some examples of the transformations that can be performed at different levels in our program transformation hierarchy.

Example 6. Consider the following program from [6]:

$$
\begin{aligned}
&f\ x\ x\\
&\textbf{where}\\
&f\ x\ y = \textbf{case }x\textbf{ of}\\
&\qquad\qquad Zero\ \ \Rightarrow y\\
&\qquad\qquad Succ(x) \Rightarrow f\ (f\ x\ x)\ (f\ x\ x)
\end{aligned}
$$

This program takes exponential time $O(2^n)$, where n is the size of the input value x. If we transform this program at level 1 in our hierarchy, we obtain the following program:

$$
\begin{aligned}
&f\ x\\
&\textbf{where}\\
&f\ x = \textbf{case }x\textbf{ of}\\
&\qquad\qquad Zero\ \ \Rightarrow Zero\\
&\qquad\qquad Succ(x) \Rightarrow f\ (f\ x)
\end{aligned}
$$

This program takes linear time $O(n)$ on the same input, so an exponential speedup has been achieved. If we transform the original program at level 2 in our hierarchy, we obtain the following program:

$$
\begin{aligned}
&f\ x\\
&\textbf{where}\\
&f\ x = \textbf{case }x\textbf{ of}\\
&\qquad\qquad Zero\ \ \Rightarrow Zero\\
&\qquad\qquad Succ(x) \Rightarrow f\ x
\end{aligned}
$$

A very slight further improvement has therefore been obtained. No further improvements are obtained at higher levels in the hierarchy.

Example 7. Consider the transformation of the naïve reverse program shown in Fig. 1, which has $O(n^2)$ runtime where n is the length of the list xs. If we transform this program at level 1 in our hierarchy, we obtain the following program:

```
f xs
where
f xs    = case xs of
             Nil        ⇒ Nil
             Cons x xs ⇒ case (f xs) of
                            Nil        ⇒ Cons x Nil
                            Cons x' xs ⇒ Cons x' (f' xs x)
f' xs x = case xs of
             Nil        ⇒ Cons x Nil
             Cons x' xs ⇒ Cons x' (f' xs x)
```

There is very little improvement in the performance of this program over the original; it still has $O(n^2)$ runtime. However, if we transform the naïve reverse program at level 2 in our hierarchy, we obtain the following program:

```
case xs of
   Nil        ⇒ Nil
   Cons x xs ⇒ f xs x Nil
where
f xs x ys = case xs of
               Nil        ⇒ Cons x ys
               Cons x' xs ⇒ f xs x' (Cons x ys)
```

This program takes linear time $O(n)$ on the same input, so a superlinear speedup has been achieved. No further improvements are obtained at higher levels in the hierarchy.

Example 8. Consider the following program:

```
map inc (qrev xs)
where
map f xs   = case xs of
                Nil        ⇒ Nil
                Cons x xs ⇒ Cons (f x) (map f xs)
inc n       = Succ n
qrev xs     = qrev' xs Nil
qrev' xs ys = case xs of
                 Nil        ⇒ ys
                 Cons x xs ⇒ qrev' xs (Cons x ys)
```

This program requires $2n$ allocations, where n is the length of the list xs. If we transform the original program at level 1 in our hierarchy, we obtain the following program:

$$
\begin{aligned}
&f\ xs\ Nil \\
&\textbf{where} \\
&f\ xs\ ys = \textbf{case}\ xs\ \textbf{of} \\
&\qquad\qquad Nil \qquad\ \Rightarrow f'\ ys \\
&\qquad\qquad Cons\ x\ xs \Rightarrow f\ xs\ (Cons\ x\ ys) \\
&f'\ xs \quad\ = \textbf{case}\ xs\ \textbf{of} \\
&\qquad\qquad Nil \qquad\ \Rightarrow Nil \\
&\qquad\qquad Cons\ x\ xs \Rightarrow Cons\ (Succ\ x)\ (f'\ xs)
\end{aligned}
$$

This program also requires $2n$ allocations, and not much improvement has been made. If we transform the original program at level 2 in our hierarchy, we obtain the following program:

$$
\begin{aligned}
&f\ xs\ Nil\ (\lambda xs.f'\ xs) \\
&\textbf{where} \\
&f\ xs\ ys\ g = \textbf{case}\ xs\ \textbf{of} \\
&\qquad\qquad Nil \qquad\ \Rightarrow g\ ys \\
&\qquad\qquad Cons\ x\ xs \Rightarrow f\ xs\ (Cons\ x\ ys)\ g \\
&f'\ xs \qquad = \textbf{case}\ xs\ \textbf{of} \\
&\qquad\qquad Nil \qquad\ \Rightarrow Nil \\
&\qquad\qquad Cons\ x\ xs \Rightarrow Cons\ (Succ\ x)\ (f'\ xs)
\end{aligned}
$$

This program still requires $2n$ allocations, so again not much improvement has been made. However, if we transform this program at level 3 in our hierarchy, we obtain the following program:

$$
\begin{aligned}
&f\ xs\ (\lambda xs.xs) \\
&\textbf{where} \\
&f\ xs\ g = \textbf{case}\ xs\ \textbf{of} \\
&\qquad\qquad Nil \qquad\ \Rightarrow g\ Nil \\
&\qquad\qquad Cons\ x\ xs \Rightarrow f\ xs\ (\lambda xs.Cons\ (Succ\ x)\ (g\ xs))
\end{aligned}
$$

This program now requires n allocations, so we can see that improvements can still be made as high as level 3 in our hierarchy (and indeed even higher in some cases). For this example, no further improvements are obtained at higher levels in the hierarchy.

6 Speedups

In this section, we look at the efficiency gains that can be obtained at different levels in our program transformation hierarchy.

Theorem 2 (Exponential Speedups). Exponential speedups can only be obtained above level 0 in our hierarchy if common sub-expression elimination is performed during generalisation.

Proof. An exponential speedup can only be obtained if a number of repeated computations are identified, so the computation need only be performed once. This can only happen in our transformations if the repeated computations are identified by the common sub-expression elimination that takes place during generalisation.

If we consider the transformation of the program at level 1 in our hierarchy given in Example 6, the term $(f\ x\ x)$ is extracted twice during generalisation, but then identified by common sub-expression elimination, thus allowing an exponential speedup to be achieved. In practice, we have found that such exponential improvements are obtained for very few useful programs; it is very uncommon for the same computation to be extracted more than once during generalisation to facilitate this improvement. It is also very unlikely that a programmer would write such an inefficient program when a much better solution exists.

We now look at the improvements in efficiency that can be obtained without common sub-expression elimination.

Theorem 3 (Non-Exponential Speedups). *Without the use of common sub-expression elimination, the maximum speedup factor possible at level $k > 0$ in our hierarchy for input of size n is $O(n^{k-1})$.*

Proof. The proof is by induction on the hierarchy level k. For level 1, the proof is as given in [24]; since there can only be a constant number of reduction steps removed between each successive call of a function, at most a linear speedup is possible. For level $k + 1$, there will be a constant number of calls to functions that were transformed at level k between each successive call of a level $k + 1$ function. By the inductive hypothesis, the maximum speedup factor for each level k function is $O(n^{k-1})$, so the maximum speedup factor at level $k + 1$ is $O(n^k)$.

Consider the transformation of the naïve reverse program at level 2 in our hierarchy given in Example 7. During this transformation, we end up having to transform a term equivalent to the following at level 1:

$$append\ (append\ xs'\ (Cons\ x'\ Nil))\ (Cons\ x\ Nil)$$

Within this term, the list xs' has to be traversed twice. This term is transformed to one equivalent to the following at level 1 (process tree (2) in Fig. 4 is the process tree produced as a result of this transformation):

$$append\ xs'\ (Cons\ x'\ (Cons\ x\ Nil))$$

Within this term, the list xs' has only to be traversed once, so a linear speedup has been obtained. This linear improvement will be made between each successive call of the naïve reverse function, thus giving an overall superlinear speedup and producing the resulting accumulating reverse program.

7 Termination

In order to prove that each of the transformers in our hierarchy terminate, we need to show that in any infinite sequence of process trees encountered during transformation $t_0, t_1, \ldots$ there definitely exists some $i < j$ where $t_i \preceq t_j$, so an embedding must eventually be encountered and transformation will not continue indefinitely without folding or generalising. This amounts to proving that the embedding relation $\preceq$ is a *well-quasi order*.

Lemma 1 ($\preceq$ is a Well-Quasi Order). The embedding relation $\preceq$ is a *well-quasi order* on any sequence of process trees that are encountered during transformation at level $k > 0$ in our hierarchy.

Proof. The proof is by induction on the hierarchy level k.

For level 1, the proof is similar to that given in [15]. This involves showing that there are a finite number of syntactic constructors in the language. The process trees encountered during transformation are those produced at level 0, so the function names will be those from the original program, so must be finite. Applications of different arities are replaced with separate constructors; we prove that arities are bounded, so there are a finite number of these. We also replace **case** expressions with constructors. Since bound variables are defined using de Bruijn indices, each of these are replaced with separate constructors; we also prove that de Bruijn indices are bounded. The overall number of syntactic constructors is therefore finite, so Kruskal's tree theorem can then be applied to show that $\preceq$ is a well-quasi-order at level 1 in our hierarchy.

At level $k + 1$, the process trees encountered during transformation are those produced at level k and must be finite (by the inductive hypothesis). The number of functions in these process trees must therefore be finite, and the same argument given above for level 1 also applies here, so $\preceq$ is a well-quasi-order at level $k + 1$ in our hierarchy.

Since we only check for embeddings for expressions which have a named function as redex, we need to show that every potentially infinite sequence of expressions encountered during transformation must include expressions of this form.

Lemma 2 (Function Unfolding During Transformation). Every infinite sequence of transformation steps must include function unfolding.

Proof. Every infinite sequence of transformation steps must include either function unfolding or λ-application. Since we do not allow λ-abstractions in our input program, the only way in which new λ-abstractions can be introduced is by function unfolding. Thus, every infinite sequence of transformation steps must include function unfolding.

Theorem 4 (Termination of Transformation). The transformation algorithm always terminates.

Proof. The proof is by contradiction. If the transformation algorithm did not terminate, then the set of memoised process trees in ρ must be infinite. Every new process tree which is added to ρ cannot have any of the previous process trees in ρ embedded within it by the homeomorphic embedding relation $\preceq$, since generalisation would have been performed instead. However, this contradicts the fact that $\preceq$ is a well-quasi-order (Lemma 1).

8   Related Work

The seminal work corresponding to level 1 in our hierarchy is that of Turchin on supercompilation [27], although our level 1 transformer more closely resembles positive supercompilation [26]. There have been several previous attempts to move beyond level 1 in our transformation hierarchy, the first one by Turchin himself using *walk grammars* [28]. In this approach, traces through residual graphs are represented by regular grammars that are subsequently analysed and simplified. This approach is also capable of achieving superlinear speedups, but no automatic procedure is defined for it; the outlined heuristics and strategies may not terminate.

A hierarchy of program specialisers is described in [7] that shows how programs can be metacoded and then manipulated through a *metasystem transition*, with a number of these metasystem transitions giving a metasytem hierarchy in which the original program may have several levels of metacoding. In the work described here, a process tree can be considered to be the metacoding of a program. However, we do not have the difficulties associated with metasystem transitions and multi-level metacoding, as our process trees are residualised back to the object level.

Distillation [9, 11] is built on top of positive supercompilation, so corresponds to level 2 in our hierarchy, but does not go beyond this level. Klyuchnikov and Romanenko [16] construct a hierarchy of supercompilers in which lower level supercompilers are used to prove lemmas about term equivalences, and higher level supercompilers utilise these lemmas by rewriting according to the term equivalences (similar to the "second order replacement method" defined by Kott [18]). Transformers in this hierarchy are capable of similar speedups to those in our hierarchy, but no automatic procedure is defined for it; the need to find and apply appropriate lemmas introduces infinite branching into the search space, and various heuristics have to be used to try to limit this search.

Preliminary work on the hierarchy of transformers defined here was presented in [10]; this did not include analysis of the efficiency improvements that can be made at each level in the hierarchy. The work described here is a lot further developed than that described in [10], and we hope simpler and easier to follow.

Logic program transformation is closely related, and the equivalence of partial deduction and driving (as used in supercompilation) has been argued by Glück and Sørensen [8]. Superlinear speedups can be achieved in logic program transformation by *goal replacement* [22,23]: replacing one logical clause with another to facilitate folding. Techniques similar to the notion of "higher level supercompilation" [16] have been used to prove correctness of goal replacement, but have similar problems regarding the search for appropriate lemmas.

9   Conclusion and Further Work

We have presented a hierarchy of program transformers, capable of performing fusion to eliminate intermediate data structures, in which the transformer at each level of the hierarchy builds on top of those at lower levels. We have proved that the transformers at each level in the hierarchy terminate, and have characterised the speedups that can be obtained at each level. Previous works [1,2,17,24,31] have noted that the unfold/fold transformation methodology is incomplete; some programs cannot be synthesised from each other. It is our hope that this work will help to overcome this restriction.

There are many possible avenues for further work. Firstly, we need to determine what level in the hierarchy is sufficient to optimise a program as much as is possible using this approach. We have seen that it is not sufficient to just transform a program until no further improvement is obtained; improvements may still be still possible at higher levels. We would therefore like to find some analysis technique which would allow us to determine what level in the hierarchy is required. Ultimately, we would like the process trees produced by our transformers to be in what we call *distilled form* $t^{\{\}}$, which is defined as follows:

$$
\begin{aligned}
t^\rho ::= & (x_0\ x_1 \ldots x_n) \to t_0^{(\rho \cup \{x_1,\ldots,x_n\})}, t_1^\rho, \ldots, t_n^\rho \\
& |\ (\textbf{case}\ x_0\ \textbf{of}\ p_1 \Rightarrow e_1 \ldots p_n \Rightarrow e_n) \to (x_0 \to \epsilon), t_1^\rho, \ldots, t_n^\rho\ (x_0 \notin \rho) \\
& |\ \phi(e_1 \ldots e_n) \to t_1^\rho, \ldots, t_n^\rho
\end{aligned}
$$

Within this definition, generalisation variables are added to the set ρ, and cannot be used in the selectors of **case** expressions, so the resulting programs must not create any intermediate data structures. Each of the example programs that we transformed using our transformation hierarchy are ultimately transformed into distilled form before no further improvement is obtained. We could therefore apply successively higher levels in our hierarchy until a process tree in distilled form is obtained. However, at present, we have no proof that this must eventually happen. Work is continuing in this area.

If we can obtain process trees that are in distilled form, then there are many areas in which our work can be applied, as distilled form is much easier to analyse and reason about. These areas include termination analysis, computational complexity analysis, theorem proving, program verification and constructing programs from specifications. Work is also continuing in all of these areas.

Acknowledgements. The author would like to thank the anonymous referees, who provided very useful feedback and suggested improvements to this paper. This work owes a lot to the input of Neil D. Jones, who provided many useful insights and ideas on the subject matter presented here.

References

1. Amtoft, T.: Sharing of Computations. Ph.D. thesis, DAIMI, Aarhus University (1993)
2. Andersen, L.O., Gomard, C.K.: Speedup analysis in partial evaluation: preliminary results. In: ACM SIGPLAN Workshop on Partial Evaluation and Semantics-Based Program Manipulation, pp. 1–7 (1992)
3. Bol, R.: Loop checking in partial deduction. J. Log. Program. 16(1–2), 25–46 (1993)
4. Burstall, R., Darlington, J.: A transformation system for developing recursive programs. J. ACM 24(1), 44–67 (1977)
5. Dershowitz, N., Jouannaud, J.P.: Rewrite systems. In: van Leeuwen, J. (ed.) Handbook of Theoretical Computer Science, pp. 243–320. Elsevier, MIT Press (1990)
6. Glück, R., Klimov, A., Nepeivoda, A.: Non-linear configurations for superlinear speedup by supercompilation. In: Proceedings of the Fifth International Workshop on Metacomputation in Russia (2016)
7. Glück, R., Hatcliff, J., Jørgensen, J.: Generalization in hierarchies of online program specialization systems. In: Flener, P. (ed.) LOPSTR 1998. LNCS, vol. 1559, pp. 179–198. Springer, Heidelberg (1999). https://doi.org/10.1007/3-540-48958-4_10
8. Glück, R., Jørgensen, J.: Generating transformers for deforestation and supercompilation. In: Le Charlier, B. (ed.) SAS 1994. LNCS, vol. 864, pp. 432–448. Springer, Heidelberg (1994). https://doi.org/10.1007/3-540-58485-4_57
9. Hamilton, G.W.: Distillation: extracting the essence of programs. In: Proceedings of the ACM SIGPLAN Symposium on Partial Evaluation and Semantics-Based Program Manipulation, pp. 61–70 (2007)
10. Hamilton, G.W.: A hierarchy of program transformers. In: Proceedings of the Second International Workshop on Metacomputation in Russia (2012)
11. Hamilton, G.W., Jones, N.D.: Distillation with labelled transition systems. In: Proceedings of the ACM Workshop on Partial Evaluation and Program Manipulation, pp. 15–24. ACM (2012)
12. Higman, G.: Ordering by divisibility in abstract algebras. Proc. Lond. Math. Soc. 2, 326–336 (1952)
13. Huet, G.: The zipper. J. Funct. Program. 7(5), 549–554 (1997)
14. Jones, N.D., Gomard, C.K., Sestoft, P.: Partial Evaluation and Automatic Program Generation. Prentice Hall, Hoboken (1993)
15. Klyuchnikov, I.: Supercompiler HOSC 1.1: Proof of Termination. Preprint 21, Keldysh Institute of Applied Mathematics, Moscow (2010)
16. Klyuchnikov, I.: Towards higher-level supercompilation. In: Proceedings of the Second International Workshop on Metacomputation in Russia, pp. 82–101 (2010)
17. Kott, L.: A system for proving equivalences of recursive programs. In: 5th Conference on Automated Deduction, pp. 63–69 (1980)
18. Kott, L.: Unfold/fold transformations. In: Nivat, M., Reynolds, J. (eds.) Algebraic Methods in Semantics, chap. 12, pp. 412–433. CUP (1985)
19. Kruskal, J.: Well-quasi ordering, the tree theorem, and vazsonyi's conjecture. Trans. Am. Math. Soc. 95, 210–225 (1960)
20. Leuschel, M.: On the power of homeomorphic embedding for online termination. In: Levi, G. (ed.) SAS 1998. LNCS, vol. 1503, pp. 230–245. Springer, Heidelberg (1998). https://doi.org/10.1007/3-540-49727-7_14
21. Marlet, R.: Vers une Formalisation de l'Évaluation Partielle. Ph.D. thesis, Université de Nice - Sophia Antipolis (1994)

22. Pettorossi, A., Proietti, M.: A theory of totally correct logic program transformations. In: Proceedings of the ACM SIGPLAN Workshop on Partial Evaluation and Semantics-Based Program Manipulation (PEPM), pp. 159–168 (2004)
23. Roychoudhury, A., Kumar, K., Ramakrishnan, C., Ramakrishnan, I.: An unfold/fold transformation framework for definite logic programs. ACM Trans. Program. Lang. Syst. **26**(3), 464–509 (2004)
24. Sørensen, M.H.: Turchin's Supercompiler Revisited. Master's thesis, Department of Computer Science, University of Copenhagen (1994). dIKU-rapport 94/17
25. Sørensen, M.H., Glück, R.: An algorithm of generalization in positive supercompilation. Lect. Notes Comput. Sci. **787**, 335–351 (1994)
26. Sørensen, M.H., Glück, R., Jones, N.D.: A positive supercompiler. J. Funct. Program. **6**(6), 811–838 (1996)
27. Turchin, V.F.: The concept of a supercompiler. ACM Trans. Program. Lang. Syst. **8**(3), 90–121 (1986)
28. Turchin, V.F.: Program transformation with metasystem transitions. ACM Trans. Program. Lang. Syst. **3**(3), 283–313 (1993)
29. Wadler, P.: The Concatenate Vanishes (December 1987). fP Electronic Mailing List
30. Wadler, P.: Deforestation: transforming programs to eliminate trees. In: Ganzinger, H. (ed.) ESOP 1988. LNCS, vol. 300, pp. 344–358. Springer, Heidelberg (1988). https://doi.org/10.1007/3-540-19027-9_23
31. Zhu, H.: How powerful are folding/unfolding transformations? J. Funct. Program. **4**(1), 89–112 (1994)

Representation and Processing of Instantaneous and Durative Temporal Phenomena

Manolis Pitsikalis$^{(\boxtimes)}$ (iD), Alexei Lisitsa (iD), and Shan Luo (iD)

Department of Computer Science, University of Liverpool, Liverpool, UK
{e.pitsikalis,a.lisitsa,shan.luo}@liverpool.ac.uk

Abstract. Event definitions in Complex Event Processing systems are constrained by the expressiveness of each system's language. Some systems allow the definition of instantaneous complex events, while others allow the definition of durative complex events. While there are exceptions that offer both options, they often lack of intervals relations such as those specified by the Allen's interval algebra. In this paper, we propose a new logic based temporal phenomena definition language, specifically tailored for Complex Event Processing. Our proposed language allows the representation of both instantaneous and durative phenomena and the temporal relations between them. Moreover, we demonstrate the expressiveness of our proposed language by employing a maritime use case where we define maritime events of interest. We analyse the execution semantics of our proposed language for stream processing and finally, we introduce and evaluate on real world data, Phenesthe, our open-source Complex Event Processing system.

Keywords: Event definition language · Temporal logic · Stream processing · Event recognition

1 Introduction

There are numerous event description languages, each with its own formal description and expressiveness. Event description languages allow the representation and the specification of temporal phenomena. They have been used widely in, among others, Complex Event Processing and Recognition [3,5,7,12], and System Analysis and Verification [8,14]. In the case of Complex Event Processing, which is the focus of this paper, users with expert knowledge, or machine learning algorithms, provide definitions of events of interest i.e., complex events that are represented in an event definition language. The Complex Event Processing system accepts as input a single or multiple streams of low level events, such as the timestamped transmitted values of a sensor and by continuously

This work has been funded by the Engineering and Physical Sciences Research Council (EPSRC) Centre for Doctoral Training in Distributed Algorithms at the University of Liverpool, and Denbridge Marine Limited, United Kingdom.

© Springer Nature Switzerland AG 2022
E. De Angelis and W. Vanhoof (Eds.): LOPSTR 2021, LNCS 13290, pp. 135–156, 2022.
https://doi.org/10.1007/978-3-030-98869-2_8

applying temporal queries that involve the provided event definitions, it will produce a stream of complex events associated with some temporal information.

However, the set of events that can be represented in the language of a Complex Event Processing system is constrained by the expressiveness of its event definition language. For example, languages with a point-based temporal model associate facts to instants of time while languages with an interval-based temporal model associate facts with intervals [11]. Consequently, the representation of durative and instantaneous entities in each case respectively is sometimes impossible or not straightforward. Event Calculus [16] approaches [5,10,15] allow the representation of both instantaneous and durative entities, however they lack of interval relations such as those specified by the Allen's interval algebra [2].

In this paper, we formally present a logic based language for Complex Event Processing that allows the description of both instantaneous and durative temporal phenomena and the relations between them. We demonstrate the expressiveness of the language by employing a maritime use-case scenario where the goal is to describe maritime activities of interest. Moreover, we present the execution semantics for stream processing. Finally, we introduce and evaluate the Phenesthe[1] Complex Event Processing system. Thus, the contributions of this paper are the following:

- a formally described language for the representation of both instantaneous and durative temporal phenomena and their relations,
- a demonstration of the expressiveness of the language in the maritime use case,
- the execution semantics for stream processing,
- and finally, the open-source Complex Event Processing system Phenesthe that utilises the language of this paper.

The paper is organised as follows, in Sect. 2 we present the syntax, the grammar and the semantics of our language. Next, in Sect. 3 we demonstrate its expressiveness by formalising a set of maritime activities. In Sect. 4 we present the execution semantics for stream processing, while in Sect. 5 we present and evaluate empirically the Phenesthe Complex Event Processing system. Next, in Sect. 6 we compare our language with relevant works. Finally, in Sect. 7 we summarise our approach and discuss our future directions.

2   Language

The key components of our language are events, states and dynamic temporal phenomena. In what follows, 'temporal phenomena' includes all of the three aforementioned entities. Events are true at instants of time, while states and dynamic temporal phenomena hold on intervals. Events are defined in terms of logical operations between instantaneous temporal phenomena, states are defined

---

[1] Phenesthe corresponds to the Greek word 'Φαίνεσθαι' which means 'to appear'. Phenesthe (Φαίνεσθαι) and phenomenon (φαινόμενον) are different forms of the ancient Greek verb 'Φαίνω' meaning 'I cause to appear'.

using the operators of maximal range, temporal union, temporal intersection and temporal complement; finally, dynamic temporal phenomena are defined in terms of temporal relations that involve the basic seven of Allen's interval algebra [2]. In this Section, we present the syntax, the semantics and the grammar of our language.

2.1 Syntax

Formally, our language is described by the triplet $\langle \mathcal{P}, L, \Phi \rangle$, where

- $\mathcal{P}$ is a set of Predicates (atomic formulae), that may be of three types, event, state or dynamic temporal phenomenon predicates;
- L is a set defined by the union of the set of logical connectives $\{\wedge, \vee, \neg\}$, the set of temporal operators, $\{\rightarrowtail, \sqcup, \sqcap, \backslash\}$, the set of temporal relations $\{\mathsf{before}, \mathsf{meets}, \mathsf{overlaps}, \mathsf{finishes}, \mathsf{starts}, \mathsf{equals}, \mathsf{contains}\}$ and finally the set of the $\{\mathsf{start}, \mathsf{end}\}$ operators.
- Φ is the set of formulae defined by the union of the formulae sets $\Phi^{\bullet}$, Φ^{-} and $\Phi^{=}$, that we will present below.

Formulae of $\Phi^{\bullet}$ describe instantaneous temporal phenomena, formulae of Φ^{-} describe durative temporal phenomena that hold (are true) in disjoint maximal intervals, finally formulae of $\Phi^{=}$ describe durative temporal phenomena that may hold in non-disjoint intervals. Atomic formulae of $\Phi^{\square}$ where $\square \in \{\bullet, -, =\}$ are denoted as $\Phi_{o}^{\square}$. Terms are defined as follows:

- Each variable is a term.
- Each constant is a term.

Events, states and dynamic temporal phenomena are expressed as n-ary predicate symbols, of the corresponding type (event, state or dynamic temporal phenomenon), $P(a_1, ..., a_n)$, where P is the associated name and $a_1, ..., a_n$ are terms corresponding to atemporal properties. Moreover, we assume that the set of predicate symbols includes those with atemporal and fixed semantics, such as arithmetic comparison operators etc., however for simplification reasons in what follows we omit their presentation. The set of formulae $\Phi^{\bullet}$ is defined as follows:

- (Event predicate) If P is an n-ary event predicate and $a_1, ..., a_n$ are terms then $P(a_1, ..., a_n)$ is a formula of $\Phi^{\bullet}$.
- (Negation) If ϕ is a formula of $\Phi^{\bullet}$ then $\neg\phi$ is a formula of $\Phi^{\bullet}$.
- (Conjunction/disjunction) If ϕ and ψ are formulae of $\Phi^{\bullet}$ then ϕ op ψ, where op is the conjunction ($\wedge$) or disjunction ($\vee$) connective, is a formula of $\Phi^{\bullet}$.
- (start/end) If ϕ is a formula of Φ^{-} then $\mathsf{start}(\phi)$ and $\mathsf{end}(\phi)$ are formulae of $\Phi^{\bullet}$.

Following, we define the set of formulae Φ^{-}:

- (State predicate) If P is an n-ary state predicate and $a_1, ..., a_n$ are terms then $P(a_1, ..., a_n)$ is a formula of Φ^{-}.
- (Maximal range) If ϕ and ψ are formulae of $\Phi^{\bullet}$ then $\phi \rightarrowtail \psi$ is a formula of Φ^{-}.

- (Temporal union, intersection & complement) If ϕ and ψ are formulae of Φ^- then $\phi \ \square \ \psi$, where $\square \in \{\sqcup, \sqcap, \backslash\}$, is a formula of Φ^-. The temporal operators $\sqcup, \sqcap$ and $\backslash$ correspond to temporal union, intersection and complement respectively.

Finally, we define the set of formulae $\Phi^=$ as follows:

- (Dynamic temporal phenomenon predicate) If P is an n-ary dynamic temporal phenomenon predicate and $a_1, ..., a_n$ are terms then $P(a_1, ..., a_n)$ is a formula of $\Phi^=$.
- (Temporal relation)
  - If ϕ and ψ are formulae of $\Phi^- \cup \Phi^=$ then $\phi \ tr \ \psi$, where $tr \in \{$meets, overlaps, equals$\}$, is a formula of $\Phi^=$.
  - If ϕ is a formula of $\Phi^\bullet \cup \Phi^- \cup \Phi^=$ and ψ is a formula of $\Phi^- \cup \Phi^=$ then $\phi \ tr \ \psi$, where $tr \in \{$finishes, starts$\}$, is a formula of $\Phi^=$.
  - If ϕ is a formula of $\Phi^- \cup \Phi^=$ and ψ is a formula of $\Phi^\bullet \cup \Phi^- \cup \Phi^=$ then ϕ contains ψ is a formula of $\Phi^=$.
  - If ϕ is a formula of $\Phi^\bullet \cup \Phi^- \cup \Phi^=$ and ψ is a formula of $\Phi^\bullet \cup \Phi^- \cup \Phi^=$ then ϕ before ψ is a formula of $\Phi^=$.

2.2   Grammar

In addition to the elements described above, our language includes temporal phenomena definitions that specify new event, state and dynamic temporal phenomena predicates. The production rule-set (1) presents the complete grammar of the language in the Extended Backus-Naur Form (EBNF).

$$
\begin{aligned}
&\langle event \rangle ::= \ eventName(...); \\
&\langle state \rangle ::= \ stateName(...); \\
&\langle dynamic \rangle ::= \ dynamicPhenomenonName(...); \\
&\langle temporalExpression \rangle ::= \langle instantExpression \rangle \mid \langle intervalExpression \rangle; \\
&\langle instantExpression \rangle ::= \ '(' \langle instantExpresstion \rangle ')' \mid \neg \ \langle instantExpression \rangle \\
&\qquad\qquad \mid \langle instantExpression \rangle \ (' \wedge ' \mid ' \vee ') \ \langle instantExpression \rangle \\
&\qquad\qquad \mid \langle startEndOp \rangle \mid \langle event \rangle; \\
&\langle intervalExpression \rangle ::= \langle intervalOperation \rangle \mid \langle intervalRelation \rangle; \\
&\langle intervalOperation \rangle ::= \langle intervalOperation \rangle \ (' \sqcup ' \mid ' \sqcap ' \mid ' \backslash ') \ \langle intervalOperation \rangle \\
&\qquad\qquad \mid \langle instantExpression \rangle \ ' \rightarrowtail ' \ \langle instantExpression \rangle \\
&\qquad\qquad \mid \ '(' \langle intervalOperation \rangle ')' \mid \langle state \rangle; \\
&\langle intervalRelation \rangle ::= \langle temporalExpression \rangle \ \text{'before'} \ \langle temporalExpression \rangle \\
&\qquad\qquad \mid \langle intervalExpression \rangle \ \text{'overlaps'} \ \langle intervalExpression \rangle \\
&\qquad\qquad \mid \langle intervalExpression \rangle \ \text{'meets'} \ \langle intervalExpression \rangle \\
&\qquad\qquad \mid \langle temporalExpression \rangle \ \text{'finishes'} \ \langle intervalExpression \rangle \\
&\qquad\qquad \mid \langle temporalExpression \rangle \ \text{'starts'} \ \langle intervalExpression \rangle \\
&\qquad\qquad \mid \langle intervalExpression \rangle \ \text{'contains'} \ \langle temporalExpression \rangle \\
&\qquad\qquad \mid \langle intervalExpression \rangle \ \text{'equals'} \ \langle intervalExpression \rangle \\
&\qquad\qquad \mid \ '(' \langle intervalRelation \rangle ')' \mid \langle dynamic \rangle; \\
&\langle startEndOp \rangle ::= (\text{'start'} \mid \text{'end'}) '(' \langle intervalOperation \rangle ')'; \\
&\langle definitions \rangle ::= \langle eventDefinition \rangle \mid \langle stateDefinition \rangle \\
&\qquad\qquad \mid \langle dynamicDefinition \rangle; \\
&\langle eventDefinition \rangle ::= \text{'event\_phenomenon'} \ \langle event \rangle ' : ' \ \langle instantExpression \rangle '.'; \\
&\langle stateDefinition \rangle ::= \text{'state\_phenomenon'} \ \langle state \rangle ' : ' \langle intervalOperation \rangle '.'; \\
&\langle dynamicDefinition \rangle ::= \text{'dynamic\_phenomenon'} \ \langle dynamic \rangle ' : ' \langle intervalRelation \rangle '.';
\end{aligned}
$$

(1)

Phenomena definitions are specified by the production rule $\langle definitions \rangle$ of the grammar. Event predicates are defined using expressions on instants of time, expressed via formulae of $\Phi^{\cdot}$, while state predicates are defined in terms of formulae of Φ^{-}. Finally, dynamic temporal phenomena predicates are defined in terms of temporal relations on intervals and instants, therefore specified via formulae of $\Phi^{=}$. Note, that the set of definitions allowed in the language is subject to an additional constraint: no cyclic dependencies in the definitions of temporal phenomena are allowed. A temporal phenomenon A depends from phenomenon B if B is a sub-formula of the definition of A.

2.3   Semantics

We assume time is represented by an infinite non empty set $T = \mathbb{Z}_0^+$ of non-negative integers ordered via the '$<$' relation, formally $T = \langle T, < \rangle$. For the formulae sets $\Phi^{\cdot}, \Phi^{-}$ and $\Phi^{=}$ we define the model $\mathcal{M} = \langle T, I, <, V^{\cdot}, V^{-}, V^{=} \rangle$ where $V^{\cdot} : \Phi_o^{\cdot} \to 2^T$, $V^{-} : \Phi_o^{-} \to 2^I$, $V^{=} : \Phi_o^{=} \to 2^I$ are valuations of atomic formulae and $I = \{[ts, te] : ts < te$ and $ts, te \in T\} \cup \{[ts, \infty) : ts \in T\}$ is the set of the accepted time intervals of T. Given a model $\mathcal{M}$, the validity of a formula $\phi \in \Phi^{\cdot}$ at a timepoint $t \in T$ (in symbols $\mathcal{M}, t \models \phi$) is determined by the rules below:

- $\mathcal{M}, t \models P(a_1, ..., a_n)$ where P is an n-ary event predicate symbol iff $t \in V^{\cdot}(P(a_1, ..., a_n))$;
- $\mathcal{M}, t \models \neg \phi$ where $\phi \in \Phi^{\cdot}$ iff $\mathcal{M}, t \not\models \phi$;
- $\mathcal{M}, t \models \phi \wedge \psi$ where $\phi, \psi \in \Phi^{\cdot}$ iff $\mathcal{M}, t \models \phi$ and $\mathcal{M}, t \models \psi$;
- $\mathcal{M}, t \models \phi \vee \psi$ where $\phi, \psi \in \Phi^{\cdot}$ iff $\mathcal{M}, t \models \phi$ or $\mathcal{M}, t \models \psi$;
- $\mathcal{M}, t \models start(\phi)$ where $\phi \in \Phi^{-}$ iff $\exists te \in T$ and $\mathcal{M}, [t, te] \models \phi$, where $\mathcal{M}, [t, te] \models \phi$ denotes the validity of formula $\phi \in \Phi^{-}$ at an interval $[t, te]$ as defined below;
- $\mathcal{M}, t \models end(\phi)$ where $\phi \in \Phi^{-}$ iff $\exists ts \in T$ and $\mathcal{M}, [ts, t] \models \phi$;

Given a model $\mathcal{M}$, the validity of a formula $\phi \in \Phi^{-}$ at a time interval $[ts, te] \in I$ (in symbols $\mathcal{M}, [ts, te] \models \phi$) is defined as follows:

- $\mathcal{M}, [ts, te] \models P(a_1, ..., a_n)$ where P is an n-ary state predicate symbol iff $[ts, te] \in V^{-}(P(a_1, ..., a_n))$;
- $\mathcal{M}, [ts, te] \models \phi \rightarrowtail \psi$ where $\phi, \psi \in \Phi^{\cdot}$ iff:
  1. $ts \in T$ and $\mathcal{M}, ts \models \phi$,
  2. $te \in (ts, \infty) \subset T$ and $\mathcal{M}, te \models \psi \wedge \neg \phi$,
  3. $\forall ts' \in [0, ts) \subset T, \exists te' \in (ts', ts)$ where $\mathcal{M}, ts' \models \phi$ and $\mathcal{M}, te' \models \psi \wedge \neg \phi$,
  4. and finally, $\nexists te'' \in (ts, te) \subset T$ where $\mathcal{M}, te'' \models \psi \wedge \neg \phi$.

  Essentially, $\phi \rightarrowtail \psi$ holds for the disjoint maximal intervals that start at the earliest instant ts where ϕ is true (conditions 1, 3) and end at the earliest instant $te, te > ts$ (condition 4) where ψ is true and ϕ is false (condition 2, 4).
- $\mathcal{M}, [ts, \infty) \models \phi \rightarrowtail \psi$ where $\phi, \psi \in \Phi^{\cdot}$ iff conditions (1) and (3) from above hold and $\nexists te \in (ts, \infty) \subset T$ such that $\mathcal{M}, te \models \psi \wedge \neg \phi$. Therefore a formula $\phi \rightarrowtail \psi$ may hold indefinitely if there does not exist an appropriate instant

after ts at which $\phi \wedge \neg \psi$ is satisfied. This effectively implements the common-sense law of inertia [20]. For simplification reasons in the semantics below we omit intervals open at the right to infinity since they can be treated in a similar manner.

- $\mathcal{M}, [ts, te] \models \phi \sqcup \psi$ where $\phi, \psi \in \Phi^-$ iff one of the cases below holds:
  - $\exists$ a sequence of length $k > 1$ of intervals $i_1, ..., i_k \in I$ where $i_k = [ts_k, te_k]$, $ts = ts_1$ and $te = te_k$ s.t.:
    1. $\forall \alpha \in [1, k-1]: te_\alpha \in i_{\alpha+1}$, $ts_\alpha < ts_{\alpha+1}$ and $te_\alpha < te_{\alpha+1}$,
    2. $\forall \beta \in [1, k]: \mathcal{M}, [ts_\beta, te_\beta] \models \phi$ or $\mathcal{M}, [ts_\beta, te_\beta] \models \psi$, and
    3. $\nexists i_\gamma = [ts_\gamma, te_\gamma] \in I - \{i_1, ..., i_k\}$ where $\mathcal{M}, [ts_\gamma, te_\gamma] \models \phi$ or $\mathcal{M}, [ts_\gamma, te_\gamma] \models \psi$ and $ts_1 \in i_\gamma$ or $te_k \in i_\gamma$
  - $\mathcal{M}, [ts, te] \models \phi$ or $\mathcal{M}, [ts, te] \models \psi$ and $\nexists i_\gamma = [ts_\gamma, te_\gamma] \in I - \{[ts, te]\}$ where $\mathcal{M}, [ts_\gamma, te_\gamma] \models \phi$ or $\mathcal{M}, [ts_\gamma, te_\gamma] \models \psi$ and $ts \in i_\gamma$ or $te \in i_\gamma$.

For a sequence of intervals, conditions (1–2) ensure that intervals, at which ϕ or ψ are valid, overlap or touch will coalesce, while condition (3) ensures that the resulting interval is maximal. In the case of a single interval, the conditions ensure that at the interval $[ts, te]$ ϕ or ψ is valid, and that $[ts, te]$ is maximal. In simple terms, the temporal union $\phi \sqcup \psi$ holds for the intervals where at least one of ϕ or ψ hold. The above definition of temporal union follows the definitions of temporal coalescing presented in [9,13].

- $\mathcal{M}, [ts, te] \models \phi \setminus \psi$ where $\phi, \psi \in \Phi^-$ iff $\exists [ts', te'] \in I$ where $\mathcal{M}, [ts', te'] \models \phi$, $[ts, te] \subseteq [ts', te']$ (i.e., $[ts, te]$ subinterval of $[ts', te']$), $\forall [ts_\psi, te_\psi] \in I$ where $\mathcal{M}, [ts_\psi, te_\psi] \models \psi$, $[ts, te] \cap [ts_\psi, te_\psi] = \varnothing$ and finally $[ts, te]$ is maximal. In plain language, the temporal difference of formulae ϕ, ψ holds for the maximal subintervals of the intervals at which ϕ holds but ψ doesn't hold.

- $\mathcal{M}, [ts, te] \models \phi \sqcap \psi$ where $\phi, \psi \in \Phi^-$ iff $\exists [ts_\phi, te_\phi], [ts_\psi, te_\psi] \in I$ where $\mathcal{M}, [ts_\phi, te_\phi] \models \phi$, $\mathcal{M}, [ts_\psi, te_\psi] \models \psi$ and $\exists [ts, te] \in I$ where $[ts, te] \subseteq [ts_\phi, te_\phi]$, $[ts, te] \subseteq [ts_\psi, te_\psi]$ and $[ts, te]$ is maximal. In other words, the temporal intersection of two formulae of Φ^- holds for the intervals at which both formulae hold.

Given a model $\mathcal{M}$, the validity of a formula $\phi \in \Phi^=$ at a time interval $[ts, te] \in I$ (in symbols $\mathcal{M}, [ts, te] \models \phi$) is defined as follows:

- $\mathcal{M}, [ts, te] \models P(a_1, ..., a_n)$ where P is n-ary dynamic temporal phenomenon predicate symbol iff $[ts, te] \in V^=(P(a_1, ..., a_n))$;
- $\mathcal{M}, [ts, te] \models \phi$ before ψ iff:
  - (interval - interval) for $\phi, \psi \in \Phi^- \cup \Phi^=$, $\exists a, b \in T$, $a < b$, $\mathcal{M}, [ts, a] \models \phi$, $\mathcal{M}, [b, te] \models \psi$ and all of the conditions below hold:
    * $\nexists [ts', a'] \in I$ where $\mathcal{M}, [ts', a'] \models \phi$ and $a < a' < b$,
    * $\nexists [b', te'] \in I$ where $\mathcal{M}, [b', te'] \models \psi$ and $a < b' < b$.
  - (instant - interval) for $\phi \in \Phi^\bullet$, $\psi \in \Phi^- \cup \Phi^=$, $\mathcal{M}, ts \models \phi$, $\exists a \in T, a > ts$, $\mathcal{M}, [a, te] \models \psi$ and all the conditions below hold:
    * $\nexists ts' \in T$ where $\mathcal{M}, ts' \models \phi$ and $ts < ts' < a$,
    * $\nexists [a', te'] \in I$ where $\mathcal{M}, [a', te'] \models \psi$ and $ts < a' < a$.
  - (interval - instant) for $\phi \in \Phi^- \cup \Phi^=$ and $\psi \in \Phi^\bullet$, $\exists a \in T$, $a < te$, $\mathcal{M}, [ts, a] \models \phi$, $\mathcal{M}, te \models \psi$ and all the conditions below hold:

* $\nexists [ts', a'] \in I$ where $\mathcal{M}, [ts', a'] \models \phi$ and $a < a' < te$,
* $\nexists te' \in T$ where $\mathcal{M}, te' \models \psi$ and $a < te' < te$.
- (instant - instant) for $\phi \in \Phi^{\bullet}$ and $\psi \in \Phi^{\bullet}$, $\mathcal{M}, ts \models \phi$, $\mathcal{M}, te \models \psi$ and all the conditions below hold:
  * $\nexists ts'$ where $\mathcal{M}, ts' \models \phi$ and $ts < ts' < te$,
  * $\nexists te'$ where $\mathcal{M}, te' \models \psi$ and $ts < te' < te$.

In our approach the 'before' relation holds only for intervals where the pair of instants or intervals at which the participating formulae are true or hold, are contiguous. For example, for the intervals $[1, 2]$, $[1, 3]$ and $[5, 6]$ only $[1, 3]$ is before $[5, 6]$.

- $\mathcal{M}, [ts, te] \models \phi$ meets ψ iff $\phi, \psi \in \Phi^- \cup \Phi^=$, $\exists a \in T$, $\mathcal{M}, [ts, a] \models \phi$ and $\mathcal{M}, [a, te] \models \psi$.
- $\mathcal{M}, [ts, te] \models \phi$ overlaps ψ iff $\phi, \psi \in \Phi^- \cup \Phi^=$, $\exists a, b \in T$, $ts < b < a < te$, $\mathcal{M}, [ts, a] \models \phi$ and $\mathcal{M}, [b, te] \models \psi$.
- $\mathcal{M}, [ts, te] \models \phi$ finishes ψ iff:
  - (interval - interval) for $\phi, \psi \in \Phi^- \cup \Phi^=$, $\exists a \in T$, $ts < a$, $\mathcal{M}, [a, te] \models \phi$ and $\mathcal{M}, [ts, te] \models \psi$,
  - (instant - interval) for $\phi \in \Phi^{\bullet}$ and $\psi \in \Phi^- \cup \Phi^=$, $\mathcal{M}, te \models \Phi$ and $\mathcal{M}, [ts, te] \models \psi$.
- $\mathcal{M}, [ts, te] \models \phi$ starts ψ iff:
  - (interval - interval) for $\phi, \psi \in \Phi^- \cup \Phi^=$, $\exists a \in T$, $a < te$, $\mathcal{M}, [ts, a] \models \phi$ and $\mathcal{M}, [ts, te] \models \psi$,
  - (instant - interval) for $\phi \in \Phi^{\bullet}$, $\psi \in \Phi^- \cup \Phi^=$, $\mathcal{M}, ts \models \phi$ and $\mathcal{M}, [ts, te] \models \psi$.
- $\mathcal{M}, [ts, te] \models \phi$ equals ψ iff for $\phi, \psi \in \Phi^- \cup \Phi^=$, $\mathcal{M}, [ts, te] \models \phi$ and $\mathcal{M}, [ts, te] \models \psi$.
- $\mathcal{M}, [ts, te] \models \phi$ contains ψ iff:
  - (interval - interval) for $\phi, \psi \in \Phi^- \cup \Phi^=$, $\mathcal{M}, [ts, te] \models \phi$, $\exists [a, b] \in I$, $ts < a < b < te$ and $\mathcal{M}, [a, b] \models \psi$,
  - (interval - instant) for $\phi \in \Phi^- \cup \Phi^=$, $\psi \in \Phi^{\bullet}$, $\mathcal{M}, [ts, te] \models \phi$, $\exists a \in T$, $ts < a < te$ and $\mathcal{M}, a \models \psi$.

3   Maritime Use Case Examples

Maritime situational awareness (MSA) is of major importance for environmental and safety reasons. Maritime monitoring systems contribute in MSA by allowing the detection of possibly dangerous, or unlawful activities while also monitoring normal activities. Typically, maritime monitoring systems—as in the case of this paper—use data from the Automatic Identification System (AIS) a system that allows the transmission of timestamped positional and vessel identity data from transceivers on vessels. Additionally, they may use contextual static information such as areas of interest or historical vessel information. Logic based approaches have already been used for Maritime Monitoring. Works such as [21,25] demonstrate that maritime activities can be expressed as patterns written in some form of an event definition language and be efficiently recognised. However, as

mentioned earlier the definitions of temporal phenomena are constrained by
the expressiveness of each language. In this section, we present definitions of
maritime situations of interest written in our temporal phenomena definition
language.

3.1 Stopped Vessel

A vessel is stopped when its speed is between a range e.g., $0-0.5$ knots. Consider
the definition for stopped vessels below:

$$
\begin{aligned}
&\textsf{event\_phenomenon } stop\_start(\textit{Vessel}): \\
&\quad ais(\textit{Vessel}, \textit{Speed}, \textit{Heading}, \textit{CoG}) \land \textit{Speed} \leq 0.5 . \\
&\textsf{event\_phenomenon } stop\_end(\textit{Vessel}): \\
&\quad ais(\textit{Vessel}, \textit{Speed}, \textit{Heading}, \textit{CoG}) \land \textit{Speed} > 0.5 . \\
&\textsf{state\_phenomenon } stopped(\textit{Vessel}): \\
&\quad stop\_start(\textit{Vessel}) \rightarrowtail stop\_end(\textit{Vessel}).
\end{aligned}
\tag{2}
$$

$ais(\textit{Vessel}, \textit{Speed}, ...)$ is an input event that contains the vessel id (Maritime
Mobile Service Identity), its speed (Knots), its heading (degrees) and its course
over ground (degrees). Heading is the direction of the vessel's bow while course
over ground is the actual path of a vessel with respect to the earth. $stop\_start$ and
$stop\_end$ are user defined events that happen when an AIS message is received for
a $\textit{Vessel}$ and its speed is either ≤ 0.5 or > 0.5 respectively. $stopped/1$ is a state
defined using the maximal range operator ($\rightarrowtail$) between the events $stop\_start$
and $stop\_end$, that holds true for the maximal intervals a vessel's speed is continuously ≤ 0.5 knots. Note that the $stop\_start$ and $stop\_end$ events are optional,
since their definition could be integrated in the definition of the $stopped$ state
directly.

3.2 Moored Vessel

A vessel is considered moored when it is stopped near a port. The knowledge
of the times and the locations vessels are moored is especially important in
historical track analyses, law enforcement, etc. Below we provide the definition
for moored vessels:

$$
\begin{aligned}
&\textsf{state\_phenomenon } in\_port(\textit{Vessel}, \textit{Port}): \\
&\quad enters\_port(\textit{Vessel}, \textit{Port}) \rightarrowtail leaves\_port(\textit{Vessel}, \textit{Port}). \\
&\textsf{state\_phenomenon } moored(\textit{Vessel}, \textit{Port}): \\
&\quad stopped(\textit{Vessel}) \sqcap in\_port(\textit{Vessel}, \textit{Port}).
\end{aligned}
\tag{3}
$$

We define first the $in\_port/2$ state using the maximal range operator ($\rightarrowtail$)
between the two input events $enters\_port/2$ and $leaves\_port/2$ denoting respectively that a $\textit{Vessel}$ enters or leaves a $\textit{Port}$. $moored/2$ is a state defined
using the interval operator of intersection ($\sqcap$) between the $stopped/2$ and
the $in\_port(\textit{Vessel}, \textit{Port})$ states. Therefore, according to the rule-set (3), the
state $moored(\textit{Vessel}, \textit{Port})$ holds for the maximal intervals at which a $\textit{Vessel}$ is
stopped inside a $\textit{Port}$ (recall the semantics of the intersection operator as defined
in Sect. 2.3).

3.3 Vessel Trips

In order to ensure abidance to regulations and safety, authorities must monitor vessel trips. A trip starts when a vessel stops being moored at a port, gets underway, and finally reaches its destination port. We define vessel trips as follows:

$$
\begin{aligned}
&\mathsf{dynamic\_phenomenon}\ trip(\textit{Vessel}, \textit{PortA}, \textit{PortB}):\\
&\quad end(moored(\textit{Vessel}, \textit{PortA}))\ \mathsf{before}\\
&\quad (underway(\textit{Vessel})\ \mathsf{before}\\
&\quad \mathsf{start}(moored(\textit{Vessel}, \textit{PortB}))).
\end{aligned} \tag{4}
$$

$trip(\textit{Vessel}, \textit{PortA}, \textit{PortB})$ is defined as a dynamic temporal phenomenon, while $underway$ is a user defined state that holds for the intervals a vessel's speed is greater than 2.7 knots. The definition of $underway$ is omitted as it is defined in a similar manner with the $stopped$ state. Therefore, the $trip(\textit{Vessel}, \textit{PortA}, \textit{PortB})$ dynamic temporal phenomenon holds for the intervals that start when a $\textit{Vessel}$ stops being moored at a $\textit{PortA}$, next the $\textit{Vessel}$ is underway, and finally end when the vessel starts being moored at a $\textit{PortB}$.

3.4 Fishing Trips

Monitoring of the fishing areas a fishing vessel has been through is important for sustainability and safety reasons. Similar to regular trips, a fishing trip can be described as a series of certain maritime activities that are arranged over a long period of time. Fishing vessels leave from a port, then they are underway, they start a fishing activity in a fishing area, and then they return to the same or another port. A definition of the fishing trip temporal phenomenon is the following:

$$
\begin{aligned}
&\mathsf{dynamic\_phenomenon}\ fishing\_trip(\textit{Vessel}, \textit{PortA}, \textit{AreaID}, \textit{PortB}):\\
&\quad end(moored(\textit{Vessel}, \textit{PortA})) \wedge type(\textit{Vessel}, \textit{Fishing})\ \mathsf{before}\\
&\quad (underway(\textit{Vessel})\ \mathsf{contains}\ in\_fishing\_area(\textit{Vessel}, \textit{AreaID}))\\
&\quad \mathsf{before}\ \mathsf{start}(moored(\textit{Vessel}, \textit{PortB})).
\end{aligned} \tag{5}
$$

Similar to the in_port state of rule-set (3), $in\_fishing\_area(\textit{Vessel}, \textit{AreaID})$ is a user defined state that holds for the intervals a $\textit{Vessel}$ is within a fishing area with id $\textit{AreaID}$. $fishing\_trip(\textit{Vessel}, \textit{PortA}, \textit{AreaID}, \textit{PortB})$ as defined in rule (5), holds for the intervals that start when a fishing $\textit{Vessel}$ stops being moored at a $\textit{PortA}$, next the $\textit{Vessel}$ gets underway, during that period it passes through a fishing area with id $\textit{AreaID}$, and finally end when the fishing $\textit{Vessel}$ starts being moored at a $\textit{PortB}$.

4 Executable Semantics

Complex Event Processing refers to the processing of one or multiple streams of atomic low level entities by continuously applying temporal queries and producing a stream of time associated complex event detections. In our case, the input stream comprises time associated temporal phenomena and the detection stream comprises the detections of the user defined temporal phenomena. Below, we provide the executable semantics that describe the recognition mechanics for stream processing.

4.1 Stream Processing

A stream is an arbitrary long sequence of time associated low level entities i.e., atomic predicates of $\Phi^{\cdot}, \Phi^{-}$ and $\Phi^{=}$. A stream σ that contains time associated atomic formulae 'occurring' from the start of time t_0 up to a time t_σ can be expressed by the model $\mathcal{M}_\sigma = \langle T_\sigma, I_\sigma, <, V^{\cdot}, V^{-}, V^{=} \rangle$, where $T_\sigma = [t_0, t_\sigma] \subset T$ and $I_\sigma = \{[ts, te] : ts < te \text{ and } ts, te \in T_\sigma\} \cup \{[ts, \infty) : ts \in T_\sigma\}$ and as in Sect. 2.3 $V^{\cdot} : \Phi^{\cdot}_o \to 2^{T_\sigma}$, $V^{-} : \Phi^{-}_o \to 2^{I_\sigma}$, $V^{=} : \Phi^{=}_o \to 2^{I_\sigma}$ are valuations. Note that in the case of streams, a valuation of an atomic formula provides the ordered set of instants or intervals that the atomic formula is associated with. Sets of instants are ordered via the less than relation, while interval sets are totally ordered, in other words the ordering is applied first on the starts of intervals then the ends. This ordering allows, as discussed later, for efficient computations of the instants or the intervals at which formulae hold.

Similar to other approaches [5, 19], for efficiency reasons, we choose to use a sliding window approach, whereby recognition of user-defined temporal phenomena happens with temporal queries on a dynamically updated working memory WM that is specified by a temporal window ω. A temporal window ω is a finite sub-sequence of a stream σ, that contains low level entities with associated temporal information that falls within a time period $\omega = (t_i, t_j], t_i < t_j$ with $t_i, t_j \in T$. We denote the number of time instants included in a temporal window ω, i.e., its size, as $|\omega| = t_j - t_i$. In what follows, we present the methodology for computing the evaluation order of phenomena and the sliding window mechanics of our approach.

Evaluation Order of Temporal Phenomena. The evaluation of the temporal phenomena must be performed in an order that does not allow unmet dependencies during processing. Recall that cyclic dependencies are forbidden (see Sect. 2.2), therefore, the dependencies between a set of temporal phenomena can be represented by a directed acyclic graph $G_d = \{E, D\}$ where E is the set of input and user defined phenomena, and $D \subseteq E \times E$ is the set of dependencies. Consequently, the processing order of a set of temporal phenomena relies on finding a valid evaluation order, that is a numbering $n : E \to \mathbb{N}$ of the phenomena so that $n(A) < n(B) \Rightarrow (A, B) \notin D$, meaning that A will be evaluated before B, and that A does not depend on B. A numbering that satisfies these constraints can be acquired by applying topological sort on G_d. Phenomena in level 0—these are the input phenomena—of the topological order, have no dependencies, while phenomena in higher levels have at least one direct dependency to phenomena of the previous level, or more to phenomena of lower levels. Figure 1 illustrates the topologically sorted dependency graph of the phenomena presented in Sect. 3.

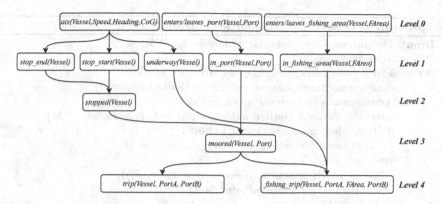

Fig. 1. Topologically sorted dependency graph of the phenomena presented in Sect. 3.

Sliding Window Mechanics. In order to deal efficiently with the input load, we adopt a sliding temporal window approach. With this approach, user defined temporal phenomena are detected using information inside a working memory set WM that contains: time associated phenomena of the input stream that take place within the current temporal window ω, time associated phenomena of previous windows that have been classified as non-redundant and finally the detections of the current query.

Recognition occurs at equally distanced times $t_q \in T$, where $t_{q+1} - t_q = s$ is the sliding step. At each t_q, the instants and the intervals at which temporal phenomena are true or hold are computed according to the evaluation order specified by the topological sorting of the G_d graph and the current working memory WM. Algorithm 1 describes the recognition process of a set of user defined phenomena 'Definitions', at a query time t_q with working memory WM, window size $|\omega|$ and sliding step set to s. The instants and intervals at which user defined temporal phenomena are true or hold are computed for each level using 'process/2'—we will describe processing of phenomena definitions in Sect. 4.2— and are asserted in the current working memory; this ensures that they will be computed only once per recognition query (lines 2–10). During the processing of the user defined temporal phenomena some instants or intervals in the WM are classified as non-redundant. We will discuss the redundancy handling mechanism shortly. When all the temporal phenomena levels have been processed, the WM is updated (lines 11–12). During this step, all redundant information that falls outside the next window, i.e., within $[t_0, t_q - \omega + s]$, will be removed from the working memory WM and the processing of the next query at $t_q + s$ will be able to commence.

A time associated phenomenon included in WM at t_q is redundant if it holds (a) for an instant or an interval that is not included or overlaps the next window $(t_q + s - \omega, t_q + s]$ and (b) does not participate in incomplete or complete evaluations of formulae that hold for intervals that overlap the next window. Consider for example the intervals of Fig. 2. During the window $\omega = (t_q - |\omega|, t_q]$,

---

Algorithm 1: Querying process for working memory WM.

    Input: Definitions; DependencyGraphLevels; t_q; WM; $|\omega|$; s

1 allNonRedundant=[];

2 **for** level **in** [1,DependencyGraphLevels] **do**

3   currentPhenomena = phenomenaOfLevel(Definitions, level);

4   **for** phenomenon **in** currentPhenomena **do**

5   intervals, instants, nonRedundant = process(phenomenon, WM);

6   **if** type(phenomenon=='event') **then**

7   WM.assert(detections(phenomenon, instants));

8   **else**

9   WM.assert(detections(phenomenon, intervals));

10   allNonRedundant.add(nonRedundant)

11 **for** element **in** WM.period(t_0, $t_q - \omega + s$) **do**

12   **if** element **not in** allNonRedundant **then** WM.remove(element);

---

the states $moored(v, a)$, $moored(v, b)$ hold for the intervals $[t_0, t_1]$ and $[t_6, t_7]$ respectively, the $underway(v)$ state holds for the intervals $\{[t_2, t_5], [t_8, \infty)\}$, the input state $in\_fishing\_area$ holds for the interval $[t_3, t_4]$ and finally the dynamic temporal phenomenon $fishing\_trip(v, a, f, b)$ holds for the interval $[t_1, t_6]$. As the window advances, all the intervals that are redundant (dashed underlined) can be discarded since they can no longer contribute in a future query and fall outside the window. However, the interval $[t_6, t_7]$ where $moored(v, b)$ holds must be retained, since at window ω it participates in the incomplete evaluations of the dynamic temporal phenomena $fishing\_trip(v, a, f, b)$ and $fishing\_trip(v, b, f, b)$. In other words, it may participate in a detection of $fishing\_trip(v, a, f, b)$ or $fishing\_trip(v, b, f, b)$ in a future query.

Incomplete evaluations can only occur for dynamic temporal phenomena as per the fact that their detection requires information that sometimes is not yet available. However, this is not the case for evaluations of events and states; since at any given query time and a working memory WM the instants or intervals at which they are true or hold can always be determined. Note though that intervals may be updated if new information allows it. For example, a formula $\phi \rightarrowtail \psi$ can be true at an interval $[ts, \infty)$ at query time t_q while at a query time $t'_q > t_q$ the interval may get updated to $[ts, te]$ if there is a satisfaction of $\psi \wedge \neg\phi$ at $te > t_q$.

The feasibility of an incomplete evaluation of a user defined dynamic temporal phenomenon is determined by propagating the temporal constraints imposed by its definition and by also taking into account the information of the current WM. If the evaluation status of a formula $\phi \in \Phi^=$ at query t_q is unknown then all the participating time associated phenomena should be retained for the re-evaluation of ϕ in future queries. Consequently, at each query time, in order to label WM elements as redundant or not, apart from evaluations of temporal phenomena that can be determined to be *true* or *false*, incomplete evaluations whose validity status is *unknown* must also be computed.

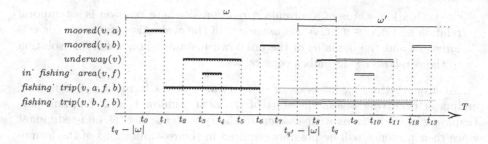

Fig. 2. Example of redundant (dashed underlined) and non redundant intervals, after the transition from window ω to ω'. Horizontal black bold and hollow lines correspond to evaluations of phenomena with all the required information, while grey lines correspond to evaluations with incomplete information. Bold black lines denote intervals that are computed during ω, while hollow black lines denote intervals that are computed during ω'.

In order to present the mechanism that classifies redundancy we introduce the concept of incomplete intervals. An incomplete interval $i_{inc} = [t, t_\circ]$ is a pair of a known time instant and an unknown value[2] $t_\circ$ with a known domain $D_{t_\circ} \subset T$. Incomplete intervals are produced when the evaluation status of a $\phi \in \Phi^=$ formula is *unknown*, while the domains of the unknown instant values are created by propagating the formula constraints. Given a working memory WM the validity status of a formula of $\Phi^=$ is *unknown* iff one of the following cases is true:

- the evaluation status of a formula ϕ before ψ is *unknown* iff for the last ending interval(s) $\{[ts_1, t], ..., [ts_k, t]\}$ where ϕ holds ($\phi \in \Phi^- \cup \Phi^=$) or the last instant t where ϕ is true ($\phi \in \Phi^\bullet$), there not exists an instant t' ($\psi \in \Phi^\bullet$) or an interval $[t', te']$ ($\psi \in \Phi^- \cup \Phi^=$) with $t' > t$ where ψ is true or holds respectively, in which case the associated incomplete intervals are $[ts_i, t_\circ]$, $i \in [1, k]$ when $\phi \in \Phi^- \cup \Phi^=$ or $[t, t_\circ]$ when $\phi \in \Phi^\bullet$ with $D_{t_\circ} = [t + 2, \infty)$,
- the evaluation status of a formula ϕ contains ψ is *unknown* iff ϕ holds for an interval $[ts, \infty)$ and there not exists an instant t, $t > ts$ ($\psi \in \Phi^\bullet$) or an interval $[ts', te']$ with $ts < ts'$ ($\psi \in \Phi^- \cup \Phi^=$) where ψ is true or holds respectively, in which case the associated incomplete interval is $[ts, t_\circ]$ with $D_{t_\circ} = (t_q, \infty)$.
- the evaluation status of a formula ϕ *relation* ψ where *relation* $\in$ {equals, starts} is *unknown* iff ϕ and ψ hold for an interval $[ts, \infty)$ in which case the associated incomplete interval is $[ts, t_\circ]$ with $D_{t_\circ} = (t_q, \infty)$.
- the evaluation status of a formula ϕ *relation* ψ where *relation* $\in$ {before, meets, overlaps, finishes}, $\phi \in \Phi^- \cup \Phi^=$ and $\psi \in \Phi$ is *unknown* iff ϕ holds for an interval $[ts, \infty)$, in which case the associated incomplete interval is $[ts, t_\circ]$ with $D_{t_\circ} = [t_q + 2, \infty)$.

---

[2] We extend the set of all allowed values with $t_\circ$ denoting a time instant that is currently not known but the domain of its possible values is known.

– the evaluation status of a formula ϕ *relation* ψ where *relation* is a temporal relation and $\phi, \psi \in \Phi^- \cup \Phi^=$, is *unknown*, iff the evaluation status of ϕ or ψ is *unknown* and the domains of the unknown instants allow a feasible solution to the ϕ *relation* ψ formula's constraints.

At a query time t_q, intervals or instants at which a formula $\phi \in \Phi$ is true, ending or occurring before the start of the next window $t_q - \omega + s$, and participating in evaluations with *unknown* validity are classified as non-redundant since their presence will be possibly required in the re-evaluations of the formulae with *unknown* validity in future recognition queries. Moreover, intervals or instants that hold or occur before the start of the next window $t_q - \omega + s$ are also retained if they participate in complete evaluations of formulae that hold for intervals that overlap $t_q - \omega + s$, therefore ensuring that recognised entities that hold on intervals that overlap the next window will also be available for processing in the next recognition query.

4.2 Processing of Temporal Phenomena

The set of time instants or intervals at which input phenomena are true or hold is provided by the input. In the case of user defined phenomena the corresponding sets have to be computed by processing their definitions. From a logical perspective, the task here is the evaluation of fixed formulae of Φ on a finite structure; since our language does not use any second or higher order logic elements, this problem is decidable and can be accomplished using polynomial time algorithms in the length of the structure [17]. In this section we present the methodology for processing the formulae that comprise temporal phenomena definitions.

Events. Events are defined by means of $\phi \in \Phi^\bullet$ formulae. The methodology for computing the set of time instants at which a formula $\phi \in \Phi^\bullet$ is true is described below.

– **Conjunction (Disjunction)** If ϕ and ψ are $\Phi^\bullet$ formulae and are true respectively at the time instants sets J and $K \subseteq \omega$ then their conjunction (disjunction) is described by the set $C = J \cap K$ $(C = J \cup K)$.
– **Negation** If ϕ is a formula of $\Phi^\bullet$ and J is the set of instants where ϕ is true in ω, then $\neg \phi$ is true in the set of instants $C = \omega \setminus J$.
– **Start (end)** Start (end) accept a formula ϕ of Φ^- and return the starting (ending) points of the intervals the formula ϕ holds.

Recall that sets of instants at which formulae are true are ordered, consequently the computation of the above operations can be accomplished in linear time relative to the evaluations of ϕ and ψ.

States. User-defined states are expressed via the formulae of Φ^-. By definition the intervals at which a state may hold are disjoint and maximal; this is because formulae of Φ^- utilise the temporal operators $\rightarrowtail, \sqcup, \sqcap$ and\which, as defined in

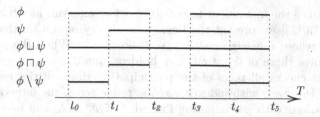

Fig. 3. Example of the resulting intervals for the temporal operators $\sqcup, \sqcap$ and\between fomulae ϕ and ψ of Φ^-.

Sect. 2.3, will always hold on disjoint maximal intervals. Below we describe the computation of these intervals for each operator.

- **Maximal range.** Given a working memory WM a formula $\phi \rightarrowtail \psi$ for $\phi, \psi \in \Phi$ holds for the intervals that start at the instant t_s where ϕ is true and continue to hold indefinitely unless at an instant $t_e > t_s$, $\psi \wedge \neg \phi$ is true. Computation of the intervals where $\phi \rightarrowtail \psi$ can be efficiently achieved by iterating over the instants where ϕ, ψ are true. In simple words, this process can be described as follows. The algorithm iterates over the instants at which formulae ϕ and $\psi \wedge \neg \phi$ are true. The start of an interval is created at the first occurrence of an instant t_s at which ϕ is true. The interval remains open at right to infinity, unless at an instant $t_e > t_s$ the formula $\phi \wedge \neg \psi$ is true, in which case an interval $[t_s, t_e]$ is created. In [23] we present in detail the single-scan algorithm that computes the intervals at which a formula $\phi \rightarrowtail \psi$ for $\phi, \psi \in \Phi^{\cdot}$ holds.
- **Temporal union, intersection and complement.** In plain language, for ϕ and ψ formulae of Φ^- the temporal operators are defined as follows. The temporal union $\phi \sqcup \psi$, holds for the maximal intervals where at least one of ϕ and ψ holds. The temporal intersection of $\phi \sqcap \psi$ formulae holds for the maximal intervals where both formulae hold together. Finally, the temporal complement $\phi \setminus \psi$ holds for the maximal sub-intervals of the intervals where ϕ holds and ψ does not hold. Figure 3 illustrates an example of these operations. The computation of the intervals resulting from temporal union, intersection and complement can be computed efficiently using single-scan, sorting-based or index-based algorithms [13]. For our setting and our implementation which we introduce below, we use single-scan algorithms, however since these algorithms appear widely in related bibliography [9,13] we omit their presentation here.

Dynamic Temporal Phenomena. Dynamic temporal phenomena are defined using formulae of $\Phi^=$ and may hold in non-disjoint intervals. Given a working memory WM, the intervals at which dynamic temporal phenomena hold can be computed using the declarative semantics. When the formulae participating in a temporal relation are either of $\Phi^{\cdot}$ or Φ^- efficient linear complexity algorithms are possible since the instants or the disjoint set of intervals at which they hold are ordered. In [23] we present the linear complexity algorithm that computes the intervals where ϕ before ψ with $\phi, \psi \in \Phi^-$ holds. When the participating formulae involve those of $\Phi^=$, that may hold on non-disjoint intervals, a naive approach that checks all pairs of the participating time entities requires polynomial time. However, with indexes such as range trees, the intervals at which temporal relations with participating formulae of $\Phi^=$ hold can be computed in linearithmic time [18].

5 Implementation

In the previous Sections, we formally presented the syntax, the semantics and the executable semantics of our proposed language. Moreover we presented some phenomena definitions inspired from the maritime domain demonstrating the usage and the expressiveness of our language. In this section we introduce and evaluate Phenesthe [22], our Complex Event Processing system that utilises the language and the executable semantics presented in this paper.

5.1 Architecture

The Complex Event Processing system Phenesthe is implemented in Prolog and follows the architecture illustrated in Fig. 4.

Input Information. The input is of two kinds; static and dynamic information. Static input refers to a set of phenomena definitions written in the language of this paper along with a declaration of the expected input phenomena. Static information may also include atemporal information such as predicates storing information regarding the elements of a specific use-case. For example in the maritime use-case an atemporal predicate can be used for storing the ship types of vessels. Dynamic input information refers to the input stream which contains input phenomena associated with some temporal information. The phenomena definitions and declarations pass through a transformation step, during which they are transformed into a standard Prolog language representation. Additionally, the dependencies between phenomena are computed and a valid evaluation order is produced as outlined in Sect. 4.1 (see 'Dependency Graph Computation' in Fig. 4).

Temporal Querying. When the transformation and the computation of the evaluation order of the user defined phenomena is complete, processing of the input stream is able to commence. As already described in Sect. 4, processing of the input stream happens in the form of temporal queries at equally distanced times specified by the value of step. During a temporal query the instants and the intervals at which user defined phenomena are true or hold are computed and printed in the output stream. Additionally, during each temporal query redundant information is discarded and non-redundant information is retained until classified otherwise via the redundancy handling mechanism.

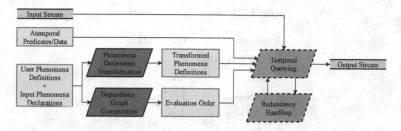

Fig. 4. Architecture of Phenesthe. Grey rectangles correspond to static information, green partial rectangles denote streams of phenomena, parallelograms correspond to offline (bold perimeter) and online (dashed perimeter) operations. (Color figure online)

Dependency-Aware Parallelisation. User defined phenomena can be processed in a sequential manner by following the evaluation order produced by the topological sort of the directed acyclic graph they form. However, if possible they can also be executed in parallel. In Phenesthe we implement dependency-aware parallelisation whereby phenomena definitions that have no pending dependencies are processed in parallel via a master-worker paradigm. Here, the master checks for phenomena definitions that do not have any unmet dependencies and inserts them in the processing queue. Workers remove phenomena definitions from the processing queue, process them, and notify the master as soon as they complete. This process goes on until all the user defined phenomena are processed. For example, in the dependency graph of Fig. 1 the master will first insert in the processing queue all the phenomena of Level 1, since those don't have any unmet dependencies. Next, as soon as both *stop_start* and *stop_end* are processed the master will add *stopped* in the processing queue and a worker, if available, will process it. It has to be noted, that the performance of the dependency-aware parallelisation cannot be better than the time required to execute the critical path, that is the longest chain of phenomena with sequential dependencies. For example in the graph of Fig. 1 one critical path is *ais*/4, *stop_end*/1, *stopped*/1, *moored*/2 and *fishing_trip*/4. Consequently, phenomena definitions sets with dependency graphs that have few operations that can be executed in parallel will have little to no gain from the dependency-aware parallelization.

5.2. Empirical Evaluation

We evaluate the efficiency of Phenesthe in the maritime use-case by performing Complex Event Processing on real world maritime data. Below we present the experimental setup and the results of our experimental evaluation.

Experimental Setup. For our experimental evaluation we used the maritime phenomena definitions presented in Sect. 3. Table 2 summarises all the input and output phenomena of our use-case. Note that the complete phenomena definition

Table 1. Dataset characteristics.

Attribute	Description
Period (months)	6
Vessels	5K
AIS messages	16M
Spatial events	89K
Fishing areas	263
Ports	222

Table 2. Description of the maritime phenomena.

	Phenomenon	Description
Input	$ais(V, S, H, CoG)$	AIS transmitted values of speed S, heading H, and course over ground CoG for a vessel V
	$enters\_\{port, fishing\_area\}(V, A)$	A vessel V enters a port/fishing area A
	$leaves\_\{port, fishing\_area\}(V, A)$	A vessel V leaves a port/fishing area A
Output	$in\_\{port, fishing\_area\}(V, A)$	A vessel V is within a port/fishing area A
	$stop\_\{start, end\}(V)$	A vessel V starts or ends a stop.
	$stopped(V)$	A vessel V has speed less than 0.5 knots.
	$underway(V)$	A vessel V is underway ($Speed > 2.7$ knots).
	$moored(V, P)$	A vessel V is moored at a port P
	$trip(V, D, A)$	A vessel V traveled from port D to port A
	$fishing\_trip(V, D, FA, A)$	A vessel V starts a fishing trip from port D, passes over fishing area FA and reaches port A

set is available in [22]. Regarding the input stream, we used a publicly available dataset containing AIS vessel data, transmitted over a period of 6 months, from October 1st, 2015 to March 31st, 2016, in the area of Brest, France [24]. Moreover, we included spatial events that occur when vessels enter or leave specific areas. These spatial events were produced by the Spatial Prepossessing module described in [21]. Table 1 presents the characteristics of the dataset we used. The experiments were conducted on a machine running macOS 10.15.7 with an Intel(R) CORE(TM) i5-7360U CPU and 8 GB 2133 MHz RAM under SWI-Prolog 8.2.4. The number of threads when running the multithreaded version of Phenesthe was set to 4.

Experimental Evaluation. The results of our experimental evaluation are presented in Fig. 5. Recall that processing of phenomena happens at equally distanced query times. For the presented experiments, the sliding step has been set to 2 h, while the window size $|\omega|$ varies from 2 to 32 h. For each window size we report the average number of input phenomena, the average number of instants and intervals at which user defined phenomena are true or hold and finally the average processing time. Moreover, in order to assess the efficiency

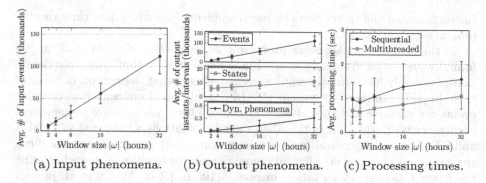

(a) Input phenomena.   (b) Output phenomena.   (c) Processing times.

Fig. 5. Results of our evaluation. The experiments were conducted for $|\omega| = \{2, 4, 8, 16, 32\}$ while the window sliding step was set to 2 h. Plots (a), (b) and (c) show the average number of input events (thousands), the average number (thousands) of instants and intervals detected for user defined phenomena, and the average processing time (sec) per temporal query, respectively.

of the dependency-aware parallelisation we perform Complex Event Processing using the sequential and the multithreaded version of Phenesthe. Figure 5(a) shows that the average number of input events ranges from 7.5 K when $|\omega| = 2$ h to 120 K input events when $|\omega| = 32$ h. Figure 5(b) shows the average number of instants or intervals at which user defined phenomena are true or hold per temporal query. In Figure 5(c) it can be seen that Phenesthe completes a temporal query on a 2 h window in approximately 0.9 (sequential) and 0.6 (multithreaded) seconds, while for a 32 h window it takes approximately 1.6 (sequential) and 1.1 (multithreaded) seconds to perform a temporal query. Expectedly, results from Fig. 5(c) show that dependency-aware parallelisation improves significantly the performance of Phenesthe. All in all, in both sequential and multithreaded version, Phenesthe is capable of providing near-instantaneous output, even when the window size is set to 32 h, thus meeting the requirements of real-time maritime monitoring applications.

6 Related Work

There are numerous languages for describing temporal phenomena with different levels of expressiveness. For example, Balbiani et al. in [6] present a two-sorted point-interval temporal logic framework where both instants and intervals can be used in formulae. However, in P. Balbiani's approach, operations such as the maximal range, union, intersection and complement are not available, therefore phenomena that utilise these operators (e.g., the definition of *moored/2* in Sect. 3) are not directly, if at all, expressible in their language. Moreover, neither executable semantics nor applications of their temporal logic are discussed. Ahmed et al. in [1] use point-based metric temporal logic that has limited interval expressivity to specify stream queries for intrusion detection. Kowalski in [16] presents the Event Calculus, a logic based formalism that deals with events (instantaneous) and their effects on inertive fluents (durative), i.e., time-varying properties.

In the field of complex event processing or recognition, Cugola et al. in [12] formally present an event specification language, TESLA, that allows the definition of possibly hierarchical complex event patterns that happen on instants of time. In [4] D. Anicic et al. present ETALIS, a rule based system where complex events are durative and their definition among others may involve sequences of events, negation and some of the Allen's algebra relations. Compared to TESLA and ETALIS our language allows the description of both instantaneous and durative temporal phenomena. Efficient complex event recognition approaches using the Event Calculus among others involve [5,10]. In [5] A. Artikis et al. present the Event Calculus for Run-Time reasoning. Their approach allows the definition and processing of possibly hierarchical events and fluents that happen on instants or hold on intervals. Compared to the Event Calculi approaches of [5,10] our language allows the expression of temporal relations between durative and instantaneous phenomena that may hold, additionally, in non-disjoint intervals.

7 Summary and Future Directions

We formally presented a language for the representation of temporal phenomena, with declarative and operational semantics. Our language allows the representation of possibly hierarchical instantaneous and durative temporal phenomena. Definitions of temporal phenomena may involve the standard logical connectives, the temporal operators of maximal range, union, intersection and complement and the seven basic temporal relations of Allen's interval algebra. We introduced the Phenesthe Complex Event Processing system and demonstrated that it can efficiently process thousands of phenomena in near instantaneous time.

Our future directions involve a theoretical study of the expressiveness of our language and a comparison with existing ones. Moreover, we plan to further improve the efficiency of Phenesthe and compare it with state of the art Complex Event Processing systems. Finally, we aim to integrate temporal stream processing with process mining techniques for the discovery of dynamic temporal phenomena.

References

1. Ahmed, A., Lisitsa, A., Dixon, C.: A misuse-based network intrusion detection system using temporal logic and stream processing. In: 2011 5th International Conference on Network and System Security, pp. 1–8 (2011). https://doi.org/10.1109/ICNSS.2011.6059953
2. Allen, J.F.: Maintaining knowledge about temporal intervals. Commun. ACM 26(11), 832–843 (1983). https://doi.org/10.1145/182.358434
3. Anicic, D., Fodor, P., Rudolph, S., Stühmer, R., Stojanovic, N., Studer, R.: A rule-based language for complex event processing and reasoning. In: Hitzler, P., Lukasiewicz, T. (eds.) RR 2010. LNCS, vol. 6333, pp. 42–57. Springer, Heidelberg (2010). https://doi.org/10.1007/978-3-642-15918-3_5

4. Anicic, D., Rudolph, S., Fodor, P., Stojanovic, N.: Stream reasoning and complex event processing in ETALIS. Semant. Web **3**(4), 397–407 (2012). https://doi.org/10.3233/SW-2011-0053
5. Artikis, A., Sergot, M., Paliouras, G.: An event calculus for event recognition. IEEE Trans. Knowl. Data Eng. **27**(4), 895–908 (2015). https://doi.org/10.1109/TKDE.2014.2356476
6. Balbiani, P., Goranko, V., Sciavicco, G.: Two-sorted point-interval temporal logics. Electron. Notes Theor. Comput. Sci. **278**, 31–45 (2011). https://doi.org/10.1016/j.entcs.2011.10.004
7. Beck, H., Dao-Tran, M., Eiter, T.: LARS: a logic-based framework for analytic reasoning over streams. Artif. Intell. **261**, 16–70 (2018). https://doi.org/10.1016/j.artint.2018.04.003
8. Bellini, P., Mattolini, R., Nesi, P.: Temporal logics for real-time system specification. ACM Comput. Surv. **32**(1), 12–42 (2000). https://doi.org/10.1145/349194.349197
9. Bohlen, M.H., Busatto, R., Jensen, C.S.: Point-versus interval-based temporal data models. In: Proceedings 14th International Conference on Data Engineering, pp. 192–200 (1998). https://doi.org/10.1109/ICDE.1998.655777
10. Chittaro, L., Montanari, A.: Efficient temporal reasoning in the cached event calculus. Comput. Intell. **12**(3), 359–382 (1996). https://doi.org/10.1111/j.1467-8640.1996.tb00267.x
11. Chomicki, J.: Temporal query languages: a survey. In: Gabbay, D.M., Ohlbach, H.J. (eds.) ICTL 1994. LNCS, vol. 827, pp. 506–534. Springer, Heidelberg (1994). https://doi.org/10.1007/BFb0014006
12. Cugola, G., Margara, A.: TESLA: a formally defined event specification language. In: DEBS '10, p. 50. ACM Press (2010). https://doi.org/10.1145/1827418.1827427
13. Dohr, A., Engels, C., Behrend, A.: Algebraic operators for processing sets of temporal intervals in relational databases. In: TIME (2018)
14. Chen, H.-Y., Tsai, J.J.P., Bi, Y.: An event-based real-time logic to specify the behavior and timing properties of real-time systems. In: Proceedings of the Third International Conference on Tools for Artificial Intelligence - TAI 91, pp. 210–219 (1991). https://doi.org/10.1109/TAI.1991.167097
15. Khan, A., Bozzato, L., Serafini, L., Lazzerini, B.: Visual reasoning on complex events in soccer videos using answer set programming. In: Calvanese, D., Iocchi, L. (eds.) GCAI 2019. Proceedings of the 5th Global Conference on Artificial Intelligence. EPiC Series in Computing, vol. 65, pp. 42–53 (2019). https://doi.org/10.29007/pjd4
16. Kowalski, R., Sergot, M.: A logic-based calculus of events. N. Gener. Comput. **4**(1), 67–95 (1986). https://doi.org/10.1007/BF03037383
17. Libkin, L.: Elements of Finite Model Theory. Springer, Heidelberg (2004). https://doi.org/10.1007/978-3-662-07003-1
18. Mao, C., Eran, A., Luo, Y.: Efficient genomic interval queries using augmented range trees. Sci. Rep. **9**(1), 5059 (2019). https://doi.org/10.1038/s41598-019-41451-3
19. Mileo, A., Abdelrahman, A., Policarpio, S., Hauswirth, M.: StreamRule: a non-monotonic stream reasoning system for the semantic web. In: Faber, W., Lembo, D. (eds.) RR 2013. LNCS, vol. 7994, pp. 247–252. Springer, Heidelberg (2013). https://doi.org/10.1007/978-3-642-39666-3_23
20. Mueller, E.T.: Chapter 5 - the commonsense law of inertia. In: Mueller, E.T. (ed.) Commonsense Reasoning (Second Edn.), pp. 77–89. Morgan Kaufmann, Boston (2015). https://doi.org/10.1016/B978-0-12-801416-5.00005-X

21. Pitsikalis, M., Artikis, A., Dreo, R., Ray, C., Camossi, E., Jousselme, A.L.: Composite event recognition for maritime monitoring. In: DEBS (2019), pp. 163–174. Association for Computing Machinery, New York, NY, USA (2019). https://doi.org/10.1145/3328905.3329762
22. Pitsikalis, M., Lisitsa, A., Luo, S.: Phenesthe (2021). https://github.com/manospits/Phenesthe
23. Pitsikalis, M., Lisitsa, A., Luo, S.: Representation and processing of instantaneous and durative temporal phenomena (2021). https://arxiv.org/abs/2108.13365
24. Ray, C., Dréo, R., Camossi, E., Jousselme, A.L., Iphar, C.: Heterogeneous integrated dataset for maritime intelligence, surveillance, and reconnaissance. Data Brief **25**, 104141 (2019). https://doi.org/10.1016/j.dib.2019.104141
25. Roy, J.: Rule-based expert system for maritime anomaly detection. In: Carapezza, E.M. (ed.) Sensors, and Command, Control, Communications, and Intelligence (C3I) Technologies for Homeland Security and Homeland Defense IX, vol. 7666, pp. 597–608. International Society for Optics and Photonics, SPIE (2010). https://doi.org/10.1117/12.849131

Prefix-Based Tracing in Message-Passing Concurrency

Juan José González-Abril and Germán Vidal(✉) (iD)

MiST, VRAIN, Universitat Politècnica de València, Valencia, Spain
juagona6@vrain.upv.es, gvidal@dsic.upv.es

Abstract. The execution of concurrent applications typically involves some degree of nondeterminism, mostly due to the relative speeds of concurrent processes. An essential task in state-space exploration techniques for the verification of concurrent programs consists in finding points in an execution where alternative actions are possible. Here, the nondeterministic executions of a program can be represented by a tree-like structure. Given the *trace* of a concrete execution, one first identifies its branching points. Then, a new execution can be steered up to one of these branching points (using, e.g., a *partial* trace), so that an unexplored branch can be considered. From this point on, the execution proceeds nondeterministically, eventually producing a trace of the complete execution as a side-effect, and the process starts again. In this paper, we formalize this operation—partially driving the execution of a program and then producing a trace of the entire execution—, which we call *prefix-based tracing*. It combines ideas from both *record-and-replay* debugging and execution tracing. We introduce a semantics-based formalization of prefix-based tracing in the context of a message-passing concurrent language like Erlang. Furthermore, we also present an implementation of prefix-based tracing by means of a program instrumentation.

1 Introduction

Message-passing concurrency mainly follows the so-called *actor model*. At runtime, concurrent processes can only interact through message sending and receiving, i.e., there is no shared memory. In this work, we further assume that communication is asynchronous and that each process has a local mailbox (a queue), so that each sent message is eventually stored in the target process' mailbox. Moreover, we consider that processes can be dynamically spawned at runtime. In particular, we consider a subset of the programming language Erlang [3] for our developments. We note that, in practice, some Erlang built-in's involve shared-memory concurrency; nevertheless, we will not consider them in this work.

This work has been partially supported by grant PID2019-104735RB-C41 funded by MCIN/AEI/ 10.13039/501100011033, by the *Generalitat Valenciana* under grant Prometeo/2019/098 (DeepTrust), and by French ANR project DCore ANR-18-CE25-0007.

© Springer Nature Switzerland AG 2022
E. De Angelis and W. Vanhoof (Eds.): LOPSTR 2021, LNCS 13290, pp. 157–175, 2022.
https://doi.org/10.1007/978-3-030-98869-2_9

In the context of a message-passing concurrent language, computations are typically nondeterministic because of the relative speeds of processes. Consider, for instance, three processes, p1, p2, and p3. If p1 and p2 both send a message to process p3, the order in which these messages are received may not be fixed (e.g., when the actions of p1 and p2 are unrelated). In such a case, we say that the messages *race* (for p3). Exploring all alternatives for message races is a key ingredient of state-space exploration techniques like *stateless model checking* [5] or *reachability testing* [13].

In order to identify message races, state-space exploration methods usually consider some kind of execution *trace* (e.g., *interleavings* in [1] or *SYN-sequences* in [13]). An execution trace can be seen as an abstraction of an execution which still contains enough information to identify sources of nondeterminism and, in particular, message races. Every time a race is identified, alternative executions are considered so that all feasible executions are systematically explored.[1] A new execution of the program should be driven in such a way that it reproduces the previous execution up to the point where the race was found (as in *record-and-replay* debugging techniques), then chooses a different message and, from this point on, follows the usual nondeterministic semantics. Furthermore, a trace of the new execution should be eventually produced as a side-effect, so that the process can start again. In the following, we refer to this operation combining replay and tracing as *prefix-based tracing*.

In this work, we formalize the notion of prefix-based tracing in the context of a message-passing concurrent language like Erlang. Despite the fact that prefix-based tracing is ubiquitous in state-space exploration methods, we are not aware of any previous semantics-based formalization. In particular, a similar operation is called *prefix-based replay* in [8], though no formal definition is given. Other approaches, like [2] in the context of stateless model checking of Erlang programs, insert preemptive points in the code and, then, force the program to follow a particular scheduling up to a given point, then proceeding nondeterministically. However, as in [8], no semantics-based formalization is presented.

We note that prefix-based tracing can be seen as a generalization of traditional tracing and replay techniques. In particular, when no input trace is provided, the technique boils down to standard tracing. On the other hand, if the trace of a complete execution is provided, then it behaves as a replay debugger, so that the entire execution follows the given trace. Therefore, both tracing and replay can be seen as particular instances of the notion of prefix-based tracing.

Furthermore, besides the instrumented semantics, we also present an implementation of prefix-based tracing as a *program instrumentation*. In this case, given a program, we produce an instrumented version that is parametric w.r.t.

---

[1] In practice, *dynamic partial order reduction* techniques [4] are used to avoid exploring alternative executions which are *causally equivalent* to an already considered execution. Loosely speaking, two executions are causally equivalent if they produce the same outcome no matter if the sequence of actions is different. See, e.g., [11,12] for a formal definition of causal equivalence in the context of the language Erlang.

a particular (possibly partial) trace.[2] Then, given a particular trace, the program can be executed in the standard runtime environment so that it follows the actions in this trace and, then, proceeds nondeterministically, eventually producing a trace of the complete execution as a side-effect.

The paper is organized as follows. Section 2 presents a summary of the concurrent features of the considered language and its semantics. Then, Sect. 3 introduces the notions of trace and log, and formalizes prefix-based tracing using an instrumented semantics. In turn, Sect. 4 presents the details of an implementation of prefix-based tracing as a program instrumentation. Finally, Sect. 5 concludes and points out some directions for future work.

2   A Message-Passing Concurrent Language

In this section, we present the semantics of a message-passing concurrent language which can be seen as a subset of the Erlang language [3]. Following [10,15], we consider a layered semantics: an *expression semantics* and a *system semantics*. The expression semantics is essentially a typical *call-by-value* functional semantics defined on *local states*, which include an environment (i.e., a mapping from variables to values), an expression (to be reduced) and a stack; see [6] for more details. Since this is orthogonal to the topics of this paper, we will only introduce the following notation: $ls \xrightarrow{z} ls'$ denotes a reduction step, where ls, ls' are *local* states and z is a label with some information associated to the reduction step.

So-called *local* steps are denoted with the label ι and do not perform any side-effect at the system level. In contrast, the reduction of some—typically concurrent—actions may require a side-effect at the system level. Here, we consider the following *global* actions with side-effects:

– spawn(*mod, fun, args*): this expression dynamically creates a new process to evaluate function *fun* (defined in module *mod*) with arguments *args* (a list). E.g., spawn(*test, client,* $[S, c1]$) spawns a process that evaluates the expression *client*$(S, c1)$, where function *client* is defined in module *test*.[3] In the expression semantics, a call to spawn reduces to a fresh identifier, called pid (for *process identifier*), that uniquely identifies the new process. The step is labeled with spawn(κ, ls_0), where ls_0 is the initial local state for the new process and κ is a special variable (a sort of *future*) that will be eventually bound—in the system semantics—to the pid of the spawned process.
– $p \,!\, v$: it sends value v (the *message*) to process p (a pid). The expression reduces to v and eventually stores this value in the mailbox of process p as a side-effect. Sending a message is an asynchronous operation, so the process

---

[2] Hence, the program is only instrumented once.
[3] As in Erlang, functions and atoms (constants) begin with a lowercase letter while variables start with an uppercase symbol. The language has no user-defined data constructors, but allows the use of *lists*—following the usual Haskell-like notation— and *tuples* of the form $\{e_1, \ldots, e_n\}$, $n \geq 1$ (a polyadic function).

```
    main() ->
      S = spawn(bank, [0]),
      spawn(customer, [S]).

    bank(B) ->
      receive
        {deposit,A}
          -> bank(B+A);
        {C,{withdraw,A}} when A=<B
          -> C ! {ok,B-A},
             bank(B-A);
        _ -> C ! error, bank(B)
      end.

    customer(S) ->
      S ! {deposit,120},
      S ! {deposit,42},
      S ! {self(),{withdraw,100}},
      receive
        {ok,B} -> io:format("Current balance: ~p~n",[B]);
        error -> io:format("Insufficient balance")
      end.
```

Fig. 1. A simple Erlang program.

continues immediately with the evaluation of the next expression. In this case, the step in the expression semantics is labeled with $\mathsf{send}(p, v)$, which suffices for the system semantics to perform the corresponding side-effect.

- receive $p_1 \to e_1; \ldots; p_n \to e_n$ end: this expression looks for the *oldest* message in the process mailbox that matches some pattern p_i and, then, continues with the evaluation of e_i. As in Erlang, messages are matched sequentially against the patterns from top to bottom. When no message matches any pattern, execution is *blocked* until a matching message reaches the mailbox of the process. In this case, the step is labeled with $\mathsf{rec}(\kappa, cs)$, where cs are the branches of the receive statement (i.e., $p_1 \to e_1; \ldots; p_n \to e_n$ above). Here, κ will be bound to the expression e_i of the selected branch in the system semantics.
- self(): it reduces to the pid of the current process. Here, the step is labeled with $\mathsf{self}(\kappa)$, so that κ is bound to the pid of the current process in the system semantics.

Example 1. Consider the simple client-server program shown in Fig. 1. Here, we consider that the execution starts with the call main(). Function main then spawns two new processes that will evaluate bank(0) and customer(S), respectively, where S is the pid of the first process (the *server*).

Function **bank** implements a simple server that takes only two types of requests: {deposit, A}, to make a deposit of amount A, and {C, {withdraw, A}}, to make a withdraw of amount A, where C is the pid of the customer that makes the request. For simplicity, we assume that the bank has only one account (that of the customer), which is initialized to zero.

Given a request of the form {deposit, A}, the server simply performs a recursive call with the updated balance. If the request has the form {C, {withdraw, A}} and the amount A is less than or equal to the current balance,[4] it sends a message {ok, B − A} back to the customer and calls function **bank** with the updated balance. In any other case (denoted with the pattern "_"), the message **error** is sent back to the customer.

The implementation of the customer is very simple. It only performs three requests to the server. Note that the third one simulates a synchronous communication since it suspends the execution until a message from the server is received. Here, the built-in function **format** (module **io**) is used for printing messages.

In the remainder of this paper, a process is denoted as follows:

Definition 1 (process). *A process is denoted by a configuration of the form $\langle p, ls, q \rangle$, where p is the pid (process identifier) of the process, which is unique in a system, ls is the local state and q is the process mailbox (a list).*

A *system* is then defined as a pair $\Gamma; \Pi$, where Γ represents the network (sometimes called the *global mailbox* [10] or the *ether* [16]) and Π is a pool of processes. In the following, we often say "process p" to mean "process with pid p".

The network, Γ, is defined as a set of queues, one per each pair of (not necessarily different) processes. For instance, if we have two processes with pids p_1 and p_2, then Γ will include four queues associated to the pairs (p_1, p_1), (p_1, p_2), (p_2, p_1), and (p_2, p_2), representing all possible communications in the system. We use the notation $\Gamma[(p, p') \mapsto qs]$ either as a condition on Γ or as a modification of Γ, where p, p' are pids and qs is a (possibly empty) queue; for simplicity, we assume that queues are initially empty for each pair of processes. Queues are denoted by (finite) sequences, which are denoted as follows: $a_1, a_2, \ldots, a_n, n \geq 0$, where [] denotes an empty sequence. Here, $es + es'$ denotes the concatenation of sequences es and es'; by abuse, we use the same notation when a sequence has only a single element, i.e., $e_1 + (e_2, \ldots, e_n) = (e_1, \ldots, e_{n-1}) + e_n = e_1, \ldots, e_n$.

The second component, Π, is denoted as $\langle p_1, ls_1, q_1 \rangle \mid \cdots \mid \langle p_n, ls_n, q_n \rangle$, where "$\mid$" represents an associative and commutative operator. We often denote a *system* as $\Gamma; \langle p, ls, q \rangle \mid \Pi$ to point out that $\langle p, ls, q \rangle$ is an arbitrary process of the pool (thanks to the fact that "$\mid$" is associative and commutative).

The rules of the system semantics can be found in Fig. 2. They are similar to the those in [10], with only a few differences:

---

[4] Here, we consider the full syntax for receive statements, receive p_1 [when g_1] → $e_1; \ldots; p_n$ [when g_n] → e_n end, where each branch might have a *guard* g_i that must be evaluated to *true* in order to select this branch.

$$(Exit) \quad \frac{final(ls)}{\Gamma; \langle p, ls, q \rangle \mid \Pi \hookrightarrow \Gamma; \Pi}$$

$$(Local) \quad \frac{ls \xrightarrow{\iota} ls\hookleftarrow}{\Gamma; \langle p, ls, q \rangle \mid \Pi \hookrightarrow \Gamma; \langle p, ls', q \rangle \mid \Pi}$$

$$(Self) \quad \frac{ls \xrightarrow{self(\kappa)} ls'}{\Gamma; \langle p, ls, q \rangle \mid \Pi \hookrightarrow \Gamma; \langle p, ls'\{\kappa \mapsto p\}, q \rangle \mid \Pi}$$

$$(Spawn) \quad \frac{ls \xrightarrow{spawn(\kappa, ls_0)} ls' \text{ and } p' \text{ is a fresh pid}}{\Gamma; \langle p, ls, q \rangle \mid \Pi \hookrightarrow \Gamma; \langle p, ls'\{\kappa \mapsto p'\}, q \rangle \mid \langle p', ls_0, [] \rangle \mid \Pi}$$

$$(Send) \quad \frac{ls \xrightarrow{send(p', v)} ls'}{\Gamma[(p, p') \mapsto qs]; \langle p, ls, q \rangle \mid \Pi \hookrightarrow \Gamma[(p, p') \mapsto qs+v]; \langle p, ls', q \rangle \mid \Pi}$$

$$(Deliver) \quad \frac{}{\Gamma[(p', p) \mapsto v+qs]; \langle p, ls, q \rangle \mid \Pi \hookrightarrow \Gamma[(p', p) \mapsto qs]; \langle p, ls, q+v \rangle \mid \Pi}$$

$$(Receive) \quad \frac{ls \xrightarrow{rec(\kappa, cs)} ls' \text{ and } \mathsf{matchrec}(ls', \kappa, cs, q) = (ls'', q')}{\Gamma; \langle p, ls, q \rangle \mid \Pi \hookrightarrow \Gamma; \langle p, ls'', q' \rangle \mid \Pi}$$

Fig. 2. System semantics

- The local state is abstracted in our semantics, so that it can be instantiated to Core Erlang (as in [10]) but also to Erlang (as in [6]).
- The network, Γ, is defined as a set of queues, so that the order of the messages between any two given processes can be preserved (while Γ was defined as a set of triples (*sender, target, message*) in [10] and the order could not be preserved).

Moreover, in contrast to the system semantics in [12], we have process' mailboxes and a rule for message delivery, which are abstracted away in [12], where messages are directly consumed from Γ by receive statements. We note that this is not a limitation of [12] since this work focuses on *replay* (reversible) debugging and the trace of an actual execution is always provided. Therefore, their system semantics needs not implement the actual semantics of the language but may rely on the order of message reception given in the considered trace.

Let us briefly explain the transiton rules of our system semantics (Fig. 2):

- Rule *Exit* removes a process from the pool when the local state is *final*, i.e., when the expression to be reduced is a data term. If Γ contains some nonempty queue for (p, p'), where p' is the removed process, these messages will never be delivered (which is coherent with the behavior of Erlang).
- Rule *Local* just updates the local state of the selected process according to a transition of the expression semantics, while rule *Self* binds κ to the pid of the current process.

– Rule *Spawn* updates the local state, binds κ to the pid of the new process and adds a new initial process configuration with local state ls_0 as a side-effect.
– Rule *Send* updates the local state and, moreover, adds a new message to the corresponding queue of the network as a side-effect. For simplicity, we implicitly assume that Γ is extended with a new queue for the pair (p, p') whenever it does not already exist.
– Rule *Deliver* nondeterministically (since Γ might contain several nonempty queues with the same target process p) takes a message from the network and moves it to the corresponding process mailbox.
– Finally, rule *Receive* consumes a message from the process mailbox using the auxiliary function matchrec that takes the local state ls', the *future* κ, the branches of the receive expression cs, and the queue q. It then selects the oldest message in q that matches a branch in cs (if any), and returns a new local state ls'' (where κ is bound to the expression in the selected branch) and a queue q' (where the selected message has been removed).

Note that the tracing semantics has two main sources of nondeterminism: selecting a process to apply a reduction rule, and selecting the message to be delivered from the network (rule *Deliver*). Regarding the first point, one can for instance implement a *round-robin* algorithm that performs a fixed number of transitions (assuming the process is not blocked), then moves to another process, etc. As for the selection of a message to be delivered, there are several possible strategies. For instance, the CauDEr debugger [6,9,10] implements both a user-driven strategy (where the user selects any of the available messages) and a random selection.

Given systems α_0, α_n, we call $\alpha_0 \hookrightarrow^* \alpha_n$ a *derivation*; it is a shorthand for

$$\alpha_0 \hookrightarrow \dots \hookrightarrow \alpha_n, \ n \geq 0$$

One-step derivations are simply called *transitions*. We use $\delta, \delta', \delta_1, \dots$ to denote derivations and $t, t', t_1, \dots$ for transitions. A system α is said *initial* if it has the form $\mathcal{E}; \langle p, ls, [\,] \rangle$, where $\mathcal{E}$ denotes a network with an empty queue for (p, p), p is the pid of some initial process and ls is an initial local state containing the expression to be evaluated. In the following, we assume that all derivations start with an initial system.

3   Prefix-Based Tracing Semantics

In this section, we formalize the notion of prefix-based tracing for message-passing concurrent programs. In order to trace a running application, [11] introduces *message tags*, so that one can identify the sender and receiver of each message, even if there are several messages with the same value. To be precise, each message value v is now wrapped in a tuple of the form $\{\ell, v\}$, where ℓ is a message tag which is unique in the considered execution.

Following [7], we consider that an execution *trace* is a mapping from pids to sequences of *terms* denoting global actions (so we often refer to these terms as

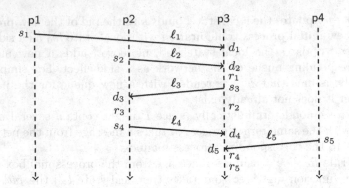

Fig. 3. Processes (pi, $i = 1, \ldots, 4$) are represented as vertical dashed arrows (time flows from top to bottom). Message sending and delivery is represented by solid arrows labeled with a message tag (ℓ_i), from a sending event (s_i) to a delivery event (d_i), $i = 1, \ldots, 5$. Receive events are denoted by r_i, $i = 1, \ldots, 5$. Note that all events associated to a message ℓ_i have the same subscript i.

actions). These terms can be seen as an abstraction of the corresponding actions, including only some minimal information (but still enough for our purposes):

Definition 2 (trace [7]). *A trace is a mapping from pids to sequences of terms of the form*

- spawn(p), *where p is the pid of the spawned process;*
- exit, *which denotes process termination;*
- send(ℓ, p), *where ℓ is the tag of the message sent (initially stored in the network) and p is the pid of the target process;*
- deliver(ℓ), *where ℓ is the tag of the delivered message (i.e., moved from the network to the mailbox of the target process);*
- rec(ℓ), *where ℓ is the tag of the message consumed from the local mailbox.*

We note that deliver *events are attributed to the target of the message. Given a trace $\mathcal{T}$, we let $\mathcal{T}(p)$ denote the sequence of actions associated to process p in $\mathcal{T}$. Also, $\mathcal{T}[p \mapsto as]$ denotes that $\mathcal{T}$ is an arbitrary trace such that $\mathcal{T}(p) = as$; we use this notation either as a condition on $\mathcal{T}$ or as a modification of $\mathcal{T}$.*

Let us consider the following trace:

$$
\begin{aligned}
[\, \mathsf{p1} &\mapsto \mathsf{spawn}(\mathsf{p3}), \mathsf{spawn}(\mathsf{p2}), \mathsf{spawn}(\mathsf{p4}), \mathsf{send}(\ell_1, \mathsf{p3}), \mathsf{exit}; \\
\mathsf{p2} &\mapsto \mathsf{send}(\ell_2, \mathsf{p3}), \mathsf{deliver}(\ell_3), \mathsf{rec}(\ell_3), \mathsf{send}(\ell_4, \mathsf{p3}), \mathsf{exit}; \\
\mathsf{p3} &\mapsto \mathsf{deliver}(\ell_1), \mathsf{deliver}(\ell_2), \mathsf{rec}(\ell_1), \mathsf{send}(\ell_3, \mathsf{p2}), \mathsf{rec}(\ell_2), \quad (1) \\
&\quad\; \mathsf{deliver}(\ell_4), \mathsf{deliver}(\ell_5), \mathsf{rec}(\ell_4), \mathsf{rec}(\ell_5), \mathsf{exit}; \\
\mathsf{p4} &\mapsto \mathsf{send}(\ell_5, \mathsf{p3}), \mathsf{exit} \qquad\qquad\qquad\qquad\qquad\quad\;\,]
\end{aligned}
$$

The associated execution can be informally represented using a simple message-passing diagram, as shown in Fig. 3, where we have skipped spawn actions for clarity.

Observe that we do not need to fix a particular (global) interleaving for all the actions in the trace. Only the order within each process matters; i.e., a trace represents a *partial order* on the possible interleavings (analogously to the SYN-sequences of [13]).

We also consider a simplification of the trace, called *log* in [11,12], where process exit and message delivery actions are skipped and message sending is represented just by $\mathsf{send}(\ell)$, without the pid of the target process.

Definition 3 (log). *A* log *is a mapping from pids to sequences of terms of the form* $\mathsf{spawn}(p)$, $\mathsf{send}(\ell)$, *and* $\mathsf{rec}(\ell)$, *where p is a pid and ℓ is a message tag. We use the same notation conventions as for traces. Moreover, given a trace $\mathcal{T}$, we let $log(\mathcal{T})$ be the log, $\mathcal{W}$, obtained from $\mathcal{T}$ by removing message delivery and exit actions, as well as by replacing every action of the form* $\mathsf{send}(\ell, p)$ *by* $\mathsf{send}(\ell)$.

For instance, the log obtained from the trace in Example 2 above is as follows:

$$
\begin{aligned}
[\,\mathsf{p1} &\mapsto \mathsf{spawn}(\mathsf{p3}), \mathsf{spawn}(\mathsf{p2}), \mathsf{spawn}(\mathsf{p4}), \mathsf{send}(\ell_1); \\
\mathsf{p2} &\mapsto \mathsf{send}(\ell_2), \mathsf{rec}(\ell_3), \mathsf{send}(\ell_4); \\
\mathsf{p3} &\mapsto \mathsf{rec}(\ell_1), \mathsf{send}(\ell_3), \mathsf{rec}(\ell_2), \mathsf{rec}(\ell_4), \mathsf{rec}(\ell_5); \\
\mathsf{p4} &\mapsto \mathsf{send}(\ell_5) \qquad\qquad\qquad\qquad\qquad\qquad]
\end{aligned}
\tag{2}
$$

Despite the simplification, the resulting log suffices to replay a given execution [12, Theorem 4.22] or a *causally equivalent* one.[5] Therefore, in the following, we distinguish *logs*, which are useful to replay a given execution, and *traces*, which can be used, e.g., to identify message races (as in [7]).

Consider, for instance, the execution of Fig. 3. Here, we might have a race for p3 between messages ℓ_1 and ℓ_2 (assuming both messages match the constraints of the receive statement r_1). If we swap the delivery of these messages, we can have a new execution which is not causally equivalent to the previous one and, thus, may give rise to a different outcome. A similar situation occurs with messages ℓ_4 and ℓ_5. See [7] for more details on the computation of message races. A typical state-space exploration method would follow these steps:

- First, one considers a random execution of the program and its associated trace.
- The trace is then analyzed and its message races are identified (if any).
- For each message race, we construct a (partial) log that can be used to drive the execution of the program to an execution point where a different choice is made. Then, execution continues nondeterministically, eventually producing a trace of the entire execution. We call this operation *prefix-based tracing*.

---

[5] We say that two actions are *causally* related when one action cannot happen without the other, e.g., message sending and receiving, spawning a process and any action of this process, etc. Causality is often defined as the transitive closure of the above relation. When two actions are not causally related, we say that they are *independent*. Two executions are *causally equivalent* if they only differ in the order of independent actions. Equivalently, two executions are causally equivalent if they have the same log [12]. Actually, logs can be seen as a representation of so-called *Mazurkiewicz traces* [14]. We refer the interested reader to [12] for more details.

- The process starts again with the new executions, and so forth. Typically, some backtracking algorithm is used in order to avoid considering the same execution (or a causally equivalent one) once and again.

For instance, given the execution of Fig. 3 and the associated trace in (1), we have a race for p3 between messages ℓ_1 and ℓ_2. Here, the following partial log could be used to drive the execution to a different choice, where message ℓ_2 is delivered to process p3 before message ℓ_1:

$$
\begin{array}{ll}
[\ \textsf{p1} \mapsto \textsf{spawn(p3)}, \textsf{spawn(p2)}, \textsf{spawn(p4)}, \textsf{send}(\ell_1); & \\
\quad \textsf{p2} \mapsto \textsf{send}(\ell_2); & \\
\quad \textsf{p3} \mapsto \textsf{rec}(\ell_2); & (3) \\
\quad \textsf{p4} \mapsto \textsf{send}(\ell_5) &]
\end{array}
$$

In the instrumented semantics, a *logged* system is now denoted by a triple $\mathcal{W}; \Gamma; \Pi$, where $\mathcal{W}$ is a (possibly partial) log. We will simply speak of *systems* when no confusion can arise between logged and non-logged systems. Furthermore, we also need some auxiliary functions. In prefix-based tracing, some steps might be driven by a log while others might not (e.g., when all the actions of a process have been already *consumed*). In order to deal with these two situations in a uniform way, we introduce the following function next:

$$
\textsf{next}(p, \mathcal{W}) = \begin{cases}
(p', \mathcal{W}) & \text{if } \mathcal{W}(p) = [\ ] \text{ and } p' \text{ is a fresh identifier} \\
(p', \mathcal{W}[p \mapsto as]) & \text{if } \mathcal{W}(p) = \textsf{spawn}(p') + as \\
(\ell, \mathcal{W}[p \mapsto as]) & \text{if } \mathcal{W}(p) = \textsf{send}(\ell) + as \\
(\ell, \mathcal{W}[p \mapsto as]) & \text{if } \mathcal{W}(p) = \textsf{rec}(\ell) + as
\end{cases}
$$

Essentially, $\textsf{next}(p, \mathcal{W})$ either *consumes* the first action of $\mathcal{W}(p)$ and returns the corresponding pid p' (if the first action is $\textsf{spawn}(p')$) or a message tag ℓ (if the first action is $\textsf{send}(\ell)$ or $\textsf{rec}(\ell)$), or returns fresh identifiers when $\mathcal{W}(p)$ is empty. It also returns the log resulting from removing the consumed action (if any). Here, we consider that pids and tags belong to the same domain for simplicity; otherwise, one would need two different functions, next_pid and next_tag, depending on the particular case.

Our second function, admissible, is used to check if delivering a message is consistent with the current system. Note that message delivery is in principle a nondeterministic operation in the standard semantics (Fig. 2) when we have messages in different queues of Γ addressed to the same target process. On the other hand, once messages are delivered, the order is fixed and the receive statements will consume them in a deterministic manner. Therefore, we should ensure that message deliveries follow the corresponding log. For this purpose, we introduce the auxiliary function admissible. Given a log $\mathcal{W}$, if $\mathcal{W}(p)$ is not empty, we have $\textsf{admissible}(p, \mathcal{W}[p \mapsto as], q, \ell) = true$ if $\textsf{rec}(\ell_1), \ldots, \textsf{rec}(\ell_n)$, $n > 0$, are the receive actions in as, q contains messages $\ell_1, \ldots, \ell_i$, $0 \le i < n$, and $\ell = \ell_{i+1}$. When $\log(p)$ is empty or contains no rec actions, function admissible simply returns *true* in order to proceed nondeterministically as in the standard semantics. Otherwise, it compares the list of messages to be received by p and the list of messages already in p's mailbox in order to determine if ℓ is indeed the next message that must be delivered in order to follow the order of message receptions given by the log.

(*Exit*)
$$\frac{final(ls)}{\mathcal{W}; \Gamma; \langle p, ls, q \rangle \mid \Pi \rightsquigarrow_{p:\mathsf{exit}} \mathcal{W}; \Gamma; \Pi}$$

(*Local*)
$$\frac{ls \xrightarrow{\iota} ls\nrightarrow}{\mathcal{W}; \Gamma; \langle p, ls, q \rangle \mid \Pi \rightsquigarrow_{\epsilon} \mathcal{W}, \Gamma; \langle p, ls', q \rangle \mid \Pi}$$

(*Self*)
$$\frac{ls \xrightarrow{\mathsf{self}(\kappa)} ls'}{\mathcal{W}; \Gamma; \langle p, ls, q \rangle \mid \Pi \rightsquigarrow_{\epsilon} \mathcal{W}; \Gamma; \langle p, ls'\{\kappa \mapsto p\}, q \rangle \mid \Pi}$$

(*Spawn*)
$$\frac{ls \xrightarrow{\mathsf{spawn}(\kappa, ls_0)} ls' \text{ and } next(p, \mathcal{W}) = (p', \mathcal{W}')}{\mathcal{W}; \Gamma; \langle p, ls, q \rangle \mid \Pi \rightsquigarrow_{p:\mathsf{spawn}(p')} \mathcal{W}'; \Gamma; \langle p, ls'\{\kappa \mapsto p'\}, q \rangle \mid \langle p', ls_0, [\,] \rangle \mid \Pi}$$

(*Send*)
$$\frac{ls \xrightarrow{\mathsf{send}(p', v)} ls' \text{ and } next(p, \mathcal{W}) = (\ell, \mathcal{W}')}{\mathcal{W}; \Gamma[(p, p') \mapsto qs]; \langle p, ls, q \rangle \mid \Pi \rightsquigarrow_{p:\mathsf{send}(\ell, p')} \mathcal{W}'; \Gamma[(p, p') \mapsto qs + \{v, \ell\}]; \langle p, ls', q \rangle \mid \Pi}$$

(*Deliver*)
$$\frac{admissible(p, \mathcal{W}, q, \ell) = true}{\mathcal{W}; \Gamma[(p', p) \mapsto \{v, \ell\} + vs]; \langle p, ls, q \rangle \mid \Pi \rightsquigarrow_{p:\mathsf{deliver}(\ell)} \mathcal{W}; \Gamma[(p', p) \mapsto vs]; \langle p, ls, q + \{v, \ell\} \rangle \mid \Pi}$$

(*Receive*)
$$\frac{ls \xrightarrow{\mathsf{rec}(\kappa, cs)} ls' \;\; matchrec(ls', \kappa, cs, q) = (ls'', q', \ell) \text{ and } next(p, \mathcal{W}) = (\ell, \mathcal{W}')}{\mathcal{W}; \Gamma; \langle p, ls, q \rangle \mid \Pi \rightsquigarrow_{p:\mathsf{rec}(\ell)} \mathcal{W}'; \Gamma; \langle p, ls'', q' \rangle \mid \Pi}$$

Fig. 4. Prefix-based tracing semantics

The instrumented semantics is defined by means of the labeled transition system shown in Fig. 4. Now, each transition is labeled with an *event* of the form $p : a$ where p is the pid of a process and a is the action performed by this process. Let us briefly explain the transition rules:

- The first three rules, *Exit*, *Local* and *Self* are similar to their counterpart in the standard semantics (Fig. 2), since the log plays no role in these cases. The only relevant difference is that we label the transition with the corresponding action, $p : \mathsf{exit}$, in the first rule, and ϵ (a null event) in the other two rules.
- Rules *Spawn* and *Send* proceed in a similar way: when $\mathcal{W}(p)$ is not empty, the pid of the new process (rule *Spawn*) or the message tag (rule *Send*) are taken from the log. Otherwise, fresh identifiers are used, as in the standard semantics of Fig. 2. The transitions are labeled with the events $p : \mathsf{spawn}(p')$ and $p : \mathsf{send}(\ell, p')$, respectively.
- Rule *Deliver* ensures that messages are delivered according to the order in $\mathcal{W}(p)$. Observe that, given a process p, the order of message deliveries is now

deterministic when $\mathcal{W}(p)$ is not empty and includes at least one rec action. Here, the transition is labeled with the event p:deliver(ℓ).

- Finally, rule *Receive* is similar to its counterpart in Fig. 2, with only a subtle difference: now, function matchrec also returns the tag of the selected message, since it is required for the label of the transition, p : rec(ℓ). We note that function next is only used to consume an action from the log (when $\mathcal{W}(p)$ is not empty) but it imposes no actual restriction on the transition, since once the messages are in the process queue, message reception becomes deterministic. This is why function admissible checks the log in order to deliver messages in the right order.

Given a sequence of events $es = (p_1\!:\!a_1, p_2\!:\!a_2, \ldots, p_n\!:\!a_n)$, we let actions$(p, es)$ denote the sequence of actions $a_1', a_2', \ldots, a_m'$ such that $p\!:\!a_1', p\!:\!a_2', \ldots, p\!:\!a_m'$ are all the events of process p in es and in the same order. Then, given a derivation $\delta = (\alpha_0 \leadsto_{e_1} \alpha_1 \leadsto_{e_2} \cdots \leadsto_{e_n} \alpha_{n+1})$, $n > 0$, the associated trace, in symbols trace(δ), is a trace $\mathcal{T}$ such that $\mathcal{T}(p_i) = $ actions(p_i, es) for each pid p_i occurring in $es = (e_1, \ldots, e_n)$.

Following [12], we say that two derivations are *causally equivalent* if their logs are the same (cf. Theorem 3.6 in [12]).[6] Now, we focus on two scenarios for prefix-based tracing: "pure tracing" and "pure replay". In the following, we say that a logged system is *initial* if it has the form $\mathcal{E}; \mathcal{E}; \langle p, ls, [\,] \rangle$. By abuse of notation, we let $\mathcal{E}$ denote both a log where pid p is mapped to an empty sequence and a network where the queue of (p, p) is empty. Similarly to the previous section, we assume that all derivations start with an initial logged system.

The following result states that prefix-based tracing is indeed a conservative extension of the standard semantics:

Theorem 1 (pure tracing). *Let $\alpha \hookrightarrow \ldots \hookrightarrow \alpha'$ be a derivation with the standard semantics (Fig. 2). Then, there is a derivation $\delta = (\mathcal{E}; \alpha \leadsto_{e_1} \ldots \leadsto_{e_n} \mathcal{E}; \alpha')$ with the prefix-based semantics of Fig. 4, where* trace(δ) *is its associated trace.*

Proof. The proof is straightforward since function next always returns a fresh pid/tag and function admissible always returns true when the log is empty. Therefore, the only difference between the rules in Fig. 2 and those in Fig. 4 when the log is empty is that the transitions are labeled with the corresponding event, so that a trace can be obtained. □

Let us now consider pure replay. In the following, we assume that all logs are *consistent*, i.e., they have been obtained from the trace of a derivation. Moreover, we say that a derivation *consumes* a log when it only performs a transition for process p if $\mathcal{W}(p)$ is not an empty sequence. In other words, it performs a replay of the execution represented by the log, and no more. The next result states that, given the log of a derivation, prefix-based tracing with this log produces a derivation which is causally equivalent to the original one.

---

[6] To be precise, the semantics in [12] does not consider process mailboxes nor message deliveries. Nevertheless, these actions are not observable in logs, and hence the property carry over easily to our case.

Theorem 2 (pure replay). *Let $\mathcal{W}$ be a nonempty log and let $\delta = (\mathcal{W}; \alpha \leadsto_{e_1}$ $\dots \leadsto_{e_n} \mathcal{E}; \alpha')$ be a derivation with the rules of Fig. 4 that consumes log $\mathcal{W}$. Then, $log(\mathsf{trace}(\delta)) = \mathcal{W}$.*

Proof (Sketch). The claim follows easily by induction on the length of the considered derivation. Since the base case is trivial, let us consider the inductive case. Here, we make a case distinction on the applied rule to system $\mathcal{W}; \alpha$:

- If we perform a step with rules *Exit, Local, Self* or *Deliver*, the claim follows trivially by induction since they have no impact on $log(\mathsf{trace}(\delta))$.
- Consider now a step with rule *Spawn* applied to a process p, and assume that the log has the form $\mathcal{W}[p \mapsto \mathsf{spawn}(p') + as]$ and the step is labeled with the event $p: \mathsf{spawn}(p')$. Hence, $\mathsf{trace}(\delta)$ associates an action $\mathsf{spawn}(p')$ to process p and so does $log(\mathsf{trace}(\delta))$. Then, the claim follows by applying the inductive hypothesis on the derived system $\mathcal{W}[p \mapsto as]; \alpha''$. A similar reasoning can be made with rule *Receive*.
- Finally, we consider rule *Send* applied to process p, and assume that the log has the form $\mathcal{W}[p \mapsto \mathsf{send}(\ell) + as]$. Here, $\mathsf{trace}(\delta)$ associates an action $\mathsf{send}(\ell, p')$ to process p and, thus, $log(\mathsf{trace}(\delta))$ will add $\mathsf{send}(\ell)$ to the sequence of actions of process p. Then, the claim follows by applying the inductive hypothesis on the derived system $\mathcal{W}[p \mapsto as]; \alpha''$.   □

In the next section, we introduce an implementation of prefix-based tracing by means of a program instrumentation.

4   A Program Instrumentation for Prefix-Based Tracing

Now, we focus on the design of a program instrumentation to perform prefix-based tracing in Erlang. In a nutshell, our program instrumentation proceeds as follows:

- First, we introduce a new process, called the *scheduler* (a server), that will be run as part of the source program.
- The scheduler ensures that the actions of a given log are followed in the same order, and that the corresponding trace is eventually computed. It also includes a data structure that corresponds to the network Γ introduced in the previous section. In the instrumented program, all messages will be sent via the scheduler.
- Finally, the sentences that correspond to the concurrent actions spawn, send and rec are instrumented in order to interact with the scheduler. The remaining code will stay untouched.

The scheduler uses several data structures called *dictionaries*, a typical key-value data structure which is commonly used in Erlang applications. Here, we consider the following standard operations on dictionaries:

- *fetch*$(k, dict)$, which returns the value *val* associated to key k in *dict*. We write *dict*$[k]$ as a shorthand for *fetch*$(k, dict)$.

- *store*(k, *val*, *dict*), which updates the dictionary by adding (or updating, if the key exists) a new pair with key k and value *val*. In this case, we write *dict*[k] := *val* as a shorthand for *store*(k, *val*, *dict*).

In particular, we consider the following dictionaries:

- Pids, which maps the pid of each process to a (unique) reference, i.e., Pids[p] denotes the reference of pid p. While pids are relative to a particular execution (i.e., the pid of the same process may change from one execution to the next one), the corresponding reference in a log or trace is permanent. This mapping is used to dynamically keep the association between pids and references in each execution. For instance, an example value for Pids is $[\{\langle 0.80.0\rangle, \mathsf{p1}\}, \langle 0.83.0\rangle, \mathsf{p2}\}]$, where $\langle 0.80.0\rangle$, $\langle 0.83.0\rangle$ are Erlang pids and $\mathsf{p1}, \mathsf{p2}$ are the corresponding references.
- LT, which is used to associate each process reference with a tuple of the form $\{ls, as\}$, where ls is a (possibly empty) list with the events of a log and as is a (possibly empty) list with the (reversed) trace of the execution so far. The log is used to drive the next steps, while the second component is used to store the execution trace so far. The list storing the trace is reversed for efficiency reasons (since it is faster to add elements to the head of the list). E.g., the initial value of LT for the partial log displayed in (3) is as follows:

$$[\{\mathsf{p1}, \{[\mathsf{spawn(p3)}, \mathsf{spawn(p2)}, \mathsf{spawn(p4)}, \mathsf{send}(\ell_1)], [\,]\}\},$$
$$\{\mathsf{p2}, \{[\mathsf{send}(\ell_2)], [\,]\}\}, \{\mathsf{p3}, \{[\mathsf{rec}(\ell_2)], [\,]\}\}, \{\mathsf{p4}, \{[\mathsf{send}(\ell_5)], [\,]\}\}]$$

- MBox, which represents the network Γ, also called global mailbox. The key of this dictionary is the pid of the target process, and the value is another dictionary in which the keys are pids (those of the sender processes) and the values are lists of (tagged) messages. For instance, the value of MBox after sending the first two messages of the execution shown in Fig. 3 could be as follows:

$$\{\langle 0.84.0\rangle, \{\langle 0.80.0\rangle, [\{\ell_1, v_1\}]\},$$
$$\{\langle 0.83.0\rangle, [\{\ell_2, v_2\}]\}\}$$

where $\langle 0.80.0\rangle$, $\langle 0.83.0\rangle$, $\langle 0.84.0\rangle$ are the pids of $\mathsf{p1}, \mathsf{p2}, \mathsf{p3}$, respectively, v_1 and v_2 are the message values and ℓ_1 and ℓ_2 are their respective tags.

Let us now describe the instrumentation of the source code. First, every expression of the form $\mathsf{spawn}(mod, fun, args)$ is replaced by a call to a new function $\mathsf{spawn\_inst}$ with the same arguments. The implementation of this function is essentially as follows:

```
spawn_inst(M, F, A) →
    Pid = self(),
    SpawnPid = spawn(fun() →
              sched ! {Pid, spawn, self()},
              apply(M, F, A)
    end),
    receive ack → ok end,
    SpawnPid.
```

where spawn takes an anonymous function as argument (so that the new process will evaluate the body of the anonymous function) and Erlang's predefined function *apply* is used to compute the application of a function to some arguments.

Intuitively speaking, the new function (1) sends the message $\{P1, \mathsf{spawn}, P2\}$ to the scheduler (here denoted by sched), where $P1$ is the pid of the current process and $P2$ is the pid of the spawned process, and (2) inserts a receive expression to make this communication *synchronous*. The reason for (2) is that every message of the form $\{P1, \mathsf{spawn}, P2\}$ must add $P2$ to the data structure Pids, either with a new reference or with the one in the current log. We require this operation to be completed before either the spawned process or the one performing the spawn can proceed with any other action. Otherwise, the scheduler could run into an inconsistent state.

The instrumentation of message sending is much simpler. We just perform the following rewriting:

$$e_1 \,!\, e_2 \quad \Rightarrow \quad \mathsf{sched}\,!\,\{\mathsf{self}(), \mathsf{send}, e_1, e_2\}$$

where sched is the pid of the scheduler and self() is a predefined function that returns the pid of the current process. Finally, the instrumentation of a receive expression rewrites the code as follows:

$$\begin{aligned}
&\mathsf{receive}\ p_1 \to e_1; \ldots; p_n \to e_n\ \mathsf{end} \\
&\quad \Rightarrow \mathsf{receive}\ \{L_1, p_1\} \to \mathsf{sched}\,!\,\{\mathsf{self}(), \mathsf{rec}, L_1\}, e_1; \ldots; \\
&\qquad\qquad\ \{L_n, p_n\} \to \mathsf{sched}\,!\,\{\mathsf{self}(), \mathsf{rec}, L_n\}, e_n\ \mathsf{end}
\end{aligned}$$

where $L_1, \ldots, L_n$ are fresh variables that are used to gather the tag of the received message and send it to the scheduler.

The main algorithm of the scheduler can be found in Algorithm 1. First, we have an initialization where the pid of the main process is associated with the reference p1 in Pids, the initial logs are assigned to LT, and the mailbox is initially empty. As is common in server processes, the scheduler is basically an infinite loop with a receive statement to process the requests. Here, we consider three requests, which correspond to the messages sent from the instrumented source code. Let us briefly explain the actions associated to each message:

- If the message received has the form $\{p, \mathsf{spawn}, p'\}$, where p, p' are pids, we look for the tuple associated to process Pids[p] in LT. If the log is empty, we can proceed nondeterministically and just need to keep a trace of the execution step. Here, we obtain a fresh reference, r', add the pair $\{p', r'\}$ to Pids, and update the trace in LT with the new action $\mathsf{spawn}(r')$. If the log is not empty, we proceed in a similar way but the reference is given in the log entry. Finally, we have to acknowledge the reception of this message since this communication is synchronous (as explained above).
- If the message received has the form $\{p, \mathsf{send}, p', v\}$, we again distinguish the case where the process log is empty. In this case, we obtain a fresh reference ℓ (the message tag) and update LT with the new action $\mathsf{send}(\ell)$. Finally, we use the auxiliary function *process_new_msg* to check the log of the target process, p', and then it proceeds as follows:

Algorithm 1. Scheduler

Initialization
    Pids := [{self(), p1}];   LT := /* *prefix logs* */;   MBox := { };
repeat
 receive
    {p, spawn, p'} →
        case LT[Pids[p]] **of**
            {[ ], as} →   /* *trace mode* */
                    r' := *new_unique_ref*();
                    update_pids(p', r', Pids);
                    LT[Pids[p]] := {[ ], [spawn(r')|as]};
            {[spawn(r')|ls], as} →   /* *replay mode* */
                    update_pids(p', r', Pids);
                    LT[Pids[p]] := {ls, [spawn(r')|as]};
        p ! *ack*;
        try_deliver(p);
    {p, send, p', v} →
        case LT[Pids[p]] **of**
            {[ ], as} →   /* *trace mode* */
                    ℓ := *new_unique_ref*();
                    LT[Pids[p]] := {[ ], [send(ℓ)|as]};
                    process_new_msg({p, p', ℓ, v}, MBox, LT);
            {[send(ℓ)|ls], as} →   /* *replay mode* */
                    LT[Pids[p]] := {ls, [send(ℓ)|as]};
                    process_msg({p, p', ℓ, v}, MBox, LT);
        try_deliver(p);
    {p, rec, ℓ} →
        case LT[Pids[p]] **of**
            {[ ], as} →   /* *trace mode* */
                    LT[Pids[p]] := {[ ], [rec(ℓ)|as]}
            {[rec(ℓ)|ls], as} →   /* *replay mode* */
                    LT[Pids[p]] := {ls, [rec(ℓ)|as]}
        try_deliver(p)
until *true*

- If the log of Pids[p'] is empty, we add the action deliver(ℓ) to the trace of Pids[p'] and then send the message to the target process: p' ! {ℓ, v}, i.e., we apply an *instant-delivery* strategy, where messages are delivered as soon as possible (this is the usual action in the Erlang runtime environment).
- If the log is not empty, we do not know when this message should be received. Hence, we add a new (tagged) message {ℓ, v} from p to p' to the mailbox MBox, and add an action deliver(ℓ) at the end of the current log. Note that computed logs (as in [11,12]) should not contain deliver actions. This one is artificially added to *force* the delivery of message ℓ as soon as possible (see function *try_deliver* below).

The pseudocode of function *process_new_msg* can be found below:

$$process\_new\_msg(\{p, p', \ell, v\}, \mathsf{MBox}, \mathsf{LT}) \rightarrow$$
case $\mathsf{LT}[\mathsf{Pids}[p']]$ **of**
$$\{[\,], as'\} \rightarrow p' \,!\, \{\ell, v\},$$
$$\mathsf{LT}[\mathsf{Pids}[p']] := \{[\,], [\mathsf{deliver}(\ell)|as']\};$$
$$\{as, as'\} \rightarrow add\_message(p, p', \{\ell, v\}, \mathsf{MBox}),$$
$$\mathsf{LT}[\mathsf{Pids}[p']] := \{as + \mathsf{deliver}(\ell), as'\}$$
end

If the log is not empty, we proceed in a similar way but the message tag is given by the log and we call the auxiliary function *process_msg* instead. This function checks the log of the target process, $\mathsf{Pids}[p']$, and then proceeds as follows:

- If the next action in the log is $\mathsf{rec}(\ell)$, we add the action $\mathsf{deliver}(\ell)$ to the trace of $\mathsf{Pids}[p']$ and send the message to the target process: $p' \,!\, \{\ell, v\}$.
- If the first action is not $\mathsf{rec}(\ell)$, we add a new (tagged) message $\{\ell, v\}$ from p to p' to the mailbox MBox. Finally, if the log of $\mathsf{Pids}[p']$ contains an action $\mathsf{rec}(\ell)$, we are done; otherwise, an action of the form $\mathsf{deliver}(\ell)$ is added to the end of the log of process $\mathsf{Pids}[p']$, as before.

The pseudocode of function *process_msg* can be found below:

$$process\_msg(\{p, p', \ell, v\}, \mathsf{MBox}, \mathsf{LT}) \rightarrow$$
case $\mathsf{LT}[\mathsf{Pids}[p']]$ **of**
$$\{[\mathsf{rec}(\ell)|as], as'\} \rightarrow p' \,!\, \{\ell, v\},$$
$$\mathsf{LT}[\mathsf{Pids}[p']] := \{as, [\mathsf{deliver}(\ell)|as']\};$$
$$\{as, as'\} \rightarrow add\_message(p, p', \{\ell, v\}, \mathsf{MBox}),$$
if $not(member(\mathsf{rec}(\ell), as))$
then $\mathsf{LT}[\mathsf{Pids}[p']] := \{as + \mathsf{deliver}(\ell), as'\}$
end

– Finally, when the received message has the form $\{p, \mathsf{rec}, \ell\}$, we just update the trace with the new action $\mathsf{rec}(\ell)$ and, if the log was not empty, we remove the first action $\mathsf{rec}(\ell)$ from the log.

Each of the above cases ends with a call *try_deliver*(p), which is basically used to deliver messages that could not be delivered before (because it would have violated the order of some log). For this purpose, this function checks the next action in the log of process $\mathsf{Pids}[p]$. If it has either the form $\mathsf{rec}(\ell)$ or $\mathsf{deliver}(\ell)$, and the message tagged with ℓ is the oldest one in one of the queues of MBox with target p, then we send the message to p, remove it from MBox and add $\mathsf{deliver}(\ell)$ to the trace of process $\mathsf{Pids}[p]$. Furthermore, in case the element of the log was $\mathsf{deliver}(\ell)$, we recursively call *try_deliver*(p) to see if there are more messages that can be delivered. In any other case, the function does nothing.

The implementation of the program instrumentation to perform prefix-based tracing is publicly available from https://github.com/mistupv/cauder.

5   Concluding Remaks

In this work, we have formalized the notion of prefix-based tracing, an essential component of state-space exploration methods, in the context of a message-passing concurrent language that can be seen as a subset of Erlang. We have proved that prefix-based tracing indeed subsumes traditional tracing and replay. Furthermore, we have implemented this operation by means of a program instrumentation which is parametric on the given input log.

We consider several interesting avenues for future work. On the one hand, we plan to extend prefix-based tracing to also consider several built-in's of the Erlang language that involve shared-memory concurrency. This extension will significantly extend the class of considered programs. On the other hand, an experimental evaluation will be carried over to determine the overhead introduced by the program instrumentation.

Acknowledgements. The authors would like to thank Ivan Lanese for his useful remarks on a preliminary version of this paper. We would also like to thank the anonymous reviewers and the participants of LOPSTR 2021 for their suggestions to improve this work.

References

1. Abdulla, P.A., Aronis, S., Jonsson, B., Sagonas, K.: Source sets: a foundation for optimal dynamic partial order reduction. J. ACM **64**(4), 25:1–25:49 (2017). https://doi.org/10.1145/3073408
2. Christakis, M., Gotovos, A., Sagonas, K.: Systematic testing for detecting concurrency errors in Erlang programs. In: Proceedings of the 6th IEEE International Conference on Software Testing, Verification and Validation (ICST 2013), pp. 154–163. IEEE Computer Society (2013). https://doi.org/10.1109/ICST.2013.50
3. Erlang website (2021). https://www.erlang.org/
4. Flanagan, C., Godefroid, P.: Dynamic partial-order reduction for model checking software. In: Palsberg, J., Abadi, M. (eds.) Proceedings of the 32nd ACM SIGPLAN-SIGACT Symposium on Principles of Programming Languages (POPL 2005), pp. 110–121. ACM (2005). https://doi.org/10.1145/1040305.1040315
5. Godefroid, P.: Model checking for programming languages using VeriSoft. In: POPL, pp. 174–186 (1997). https://doi.org/10.1145/263699.263717
6. González-Abril, J.J., Vidal, G.: Causal-consistent reversible debugging: improving CauDEr. In: Morales, J.F., Orchard, D. (eds.) PADL 2021. LNCS, vol. 12548, pp. 145–160. Springer, Cham (2021). https://doi.org/10.1007/978-3-030-67438-0_9
7. González-Abril, J.J., Vidal, G.: A lightweight approach to computing message races with an application to causal-consistent reversible debugging (2021). http://arxiv.org/abs/2112.12869
8. Hwang, G., Tai, K., Huang, T.: Reachability testing: an approach to testing concurrent software. Int. J. Softw. Eng. Knowl. Eng. **5**(4), 493–510 (1995). https://doi.org/10.1142/S0218194095000241
9. Lanese, I., Nishida, N., Palacios, A., Vidal, G.: CauDEr: a causal-consistent reversible debugger for Erlang. In: Gallagher, J.P., Sulzmann, M. (eds.) FLOPS 2018. LNCS, vol. 10818, pp. 247–263. Springer, Cham (2018). https://doi.org/10.1007/978-3-319-90686-7_16

10. Lanese, I., Nishida, N., Palacios, A., Vidal, G.: A theory of reversibility for Erlang. J. Log. Algebraic Methods Program. **100**, 71–97 (2018). https://doi.org/10.1016/j.jlamp.2018.06.004
11. Lanese, I., Palacios, A., Vidal, G.: Causal-consistent replay debugging for message passing programs. In: Pérez, J.A., Yoshida, N. (eds.) FORTE 2019. LNCS, vol. 11535, pp. 167–184. Springer, Cham (2019). https://doi.org/10.1007/978-3-030-21759-4_10
12. Lanese, I., Palacios, A., Vidal, G.: Causal-consistent replay reversible semantics for message passing concurrent programs. Fundam. Inform. **178**(3), 229–266 (2021). https://doi.org/10.3233/FI-2021-2005
13. Lei, Y., Carver, R.H.: Reachability testing of concurrent programs. IEEE Trans. Softw. Eng. **32**(6), 382–403 (2006). https://doi.org/10.1109/TSE.2006.56
14. Mazurkiewicz, A.: Trace theory. In: Brauer, W., Reisig, W., Rozenberg, G. (eds.) ACPN 1986. LNCS, vol. 255, pp. 278–324. Springer, Heidelberg (1987). https://doi.org/10.1007/3-540-17906-2_30
15. Nishida, N., Palacios, A., Vidal, G.: A reversible semantics for Erlang. In: Hermenegildo, M.V., Lopez-Garcia, P. (eds.) LOPSTR 2016. LNCS, vol. 10184, pp. 259–274. Springer, Cham (2017). https://doi.org/10.1007/978-3-319-63139-4_15
16. Svensson, H., Fredlund, L.A., Earle, C.B.: A unified semantics for future Erlang. In: 9th ACM SIGPLAN Workshop on Erlang, pp. 23–32. ACM (2010). https://doi.org/10.1145/1863509.1863514

Author Index

Printed in the United States
by Baker & Taylor Publisher Services